ISBN 0-8373-4711-4
C-4711   CAREER EXAMINATION SERIES

This is your
PASSBOOK® for...

School Bus Dispatcher

Test Preparation Study Guide
Questions & Answers

NLC

NATIONAL LEARNING CORPORATION®

Copyright © 2016 by

National Learning Corporation

212 Michael Drive, Syosset, New York 11791

All rights reserved, including the right of reproduction in whole or in part, in any form or by any means, electronic or mechanical, including photocopying, recording, or by any information storage and retrieval system, without permission in writing from the Publisher.

(516) 921-8888
(800) 645-6337
FAX: (516) 921-8743
www.passbooks.com
sales @ passbooks.com
info @ passbooks.com

PRINTED IN THE UNITED STATES OF AMERICA

PASSBOOK®
NOTICE

This book is SOLELY intended for, is sold ONLY to, and its use is RESTRICTED to *individual*, bona fide applicants or candidates who qualify by virtue of having seriously filed applications for appropriate license, certificate, professional and/or promotional advancement, higher school matriculation, scholarship, or other legitimate requirements of educational and/or governmental authorities.

This book is NOT intended for use, class instruction, tutoring, training, duplication, copying, reprinting, excerption, or adaptation, etc., by:

(1) Other publishers

(2) Proprietors and/or Instructors of "Coaching" and/or Preparatory Courses

(3) Personnel and/or Training Divisions of commercial, industrial, and governmental organizations

(4) Schools, colleges, or universities and/or their departments and staffs, including teachers and other personnel

(5) Testing Agencies or Bureaus

(6) Study groups which seek by the purchase of a single volume to copy and/or duplicate and/or adapt this material for use by the group as a whole without having purchased individual volumes for each of the members of the group

(7) Et al.

Such persons would be in violation of appropriate Federal and State statutes.

PROVISION OF LICENSING AGREEMENTS. — Recognized educational commercial, industrial, and governmental institutions and organizations, and others legitimately engaged in educational pursuits, including training, testing, and measurement activities, may address a request for a licensing agreement to the copyright owners, who will determine whether, and under what conditions, including fees and charges, the materials in this book may be used by them. In other words, a licensing facility exists for the legitimate use of the material in this book on other than an individual basis. However, it is asseverated and affirmed here that the material in this book *CANNOT* be used without the receipt of the express permission of such a licensing agreement from the Publishers.

NATIONAL LEARNING CORPORATION
212 Michael Drive
Syosset, New York 11791

Inquiries re licensing agreements should be addressed to:
The President
National Learning Corporation
212 Michael Drive
Syosset, New York 11791

PASSBOOK® SERIES

THE *PASSBOOK® SERIES* has been created to prepare applicants and candidates for the ultimate academic battlefield – the examination room.

At some time in our lives, each and every one of us may be required to take an examination – for validation, matriculation, admission, qualification, registration, certification, or licensure.

Based on the assumption that every applicant or candidate has met the basic formal educational standards, has taken the required number of courses, and read the necessary texts, the *PASSBOOK® SERIES* furnishes the one special preparation which may assure passing with confidence, instead of failing with insecurity. Examination questions – together with answers – are furnished as the basic vehicle for study so that the mysteries of the examination and its compounding difficulties may be eliminated or diminished by a sure method.

This book is meant to help you pass your examination provided that you qualify and are serious in your objective.

The entire field is reviewed through the huge store of content information which is succinctly presented through a provocative and challenging approach – the question-and-answer method.

A climate of success is established by furnishing the correct answers at the end of each test.

You soon learn to recognize types of questions, forms of questions, and patterns of questioning. You may even begin to anticipate expected outcomes.

You perceive that many questions are repeated or adapted so that you can gain acute insights, which may enable you to score many sure points.

You learn how to confront new questions, or types of questions, and to attack them confidently and work out the correct answers.

You note objectives and emphases, and recognize pitfalls and dangers, so that you may make positive educational adjustments.

Moreover, you are kept fully informed in relation to new concepts, methods, practices, and directions in the field.

You discover that you are actually taking the examination all the time: you are preparing for the examination by "taking" an examination, not by reading extraneous and/or supererogatory textbooks.

In short, this PASSBOOK®, used directedly, should be an important factor in helping you to pass your test.

SCHOOL BUS DISPATCHER

DUTIES:
This position involves responsibility for scheduling bus assignments and efficiently maintaining a system of bus routing in a school transportation system. The position may also involve duties pertaining to the operation of a transportation system, including record keeping, payroll maintenance, occasional driving, and other duties as may be required. Depending on the organizational structure of the school district, incumbents may be required to obtain certification as an examiner from the State Department of Motor Vehicles in order to provide bus driver testing and examination functions in accordance with the provisions of the Vehicle and Traffic Law. Supervision is exercised over bus drivers. Work is performed under general direction of a Transportation Supervisor or other administrative person in the school district.

SCOPE OF THE EXAMINATION
The written test is designed to evaluate knowledge, skills and/or abilities in the following areas:
1. **Bus driving practices, techniques and traffic laws** - These questions test for knowledge of the principles and practices involved in the proper and safe operation of passenger buses; the rules and regulations of the Motor Vehicle and Traffic law governing passenger bus operation, highway safety, and rules of the road.
2. **Bus driver record keeping and scheduling** - A test that requires candidates to work with simple records using general record-book or card-type formats. Questions are based on given records, which usually must be completed by the candidate before questions can be answered. In order to answer all the questions in this subtest correctly, the candidate generally must:
   - Follow written directions to understand the purpose and use of the record, and to understand the question;
   - Make correct entries in appropriate sections of the record;
   - Identify which entries are required to answer the question;
   - Knowledge of bookkeeping, account keeping, or other technical information or terminology is not necessary to answer these questions. A knowledge of simple arithmetic functions may be required.
3. **Follow directions (maps)** - These questions test your ability to follow physical/geographic directions using street maps or building maps. You will have to read and understand a set of directions and then use them on a simple map.
4. **School bus driving practices, techniques and traffic laws** -These questions test for knowledge of the principles and practices involved in the proper and safe operation of school buses; and the rules and regulations of the New York Motor Vehicle and Traffic Law governing school bus operation, highway safety, and rules of the road.
5. **Supervision** -These questions test for knowledge of the principles and practices employed in planning, organizing, and controlling the activities of a work unit toward predetermined objectives. The concepts covered, usually in a situational question format, include such topics as assigning and reviewing work; evaluating performance; maintaining work standards; motivating and developing subordinates; implementing procedural change; increasing efficiency; and dealing with problems of absenteeism, morale, and discipline.

HOW TO TAKE A TEST

I. YOU MUST PASS AN EXAMINATION

A. WHAT EVERY CANDIDATE SHOULD KNOW

Examination applicants often ask us for help in preparing for the written test. What can I study in advance? What kinds of questions will be asked? How will the test be given? How will the papers be graded?

As an applicant for a civil service examination, you may be wondering about some of these things. Our purpose here is to suggest effective methods of advance study and to describe civil service examinations.

Your chances for success on this examination can be increased if you know how to prepare. Those "pre-examination jitters" can be reduced if you know what to expect. You can even experience an adventure in good citizenship if you know why civil service exams are given.

B. WHY ARE CIVIL SERVICE EXAMINATIONS GIVEN?

Civil service examinations are important to you in two ways. As a citizen, you want public jobs filled by employees who know how to do their work. As a job seeker, you want a fair chance to compete for that job on an equal footing with other candidates. The best-known means of accomplishing this two-fold goal is the competitive examination.

Exams are widely publicized throughout the nation. They may be administered for jobs in federal, state, city, municipal, town or village governments or agencies.

Any citizen may apply, with some limitations, such as the age or residence of applicants. Your experience and education may be reviewed to see whether you meet the requirements for the particular examination. When these requirements exist, they are reasonable and applied consistently to all applicants. Thus, a competitive examination may cause you some uneasiness now, but it is your privilege and safeguard.

C. HOW ARE CIVIL SERVICE EXAMS DEVELOPED?

Examinations are carefully written by trained technicians who are specialists in the field known as "psychological measurement," in consultation with recognized authorities in the field of work that the test will cover. These experts recommend the subject matter areas or skills to be tested; only those knowledges or skills important to your success on the job are included. The most reliable books and source materials available are used as references. Together, the experts and technicians judge the difficulty level of the questions.

Test technicians know how to phrase questions so that the problem is clearly stated. Their ethics do not permit "trick" or "catch" questions. Questions may have been tried out on sample groups, or subjected to statistical analysis, to determine their usefulness.

Written tests are often used in combination with performance tests, ratings of training and experience, and oral interviews. All of these measures combine to form the best-known means of finding the right person for the right job.

II. HOW TO PASS THE WRITTEN TEST

A. NATURE OF THE EXAMINATION

To prepare intelligently for civil service examinations, you should know how they differ from school examinations you have taken. In school you were assigned certain definite pages to read or subjects to cover. The examination questions were quite detailed and usually emphasized memory. Civil service exams, on the other hand, try to discover your present ability to perform the duties of a position, plus your potentiality to learn these duties. In other words, a civil service exam attempts to predict how successful you will be. Questions cover such a broad area that they cannot be as minute and detailed as school exam questions.

In the public service similar kinds of work, or positions, are grouped together in one "class." This process is known as *position-classification*. All the positions in a class are paid according to the salary range for that class. One class title covers all of these positions, and they are all tested by the same examination.

B. FOUR BASIC STEPS

1) Study the announcement

How, then, can you know what subjects to study? Our best answer is: "Learn as much as possible about the class of positions for which you've applied." The exam will test the knowledge, skills and abilities needed to do the work.

Your most valuable source of information about the position you want is the official exam announcement. This announcement lists the training and experience qualifications. Check these standards and apply only if you come reasonably close to meeting them.

The brief description of the position in the examination announcement offers some clues to the subjects which will be tested. Think about the job itself. Review the duties in your mind. Can you perform them, or are there some in which you are rusty? Fill in the blank spots in your preparation.

Many jurisdictions preview the written test in the exam announcement by including a section called "Knowledge and Abilities Required," "Scope of the Examination," or some similar heading. Here you will find out specifically what fields will be tested.

2) Review your own background

Once you learn in general what the position is all about, and what you need to know to do the work, ask yourself which subjects you already know fairly well and which need improvement. You may wonder whether to concentrate on improving your strong areas or on building some background in your fields of weakness. When the announcement has specified "some knowledge" or "considerable knowledge," or has used adjectives like "beginning principles of…" or "advanced … methods," you can get a clue as to the number and difficulty of questions to be asked in any given field. More questions, and hence broader coverage, would be included for those subjects which are more important in the work. Now weigh your strengths and weaknesses against the job requirements and prepare accordingly.

3) Determine the level of the position

Another way to tell how intensively you should prepare is to understand the level of the job for which you are applying. Is it the entering level? In other words, is this the position in which beginners in a field of work are hired? Or is it an intermediate or advanced level? Sometimes this is indicated by such words as "Junior" or "Senior" in the class title. Other jurisdictions use Roman numerals to designate the level – Clerk I, Clerk II, for example. The word "Supervisor" sometimes appears in the title. If the level is not indicated by the title, check the description of duties. Will you be working under very close supervision, or will you have responsibility for independent decisions in this work?

4) Choose appropriate study materials

Now that you know the subjects to be examined and the relative amount of each subject to be covered, you can choose suitable study materials. For beginning level jobs, or even advanced ones, if you have a pronounced weakness in some aspect of your training, read a modern, standard textbook in that field. Be sure it is up to date and has general coverage. Such books are normally available at your library, and the librarian will be glad to help you locate one. For entry-level positions, questions of appropriate difficulty are chosen – neither highly advanced questions, nor those too simple. Such questions require careful thought but not advanced training.

If the position for which you are applying is technical or advanced, you will read more advanced, specialized material. If you are already familiar with the basic principles of your field, elementary textbooks would waste your time. Concentrate on advanced textbooks and technical periodicals. Think through the concepts and review difficult problems in your field.

These are all general sources. You can get more ideas on your own initiative, following these leads. For example, training manuals and publications of the government agency which employs workers in your field can be useful, particularly for technical and professional positions. A letter or visit to the government department involved may result in more specific study suggestions, and certainly will provide you with a more definite idea of the exact nature of the position you are seeking.

III. KINDS OF TESTS

Tests are used for purposes other than measuring knowledge and ability to perform specified duties. For some positions, it is equally important to test ability to make adjustments to new situations or to profit from training. In others, basic mental abilities not dependent on information are essential. Questions which test these things may not appear as pertinent to the duties of the position as those which test for knowledge and information. Yet they are often highly important parts of a fair examination. For very general questions, it is almost impossible to help you direct your study efforts. What we can do is to point out some of the more common of these general abilities needed in public service positions and describe some typical questions.

1) General information

Broad, general information has been found useful for predicting job success in some kinds of work. This is tested in a variety of ways, from vocabulary lists to questions about current events. Basic background in some field of work, such as sociology or economics, may be sampled in a group of questions. Often these are principles which have become familiar to most persons through exposure rather than through formal training. It is difficult to advise you how to study for these questions; being alert to the world around you is our best suggestion.

2) Verbal ability

An example of an ability needed in many positions is verbal or language ability. Verbal ability is, in brief, the ability to use and understand words. Vocabulary and grammar tests are typical measures of this ability. Reading comprehension or paragraph interpretation questions are common in many kinds of civil service tests. You are given a paragraph of written material and asked to find its central meaning.

3) Numerical ability

Number skills can be tested by the familiar arithmetic problem, by checking paired lists of numbers to see which are alike and which are different, or by interpreting charts and graphs. In the latter test, a graph may be printed in the test booklet which you are asked to use as the basis for answering questions.

4) Observation

A popular test for law-enforcement positions is the observation test. A picture is shown to you for several minutes, then taken away. Questions about the picture test your ability to observe both details and larger elements.

5) Following directions

In many positions in the public service, the employee must be able to carry out written instructions dependably and accurately. You may be given a chart with several columns, each column listing a variety of information. The questions require you to carry out directions involving the information given in the chart.

6) Skills and aptitudes

Performance tests effectively measure some manual skills and aptitudes. When the skill is one in which you are trained, such as typing or shorthand, you can practice. These tests are often very much like those given in business school or high school courses. For many of the other skills and aptitudes, however, no short-time preparation can be made. Skills and abilities natural to you or that you have developed throughout your lifetime are being tested.

Many of the general questions just described provide all the data needed to answer the questions and ask you to use your reasoning ability to find the answers. Your best preparation for these tests, as well as for tests of facts and ideas, is to be at your physical and mental best. You, no doubt, have your own methods of getting into an exam-taking mood and keeping "in shape." The next section lists some ideas on this subject.

IV. KINDS OF QUESTIONS

Only rarely is the "essay" question, which you answer in narrative form, used in civil service tests. Civil service tests are usually of the short-answer type. Full instructions for answering these questions will be given to you at the examination. But in case this is your first experience with short-answer questions and separate answer sheets, here is what you need to know:

1) Multiple-choice Questions

Most popular of the short-answer questions is the "multiple choice" or "best answer" question. It can be used, for example, to test for factual knowledge, ability to solve problems or judgment in meeting situations found at work.

A multiple-choice question is normally one of three types—
- It can begin with an incomplete statement followed by several possible endings. You are to find the one ending which *best* completes the statement, although some of the others may not be entirely wrong.
- It can also be a complete statement in the form of a question which is answered by choosing one of the statements listed.

- It can be in the form of a problem – again you select the best answer.

Here is an example of a multiple-choice question with a discussion which should give you some clues as to the method for choosing the right answer:

When an employee has a complaint about his assignment, the action which will *best* help him overcome his difficulty is to
    A. discuss his difficulty with his coworkers
    B. take the problem to the head of the organization
    C. take the problem to the person who gave him the assignment
    D. say nothing to anyone about his complaint

In answering this question, you should study each of the choices to find which is best. Consider choice "A" – Certainly an employee may discuss his complaint with fellow employees, but no change or improvement can result, and the complaint remains unresolved. Choice "B" is a poor choice since the head of the organization probably does not know what assignment you have been given, and taking your problem to him is known as "going over the head" of the supervisor. The supervisor, or person who made the assignment, is the person who can clarify it or correct any injustice. Choice "C" is, therefore, correct. To say nothing, as in choice "D," is unwise. Supervisors have and interest in knowing the problems employees are facing, and the employee is seeking a solution to his problem.

2) True/False Questions

The "true/false" or "right/wrong" form of question is sometimes used. Here a complete statement is given. Your job is to decide whether the statement is right or wrong.

SAMPLE: A roaming cell-phone call to a nearby city costs less than a non-roaming call to a distant city.

This statement is wrong, or false, since roaming calls are more expensive.

This is not a complete list of all possible question forms, although most of the others are variations of these common types. You will always get complete directions for answering questions. Be sure you understand *how* to mark your answers – ask questions until you do.

V. RECORDING YOUR ANSWERS

Computer terminals are used more and more today for many different kinds of exams.

For an examination with very few applicants, you may be told to record your answers in the test booklet itself. Separate answer sheets are much more common. If this separate answer sheet is to be scored by machine – and this is often the case – it is highly important that you mark your answers correctly in order to get credit.

An electronic scoring machine is often used in civil service offices because of the speed with which papers can be scored. Machine-scored answer sheets must be marked with a pencil, which will be given to you. This pencil has a high graphite content which responds to the electronic scoring machine. As a matter of fact, stray dots may register as answers, so do not let your pencil rest on the answer sheet while you are pondering the correct answer. Also, if your pencil lead breaks or is otherwise defective, ask for another.

Since the answer sheet will be dropped in a slot in the scoring machine, be careful not to bend the corners or get the paper crumpled.

The answer sheet normally has five vertical columns of numbers, with 30 numbers to a column. These numbers correspond to the question numbers in your test booklet. After each number, going across the page are four or five pairs of dotted lines. These short dotted lines have small letters or numbers above them. The first two pairs may also have a "T" or "F" above the letters. This indicates that the first two pairs only are to be used if the questions are of the true-false type. If the questions are multiple choice, disregard the "T" and "F" and pay attention only to the small letters or numbers.

Answer your questions in the manner of the sample that follows:

32. The largest city in the United States is
    A. Washington, D.C.
    B. New York City
    C. Chicago
    D. Detroit
    E. San Francisco

1) Choose the answer you think is best. (New York City is the largest, so "B" is correct.)
2) Find the row of dotted lines numbered the same as the question you are answering. (Find row number 32)
3) Find the pair of dotted lines corresponding to the answer. (Find the pair of lines under the mark "B.")
4) Make a solid black mark between the dotted lines.

VI. BEFORE THE TEST

Common sense will help you find procedures to follow to get ready for an examination. Too many of us, however, overlook these sensible measures. Indeed, nervousness and fatigue have been found to be the most serious reasons why applicants fail to do their best on civil service tests. Here is a list of reminders:

- Begin your preparation early – Don't wait until the last minute to go scurrying around for books and materials or to find out what the position is all about.
- Prepare continuously – An hour a night for a week is better than an all-night cram session. This has been definitely established. What is more, a night a week for a month will return better dividends than crowding your study into a shorter period of time.
- Locate the place of the exam – You have been sent a notice telling you when and where to report for the examination. If the location is in a different town or otherwise unfamiliar to you, it would be well to inquire the best route and learn something about the building.
- Relax the night before the test – Allow your mind to rest. Do not study at all that night. Plan some mild recreation or diversion; then go to bed early and get a good night's sleep.
- Get up early enough to make a leisurely trip to the place for the test – This way unforeseen events, traffic snarls, unfamiliar buildings, etc. will not upset you.
- Dress comfortably – A written test is not a fashion show. You will be known by number and not by name, so wear something comfortable.

- Leave excess paraphernalia at home – Shopping bags and odd bundles will get in your way. You need bring only the items mentioned in the official notice you received; usually everything you need is provided. Do not bring reference books to the exam. They will only confuse those last minutes and be taken away from you when in the test room.
- Arrive somewhat ahead of time – If because of transportation schedules you must get there very early, bring a newspaper or magazine to take your mind off yourself while waiting.
- Locate the examination room – When you have found the proper room, you will be directed to the seat or part of the room where you will sit. Sometimes you are given a sheet of instructions to read while you are waiting. Do not fill out any forms until you are told to do so; just read them and be prepared.
- Relax and prepare to listen to the instructions
- If you have any physical problem that may keep you from doing your best, be sure to tell the test administrator. If you are sick or in poor health, you really cannot do your best on the exam. You can come back and take the test some other time.

VII. AT THE TEST

The day of the test is here and you have the test booklet in your hand. The temptation to get going is very strong. Caution! There is more to success than knowing the right answers. You must know how to identify your papers and understand variations in the type of short-answer question used in this particular examination. Follow these suggestions for maximum results from your efforts:

1) Cooperate with the monitor

The test administrator has a duty to create a situation in which you can be as much at ease as possible. He will give instructions, tell you when to begin, check to see that you are marking your answer sheet correctly, and so on. He is not there to guard you, although he will see that your competitors do not take unfair advantage. He wants to help you do your best.

2) Listen to all instructions

Don't jump the gun! Wait until you understand all directions. In most civil service tests you get more time than you need to answer the questions. So don't be in a hurry. Read each word of instructions until you clearly understand the meaning. Study the examples, listen to all announcements and follow directions. Ask questions if you do not understand what to do.

3) Identify your papers

Civil service exams are usually identified by number only. You will be assigned a number; you must not put your name on your test papers. Be sure to copy your number correctly. Since more than one exam may be given, copy your exact examination title.

4) Plan your time

Unless you are told that a test is a "speed" or "rate of work" test, speed itself is usually not important. Time enough to answer all the questions will be provided, but this does not mean that you have all day. An overall time limit has been set. Divide the total time (in minutes) by the number of questions to determine the approximate time you have for each question.

5) Do not linger over difficult questions

If you come across a difficult question, mark it with a paper clip (useful to have along) and come back to it when you have been through the booklet. One caution if you do this – be sure to skip a number on your answer sheet as well. Check often to be sure that you have not lost your place and that you are marking in the row numbered the same as the question you are answering.

6) Read the questions

Be sure you know what the question asks! Many capable people are unsuccessful because they failed to *read* the questions correctly.

7) Answer all questions

Unless you have been instructed that a penalty will be deducted for incorrect answers, it is better to guess than to omit a question.

8) Speed tests

It is often better NOT to guess on speed tests. It has been found that on timed tests people are tempted to spend the last few seconds before time is called in marking answers at random – without even reading them – in the hope of picking up a few extra points. To discourage this practice, the instructions may warn you that your score will be "corrected" for guessing. That is, a penalty will be applied. The incorrect answers will be deducted from the correct ones, or some other penalty formula will be used.

9) Review your answers

If you finish before time is called, go back to the questions you guessed or omitted to give them further thought. Review other answers if you have time.

10) Return your test materials

If you are ready to leave before others have finished or time is called, take ALL your materials to the monitor and leave quietly. Never take any test material with you. The monitor can discover whose papers are not complete, and taking a test booklet may be grounds for disqualification.

VIII. EXAMINATION TECHNIQUES

1) Read the general instructions carefully. These are usually printed on the first page of the exam booklet. As a rule, these instructions refer to the timing of the examination; the fact that you should not start work until the signal and must stop work at a signal, etc. If there are any *special* instructions, such as a choice of questions to be answered, make sure that you note this instruction carefully.

2) When you are ready to start work on the examination, that is as soon as the signal has been given, read the instructions to each question booklet, underline any key words or phrases, such as *least, best, outline, describe* and the like. In this way you will tend to answer as requested rather than discover on reviewing your paper that you *listed without describing*, that you selected the *worst* choice rather than the *best* choice, etc.

3) If the examination is of the objective or multiple-choice type – that is, each question will also give a series of possible answers: A, B, C or D, and you are called upon to select the best answer and write the letter next to that answer on your answer paper – it is advisable to start answering each question in turn. There may be anywhere from 50 to 100 such questions in the three or four hours allotted and you can see how much time would be taken if you read through all the questions before beginning to answer any. Furthermore, if you come across a question or group of questions which you know would be difficult to answer, it would undoubtedly affect your handling of all the other questions.

4) If the examination is of the essay type and contains but a few questions, it is a moot point as to whether you should read all the questions before starting to answer any one. Of course, if you are given a choice – say five out of seven and the like – then it is essential to read all the questions so you can eliminate the two that are most difficult. If, however, you are asked to answer all the questions, there may be danger in trying to answer the easiest one first because you may find that you will spend too much time on it. The best technique is to answer the first question, then proceed to the second, etc.

5) Time your answers. Before the exam begins, write down the time it started, then add the time allowed for the examination and write down the time it must be completed, then divide the time available somewhat as follows:
    - If 3-1/2 hours are allowed, that would be 210 minutes. If you have 80 objective-type questions, that would be an average of 2-1/2 minutes per question. Allow yourself no more than 2 minutes per question, or a total of 160 minutes, which will permit about 50 minutes to review.
    - If for the time allotment of 210 minutes there are 7 essay questions to answer, that would average about 30 minutes a question. Give yourself only 25 minutes per question so that you have about 35 minutes to review.

6) The most important instruction is to *read each question* and make sure you know what is wanted. The second most important instruction is to *time yourself properly* so that you answer every question. The third most important instruction is to *answer every question*. Guess if you have to but include something for each question. Remember that you will receive no credit for a blank and will probably receive some credit if you write something in answer to an essay question. If you guess a letter – say "B" for a multiple-choice question – you may have guessed right. If you leave a blank as an answer to a multiple-choice question, the examiners may respect your feelings but it will not add a point to your score. Some exams may penalize you for wrong answers, so in such cases *only*, you may not want to guess unless you have some basis for your answer.

7) Suggestions
   a. Objective-type questions
      1. Examine the question booklet for proper sequence of pages and questions
      2. Read all instructions carefully
      3. Skip any question which seems too difficult; return to it after all other questions have been answered
      4. Apportion your time properly; do not spend too much time on any single question or group of questions

5. Note and underline key words – *all, most, fewest, least, best, worst, same, opposite,* etc.
6. Pay particular attention to negatives
7. Note unusual option, e.g., unduly long, short, complex, different or similar in content to the body of the question
8. Observe the use of "hedging" words – *probably, may, most likely,* etc.
9. Make sure that your answer is put next to the same number as the question
10. Do not second-guess unless you have good reason to believe the second answer is definitely more correct
11. Cross out original answer if you decide another answer is more accurate; do not erase until you are ready to hand your paper in
12. Answer all questions; guess unless instructed otherwise
13. Leave time for review

b. Essay questions
1. Read each question carefully
2. Determine exactly what is wanted. Underline key words or phrases.
3. Decide on outline or paragraph answer
4. Include many different points and elements unless asked to develop any one or two points or elements
5. Show impartiality by giving pros and cons unless directed to select one side only
6. Make and write down any assumptions you find necessary to answer the questions
7. Watch your English, grammar, punctuation and choice of words
8. Time your answers; don't crowd material

8) Answering the essay question

Most essay questions can be answered by framing the specific response around several key words or ideas. Here are a few such key words or ideas:

M's: manpower, materials, methods, money, management
P's: purpose, program, policy, plan, procedure, practice, problems, pitfalls, personnel, public relations

a. Six basic steps in handling problems:
1. Preliminary plan and background development
2. Collect information, data and facts
3. Analyze and interpret information, data and facts
4. Analyze and develop solutions as well as make recommendations
5. Prepare report and sell recommendations
6. Install recommendations and follow up effectiveness

b. Pitfalls to avoid
1. *Taking things for granted* – A statement of the situation does not necessarily imply that each of the elements is necessarily true; for example, a complaint may be invalid and biased so that all that can be taken for granted is that a complaint has been registered

2. *Considering only one side of a situation* – Wherever possible, indicate several alternatives and then point out the reasons you selected the best one
3. *Failing to indicate follow up* – Whenever your answer indicates action on your part, make certain that you will take proper follow-up action to see how successful your recommendations, procedures or actions turn out to be
4. *Taking too long in answering any single question* – Remember to time your answers properly

IX. AFTER THE TEST

Scoring procedures differ in detail among civil service jurisdictions although the general principles are the same. Whether the papers are hand-scored or graded by machine we have described, they are nearly always graded by number. That is, the person who marks the paper knows only the number – never the name – of the applicant. Not until all the papers have been graded will they be matched with names. If other tests, such as training and experience or oral interview ratings have been given, scores will be combined. Different parts of the examination usually have different weights. For example, the written test might count 60 percent of the final grade, and a rating of training and experience 40 percent. In many jurisdictions, veterans will have a certain number of points added to their grades.

After the final grade has been determined, the names are placed in grade order and an eligible list is established. There are various methods for resolving ties between those who get the same final grade – probably the most common is to place first the name of the person whose application was received first. Job offers are made from the eligible list in the order the names appear on it. You will be notified of your grade and your rank as soon as all these computations have been made. This will be done as rapidly as possible.

People who are found to meet the requirements in the announcement are called "eligibles." Their names are put on a list of eligible candidates. An eligible's chances of getting a job depend on how high he stands on this list and how fast agencies are filling jobs from the list.

When a job is to be filled from a list of eligibles, the agency asks for the names of people on the list of eligibles for that job. When the civil service commission receives this request, it sends to the agency the names of the three people highest on this list. Or, if the job to be filled has specialized requirements, the office sends the agency the names of the top three persons who meet these requirements from the general list.

The appointing officer makes a choice from among the three people whose names were sent to him. If the selected person accepts the appointment, the names of the others are put back on the list to be considered for future openings.

That is the rule in hiring from all kinds of eligible lists, whether they are for typist, carpenter, chemist, or something else. For every vacancy, the appointing officer has his choice of any one of the top three eligibles on the list. This explains why the person whose name is on top of the list sometimes does not get an appointment when some of the persons lower on the list do. If the appointing officer chooses the second or third eligible, the No. 1 eligible does not get a job at once, but stays on the list until he is appointed or the list is terminated.

X. HOW TO PASS THE INTERVIEW TEST

The examination for which you applied requires an oral interview test. You have already taken the written test and you are now being called for the interview test – the final part of the formal examination.

You may think that it is not possible to prepare for an interview test and that there are no procedures to follow during an interview. Our purpose is to point out some things you can do in advance that will help you and some good rules to follow and pitfalls to avoid while you are being interviewed.

What is an interview supposed to test?

The written examination is designed to test the technical knowledge and competence of the candidate; the oral is designed to evaluate intangible qualities, not readily measured otherwise, and to establish a list showing the relative fitness of each candidate – as measured against his competitors – for the position sought. Scoring is not on the basis of "right" and "wrong," but on a sliding scale of values ranging from "not passable" to "outstanding." As a matter of fact, it is possible to achieve a relatively low score without a single "incorrect" answer because of evident weakness in the qualities being measured.

Occasionally, an examination may consist entirely of an oral test – either an individual or a group oral. In such cases, information is sought concerning the technical knowledges and abilities of the candidate, since there has been no written examination for this purpose. More commonly, however, an oral test is used to supplement a written examination.

Who conducts interviews?

The composition of oral boards varies among different jurisdictions. In nearly all, a representative of the personnel department serves as chairman. One of the members of the board may be a representative of the department in which the candidate would work. In some cases, "outside experts" are used, and, frequently, a businessman or some other representative of the general public is asked to serve. Labor and management or other special groups may be represented. The aim is to secure the services of experts in the appropriate field.

However the board is composed, it is a good idea (and not at all improper or unethical) to ascertain in advance of the interview who the members are and what groups they represent. When you are introduced to them, you will have some idea of their backgrounds and interests, and at least you will not stutter and stammer over their names.

What should be done before the interview?

While knowledge about the board members is useful and takes some of the surprise element out of the interview, there is other preparation which is more substantive. It *is* possible to prepare for an oral interview – in several ways:

1) Keep a copy of your application and review it carefully before the interview

This may be the only document before the oral board, and the starting point of the interview. Know what education and experience you have listed there, and the sequence and dates of all of it. Sometimes the board will ask you to review the highlights of your experience for them; you should not have to hem and haw doing it.

2) Study the class specification and the examination announcement

Usually, the oral board has one or both of these to guide them. The qualities, characteristics or knowledges required by the position sought are stated in these documents. They offer valuable clues as to the nature of the oral interview. For example, if the job involves supervisory responsibilities, the announcement will usually indicate that knowledge of modern supervisory methods and the qualifications of the candidate as a supervisor will be tested. If so, you can expect such questions, frequently in the form of a hypothetical situation which you are expected to solve. NEVER go into an oral without knowledge of the duties and responsibilities of the job you seek.

3) Think through each qualification required

Try to visualize the kind of questions you would ask if you were a board member. How well could you answer them? Try especially to appraise your own knowledge and background in each area, *measured against the job sought*, and identify any areas in which you are weak. Be critical and realistic – do not flatter yourself.

4) Do some general reading in areas in which you feel you may be weak

For example, if the job involves supervision and your past experience has NOT, some general reading in supervisory methods and practices, particularly in the field of human relations, might be useful. Do NOT study agency procedures or detailed manuals. The oral board will be testing your understanding and capacity, not your memory.

5) Get a good night's sleep and watch your general health and mental attitude

You will want a clear head at the interview. Take care of a cold or any other minor ailment, and of course, no hangovers.

What should be done on the day of the interview?

Now comes the day of the interview itself. Give yourself plenty of time to get there. Plan to arrive somewhat ahead of the scheduled time, particularly if your appointment is in the fore part of the day. If a previous candidate fails to appear, the board might be ready for you a bit early. By early afternoon an oral board is almost invariably behind schedule if there are many candidates, and you may have to wait. Take along a book or magazine to read, or your application to review, but leave any extraneous material in the waiting room when you go in for your interview. In any event, relax and compose yourself.

The matter of dress is important. The board is forming impressions about you – from your experience, your manners, your attitude, and your appearance. Give your personal appearance careful attention. Dress your best, but not your flashiest. Choose conservative, appropriate clothing, and be sure it is immaculate. This is a business interview, and your appearance should indicate that you regard it as such. Besides, being well groomed and properly dressed will help boost your confidence.

Sooner or later, someone will call your name and escort you into the interview room. *This is it.* From here on you are on your own. It is too late for any more preparation. But remember, you asked for this opportunity to prove your fitness, and you are here because your request was granted.

What happens when you go in?

The usual sequence of events will be as follows: The clerk (who is often the board stenographer) will introduce you to the chairman of the oral board, who will introduce you to the other members of the board. Acknowledge the introductions before you sit down. Do not be surprised if you find a microphone facing you or a stenotypist sitting by. Oral interviews are usually recorded in the event of an appeal or other review.

Usually the chairman of the board will open the interview by reviewing the highlights of your education and work experience from your application – primarily for the benefit of the other members of the board, as well as to get the material into the record. Do not interrupt or comment unless there is an error or significant misinterpretation; if that is the case, do not hesitate. But do not quibble about insignificant matters. Also, he will usually ask you some question about your education, experience or your present job – partly to get you to start talking and to establish the interviewing "rapport." He may start the actual questioning, or turn it over to one of the other members. Frequently, each member undertakes the questioning on a particular area, one in which he is perhaps most competent, so you can expect each member to participate in the examination. Because time is limited, you may also expect some rather abrupt switches in the direction the questioning takes, so do not be upset by it. Normally, a board member will not pursue a single line of questioning unless he discovers a particular strength or weakness.

After each member has participated, the chairman will usually ask whether any member has any further questions, then will ask you if you have anything you wish to add. Unless you are expecting this question, it may floor you. Worse, it may start you off on an extended, extemporaneous speech. The board is not usually seeking more information. The question is principally to offer you a last opportunity to present further qualifications or to indicate that you have nothing to add. So, if you feel that a significant qualification or characteristic has been overlooked, it is proper to point it out in a sentence or so. Do not compliment the board on the thoroughness of their examination – they have been sketchy, and you know it. If you wish, merely say, "No thank you, I have nothing further to add." This is a point where you can "talk yourself out" of a good impression or fail to present an important bit of information. Remember, *you close the interview yourself.*

The chairman will then say, "That is all, Mr. _____, thank you." Do not be startled; the interview is over, and quicker than you think. Thank him, gather your belongings and take your leave. Save your sigh of relief for the other side of the door.

How to put your best foot forward

Throughout this entire process, you may feel that the board individually and collectively is trying to pierce your defenses, seek out your hidden weaknesses and embarrass and confuse you. Actually, this is not true. They are obliged to make an appraisal of your qualifications for the job you are seeking, and they want to see you in your best light. Remember, they must interview all candidates and a non-cooperative candidate may become a failure in spite of their best efforts to bring out his qualifications. Here are 15 suggestions that will help you:

1) Be natural – Keep your attitude confident, not cocky

If you are not confident that you can do the job, do not expect the board to be. Do not apologize for your weaknesses, try to bring out your strong points. The board is interested in a positive, not negative, presentation. Cockiness will antagonize any board member and make him wonder if you are covering up a weakness by a false show of strength.

2) Get comfortable, but don't lounge or sprawl

Sit erectly but not stiffly. A careless posture may lead the board to conclude that you are careless in other things, or at least that you are not impressed by the importance of the occasion. Either conclusion is natural, even if incorrect. Do not fuss with your clothing, a pencil or an ashtray. Your hands may occasionally be useful to emphasize a point; do not let them become a point of distraction.

3) Do not wisecrack or make small talk

This is a serious situation, and your attitude should show that you consider it as such. Further, the time of the board is limited – they do not want to waste it, and neither should you.

4) Do not exaggerate your experience or abilities

In the first place, from information in the application or other interviews and sources, the board may know more about you than you think. Secondly, you probably will not get away with it. An experienced board is rather adept at spotting such a situation, so do not take the chance.

5) If you know a board member, do not make a point of it, yet do not hide it

Certainly you are not fooling him, and probably not the other members of the board. Do not try to take advantage of your acquaintanceship – it will probably do you little good.

6) Do not dominate the interview

Let the board do that. They will give you the clues – do not assume that you have to do all the talking. Realize that the board has a number of questions to ask you, and do not try to take up all the interview time by showing off your extensive knowledge of the answer to the first one.

7) Be attentive

You only have 20 minutes or so, and you should keep your attention at its sharpest throughout. When a member is addressing a problem or question to you, give him your undivided attention. Address your reply principally to him, but do not exclude the other board members.

8) Do not interrupt

A board member may be stating a problem for you to analyze. He will ask you a question when the time comes. Let him state the problem, and wait for the question.

9) Make sure you understand the question

Do not try to answer until you are sure what the question is. If it is not clear, restate it in your own words or ask the board member to clarify it for you. However, do not haggle about minor elements.

10) Reply promptly but not hastily

A common entry on oral board rating sheets is "candidate responded readily," or "candidate hesitated in replies." Respond as promptly and quickly as you can, but do not jump to a hasty, ill-considered answer.

11) Do not be peremptory in your answers

A brief answer is proper – but do not fire your answer back. That is a losing game from your point of view. The board member can probably ask questions much faster than you can answer them.

12) Do not try to create the answer you think the board member wants

He is interested in what kind of mind you have and how it works – not in playing games. Furthermore, he can usually spot this practice and will actually grade you down on it.

13) Do not switch sides in your reply merely to agree with a board member

Frequently, a member will take a contrary position merely to draw you out and to see if you are willing and able to defend your point of view. Do not start a debate, yet do not surrender a good position. If a position is worth taking, it is worth defending.

14) Do not be afraid to admit an error in judgment if you are shown to be wrong

The board knows that you are forced to reply without any opportunity for careful consideration. Your answer may be demonstrably wrong. If so, admit it and get on with the interview.

15) Do not dwell at length on your present job

The opening question may relate to your present assignment. Answer the question but do not go into an extended discussion. You are being examined for a *new* job, not your present one. As a matter of fact, try to phrase ALL your answers in terms of the job for which you are being examined.

Basis of Rating

Probably you will forget most of these "do's" and "don'ts" when you walk into the oral interview room. Even remembering them all will not ensure you a passing grade. Perhaps you did not have the qualifications in the first place. But remembering them will help you to put your best foot forward, without treading on the toes of the board members.

Rumor and popular opinion to the contrary notwithstanding, an oral board wants you to make the best appearance possible. They know you are under pressure – but they also want to see how you respond to it as a guide to what your reaction would be under the pressures of the job you seek. They will be influenced by the degree of poise you display, the personal traits you show and the manner in which you respond.

ABOUT THIS BOOK

This book contains tests divided into Examination Sections. Go through each test, answering every question in the margin. We have also attached a sample answer sheet at the back of the book that can be removed and used. At the end of each test look at the answer key and check your answers. On the ones you got wrong, look at the right answer choice and learn. Do not fill in the answers first. Do not memorize the questions and answers, but understand the answer and principles involved. On your test, the questions will likely be different from the samples. Questions are changed and new ones added. If you understand these past questions you should have success with any changes that arise. Tests may consist of several types of questions. We have additional books on each subject should more study be advisable or necessary for you. Finally, the more you study, the better prepared you will be. This book is intended to be the last thing you study before you walk into the examination room. Prior study of relevant texts is also recommended. NLC publishes some of these in our Fundamental Series. Knowledge and good sense are important factors in passing your exam. Good luck also helps. So now study this Passbook, absorb the material contained within and take that knowledge into the examination. Then do your best to pass that exam.

EXAMINATION SECTION

EXAMINATION SECTION
TEST 1

DIRECTIONS: Each question or incomplete statement is followed by several suggested answers or completions. Select the one that BEST answers the question or completes the statement. *PRINT THE LETTER OF THE CORRECT ANSWER IN THE SPACE AT THE RIGHT.*

1. Pick-up and delivery points in suburban districts should include the following EXCEPT: 1____

   A. Corner pick-ups at traffic-controlled locations should be discouraged
   B. Young passengers should cross streets at locations where protection is a community responsibility
   C. There should be minimum interference with traffic on arterial or collector streets
   D. Area discharge points away from the heavy traffic should be designated
   E. Personalized bus stops should not be permitted

2. The success of safety programs depends on involvement beginning at the _____ level. 2____

   A. county   B. state   C. district
   D. individual   E. national

3. Fleet accidents and costs are MOST affected by 3____

   A. bus selection and equipment
   B. operating maintenance policies
   C. driver attitude
   D. bus routes and fleet utilization
   E. the fleets public image

4. Which of the following is the LEAST important consideration concerning the hiring of low I.Q. drivers? 4____

   A. Lack of accurate judgment in emergency situations
   B. Difficulty in concentrating while driving a vehicle
   C. Make poor witnesses in cases of accident
   D. Difficult to supervise
   E. Difficulty taking decisive action

5. How does the supervisor evaluate the trainees' progress? By 5____

   A. *evaluating* written test scores
   B. *observing* attitudes and safety awareness
   C. *observing* driver performance over a prescribed course
   D. *observing* driver's performance while transporting pupils
   E. *evaluating* the results of driving simulation tests

6. What type of driver testing is needed to enable the supervisor to help each driver develop the compensating habits needed to drive safely? _____ test. 6____

   A. Reaction time   B. Distance judgment
   C. Visual   D. Tunnel vision
   E. Glare recovery

7. *Protection Routes* do NOT usually consider 7____

    A. traffic volume on available alternate routes
    B. railroad crossings
    C. distance to be traveled
    D. sharp curves
    E. narrow pavements

8. Policy statements from the local school board should define all the following EXCEPT: 8____

    A. Minimum requirements for driver selection and training
    B. The extent of school bus service
    C. Factual basis for establishing transportation policies
    D. Equipment replacement schedule
    E. Provisions for extracurricular transportation

9. Driver selection, training, and motivation MUST be designed to 9____

    A. get and keep uniform standards of vehicle operation
    B. transport and supervise students
    C. the principles of defensive driving
    D. prevent accidents
    E. develop responsibility

10. What is the MOST important quality for a school bus driver? 10____

    A. Physical fitness   B. Congenial personality
    C. High intelligence   D. Neat appearance
    E. Emotional maturity

11. Drivers who complete an initial training course usually do NOT know 11____

    A. the laws and regulations applicable to school bus fleet operation
    B. how to administer first aid
    C. the flexibility of schedules
    D. how to deal with students who disobey rules
    E. how to operate a fire extinguisher

12. Which of the following motivational methods and techniques are recommended for use by supervisors? 12____

    A. Terminate the employ of any driver involved in a preventable accident
    B. Hold driver responsible for cleanliness of bus
    C. Do not publicly single out individuals for merit
    D. Do not inform drivers of the high degree of skill required before qualifying to drive in the fleet
    E. Defuse any developing spirit of competitiveness

13. Remedial training is PRIMARILY intended to instruct 13____

    A. operation of new equipment
    B. changes in policies, laws, and regulations
    C. problem drivers
    D. older drivers
    E. new drivers with previous driving experience

14. Glare recovery is an important test for anyone who drives when 14____

    A. there is strong sunlight
    B. the roads are snow-covered
    C. headlights must be used
    D. the roads are slick with rain
    E. routes involve tunnels

15. When does driver instruction begin? With the 15____

    A. first training class
    B. introduction to the vehicle
    C. orientation session
    D. first road test
    E. first contact with the supervisor

16. Which of the following factors MOST contributes to triggering accidents? 16____

    A. Weather conditions
    B. Road conditions
    C. Condition of vehicle
    D. Driving errors
    E. Student behavior

17. School bus drivers may continue to drive if they have suffered the loss of 17____

    A. a finger
    B. a hand
    C. a foot
    D. all of the above
    E. none of the above

18. Which of the following would NOT bar a person from driving a school bus? 18____

    A. Impaired use of foot or leg
    B. Any disease likely to interfere with safe driving
    C. Use of alcohol beverages
    D. Impaired use of arm or hand
    E. Addiction of habit-forming drugs

19. What factor determines the safety and efficiency of the school transportation program? 19____

    A. The vehicle
    B. The driver
    C. The maintenance of the vehicle
    D. All of the above
    E. None of the above

20. Violations of traffic laws CANNOT be condoned because they 20____

    A. cause loss of respect by motorists for school vehicles
    B. may result in reduced use of public streets
    C. may expose pupils to serious hazards
    D. increase the cost of school transportation
    E. reflect badly on the school system

21. What state department is MOST directly responsible for student transportation? 21____

    A. Transportation
    B. Motor vehicles
    C. Public welfare
    D. Public safety
    E. Education

22. What is the MOST important consideration to be included in the specifications for new vehicle purchases? 22___

    A. Ages of pupils to be transported
    B. Type of terrain in which vehicle will be used
    C. The pattern of transit operation
    D. The fleets1 safety performance
    E. The activities for which the vehicle will be used

23. What MOST motivates drivers to perform safely? 23___

    A. Recognition and appreciation by the school district
    B. Attendance at safety seminars
    C. Policy of rapid dismissal of unsafe drivers
    D. Proper pupil behavior
    E. The operating condition of the vehicle

24. All of the following are responsibilities of the school superintendent EXCEPT: 24___

    A. Show interest in good accident control program
    B. Outline responsibilities of all participants in the transportation system
    C. Provide specific guidelines for driver recruitment and training
    D. Establish standards for bus maintenance
    E. Involve schools and parents in transportation safety program

25. Which of the following is NOT an indication of substandard driver performance? 25___

    A. Inadequate maintenance
    B. Errors in the performance of work
    C. Changes in everyday behavior and manners
    D. Near accidents
    E. Changes in simple habits of a routine nature

KEY (CORRECT ANSWERS)

1. A
2. B
3. B
4. B
5. C

6. D
7. C
8. C
9. D
10. E

11. A
12. B
13. C
14. C
15. E

16. D
17. A
18. C
19. D
20. C

21. E
22. B
23. A
24. D
25. A

———

TEST 2

DIRECTIONS: Each question or incomplete statement is followed by several suggested answers or completions. Select the one that BEST answers the question or completes the statement. *PRINT THE LETTER OF THE CORRECT ANSWER IN THE SPACE AT THE RIGHT.*

1. Who should be responsible for driver selection? 1____

    A. District superintendent
    B. Transportation supervisor
    C. School office of personnel
    D. School board
    E. Contractor

2. Which of the following is LEAST important regarding the school bus driver? 2____
    Driver

    A. finds satisfaction in job
    B. gets along well with others
    C. is courteous to pedestrians and motorists
    D. is highly intelligent
    E. has neat appearance

3. What is the MOST important ingredient in an efficient school transportation service? 3____

    A. Safe driving
    B. Control of students
    C. Safe bus routes
    D. Vehicle maintenance
    E. Compliance with traffic regulations

4. The amount of time needed for initial training depends on the 4____

    A. person employed   B. selection program
    C. person's experience   D. all of the above
    E. none of the above

5. What is the purpose of refresher training? To 5____

    A. develop an appreciation of the importance of the job
    B. keep performance efficient and safe
    C. prevent accidents
    D. solves problems
    E. evaluate physical fitness of older drivers

6. What is the key to the success of a safety program? 6____

    A. Driver selection   B. Supervision
    C. Maintenance   D. Money
    E. Driver motivation

7. What instruction technique is MOST useful for remedial training? 7____

    A. Individual reading material
    B. Classroom lecture

C. Road instruction
D. Videotape
E. Group discussion

8. What is the emphasis of reaction time testing? The

   A. importance of keeping an adequate distance between moving vehicles
   B. time needed to react to an emergency situation or condition
   C. ability to evaluate distance
   D. ability to estimate the speed of approaching vehicles
   E. development of compensating habits

9. Eighty percent of the total number of accidents annually involve

   A. single cars
   B. car/truck collisions
   C. two cars
   D. multiple cars
   E. multiple trucks

10. All of the following are proper backing procedures EXCEPT:

    A. get out of bus before beginning to back
    B. backing from the passenger's side
    C. using a reliable person for guidance
    D. check both sides continually while backing
    E. backing slowly

11. Minimum visual acuity in both eyes with or without glasses should NOT be less than (Snellen)

    A. 15/20   B. 20/20   C. 20/40   D. 20/60   E. 20/200

12. Which of the following is NOT a disqualifying condition for school bus drivers?

    A. Diabetes
    B. Cardiovascular disease
    C. Hernia
    D. Pregnancy
    E. Back injury

13. What MOST determines the size requirement of the driver?

    A. Type of students to be transported
    B. Federal regulations
    C. Configuration of the driver's compartment
    D. Height of bus
    E. Type of bus

14. The catalyst to the safety and efficiency of the school bus transportation program is the

    A. local school board
    B. driver
    C. student
    D. district supervisor
    E. safety supervisor

15. In order to prepare specifications for bus purchases, what should the safety supervisor know?

    A. Knowledge of bus routes
    B. Knowledge of students to be transported

C. Knowledge of environmental conditions
D. Knowledge of operational conditions
E. All of the above

16. Which of the following necessitates the planning of *Protection Routes?*

    A. Scattered pick-up locations
    B. Inclement weather conditions
    C. Transportation of students outside the community
    D. Unexpected traffic delays
    E. Transportation of special education students

17. What qualification would MOST recommend a pupil to the position of bus monitor?

    A. Height and weight
    B. Intelligence
    C. Maturity
    D. Lives near start of bus line
    E. Lives near end of bus line

18. What is the MOST important criteria in adopting management for the special education student?

    A. Selecting the proper driver
    B. Behavior modification
    C. Providing personalized service
    D. Planning for each student's needs prior to placement
    E. Providing comfortable transportation

19. All activity trips should require the presence of

    A. adult chaperone   B. teacher
    C. school official   D. parent
    E. all of the above

20. Under what conditions may loose luggage or equipment be transported in the passenger compartment of an activity bus?

    A. When there is no danger of causing injury
    B. When it does not block passageways
    C. When the destination is a league sporting event
    D. When it can be safely secured
    E. None of the above

21. Which of the following items should be carried on the bus at all times?

    A. Instant camera for scene report
    B. Cards for witness signatures
    C. Portable, tape recorder for witness testimony
    D. Radio to summon help
    E. All of the above

22. An operational plan to provide two-way communication with parents is imperative in the event of   22____

    A. sudden disability of driver
    B. road failure
    C. strikes by school staff or drivers
    D. accident
    E. civil defense drill

23. When are standees permitted while the bus is in motion?   23____

    A. When written permission is obtained
    B. During special activity trips
    C. When safety straps are provided
    D. All of the above
    E. None of the above

24. Statistics show that automobile accidents occur MOST frequently   24____

    A. in the morning rush hours   B. around noon
    C. soon after sunset   D. near midnight
    E. just before sunrise

25. A bus driver is liable under the law to receive a traffic ticket for   25____

    A. double standing when a bus stop is occupied by a car
    B. not taking on all people waiting at a stop
    C. passing a preceding bus on a grade
    D. discharging a passenger at other than a bus stop
    E. none of the above

KEY (CORRECT ANSWERS)

1. B
2. D
3. A
4. D
5. B

6. E
7. E
8. A
9. C
10. B

11. C
12. D
13. C
14. E
15. E

16. C
17. C
18. D
19. A
20. E

21. B
22. D
23. E
24. C
25. D

———

TEST 3

DIRECTIONS: Each question or incomplete statement is followed by several suggested answers or completions. Select the one that BEST answers the question or completes the statement. *PRINT THE LETTER OF THE CORRECT ANSWER IN THE SPACE AT THE RIGHT.*

1. A transportation director who rides the school bus is NOT required to observe 1_____

    A. the conditions at the school's loading and unloading areas
    B. operation of vehicle in accordance with prescribed regulations
    C. accuracy of driver!s route and schedule
    D. driver-student ratio
    E. driver attitude toward other motorists and pedestrians

2. Which of the following would be proper procedure for conducting an emergency drill? 2_____

    A. Student may exit with lunchboxes and books.
    B. The driver should assist the students out of the bus.
    C. Drills should be held on the actual bus route.
    D. Drills should be held more often in the spring and fall.
    E. Students who ride buses on special trips may be excluded.

3. What is the goal in planning the parking of buses at the school loading zone? To 3_____

    A. accommodate the maximum number of buses
    B. exclude the necessity for backing up the buses
    C. inhibit the regular flow of traffic within the school site
    D. achieve the closest proximity to the school building
    E. accommodate student pick-up by parents

4. No portion of the bus may be driven onto railroad tracks if the view in either direction is obstructed for _____ feet. 4_____

    A. 250   B. 100   C. 2000   D. 500   E. 1000

5. A fleet's safety performance should measure the number of accidents per 5_____

    A. vehicle within a year
    B. vehicle mile within a year
    C. vehicle within a month
    D. length route and students carried
    E. vehicle mile within a month

6. Bus drills used to teach students about emergency evacuation procedures should have everyone exit through the 6_____

    A. front entrance door
    B. rear emergency door
    C. emergency window
    D. front entrance door or rear emergency door
    E. rear emergency door or emergency window

7. What sign or signal may be activated from the bus while it is stopped for a railroad crossing?

   A. Stop signal arm
   B. White flashing strobe light
   C. Yellow signal lamps
   D. Red signal lamps
   E. Turn signal lights

8. The driver must evacuate the bus if in normal traffic conditions the bus is not visible for a MINIMUM distance of _____ feet.

   A. 1000   B. 50   C. 300   D. 100   E. 500

9. What is the MINIMUM radius on the inner edge of pavement on all road curves within the school site? _____ feet.

   A. 50   B. 100   C. 60   D. 80   E. 90

10. All of the following are recommended EXCEPT:

    A. Roads should completely encircle a school
    B. Curbing should be constructed on all roads
    C. Eliminate all crossroads in front of buses
    D. A maximum standard of 5% grade is allowed on all roads
    E. Traffic control devices should be provided at all exits

11. Under what condition may a driver NOT proceed across railroad tracks unless authorized by a law enforcement officer or flagman?

    A. Tracks at which there is in operation any flashing red lights and/or bell
    B. During wet, stormy, or foggy weather
    C. Tracks controlled by crossing gate or barrier
    D. Tracks at which there is a railroad grade crossing
    E. Tracks not controlled by traffic signals

12. What is the SAFEST way to proceed if a bus stops near a precipice where it could still move and go over the cliff?

    A. Instruct students to remain in seats
    B. Redistribute carrying weight of students to area of greatest stability
    C. Driver should exit and stabilize bus with emergency equipment
    D. Instruct students to assume *crash* position
    E. Evacuate bus

13. Which of the following would NOT necessitate the evacuation of a school bus?

    A. Danger of fire
    B. Behavior control
    C. Unsafe position
    D. All of the above
    E. None of the above

14. How far from the bus should students go during an emergency drill? _____ feet.

    A. 100   B. 300   C. 25   D. 50   E. 200

15. Bus canopies have been found to be advantageous in

    A. schools with handicapped students
    B. elementary schools

C. schools with large enrollments
D. schools with small enrollments
E. schools located in cold climates

16. How far from rails nearest the front of the bus must the driver come to a complete stop? _____ feet.

    A. 25 B. 15 C. 50 D. 35 E. 60

17. Which of the following factors pertaining to school bus evacuation must be considered FIRST?

    A. Safety of students
    B. Stability of vehicle
    C. Leadership capacity of driver
    D. Communication of emergency situation to proper authority
    E. Maturity of students

18. What is the SAFEST way to park buses for loading and unloading?

    A. Perpendicular to curb, front end facing
    B. Perpendicular to curb, rear end facing
    C. Diagonal to curb, front end facing
    D. Diagonal to curb, rear end facing
    E. Bumper to bumper, alongside curb

19. Diagonal parking requires a MINIMUM width of paved surface of _____ feet.

    A. 50 B. 60 C. 30 D. 100 E. 40

20. When the bus driver is incapacitated, it is NOT necessary for the appointed student monitor to know how to

    A. turn off ignition switch
    B. set emergency brake
    C. use the fire ax
    D. set flags and flares
    E. put transmission in gear

21. If it is necessary to load or unload students on the main thoroughfare in front of the school, a paved road should be provided at least _____ feet wide.

    A. 36 B. 24 C. 48 D. 60 E. 40

22. What MINIMUM tangent section should be provided between reverse curves? _____ feet.

    A. 60 B. 50 C. 30 D. 40 E. 75

23. During an evacuation drill, the

    A. ignition should be left off
    B. transmission should be in neutral position
    C. front entrance door should be blocked
    D. emergency doors' folding stirrup step should be used
    E. all of the above

24. What is the MAXIMUM standard of grade allowed for roads on school sites? 24____

    A. 1% B. 5% C. 2% D. 7% E. 3%

25. School bus safety is BEST achieved when 25____

    A. separate loading zones accommodate two-way bus traffic
    B. intersections within school site are eliminated
    C. trees and shrubbery are not planted or eliminated
    D. island construction in driveways should be avoided
    E. all roads should be of uniform width

KEY (CORRECT ANSWERS)

1.	D	11.	A
2.	D	12.	E
3.	B	13.	B
4.	E	14.	A
5.	B	15.	A
6.	D	16.	C
7.	E	17.	A
8.	C	18.	C
9.	C	19.	B
10.	A	20.	E

21. E
22. B
23. A
24. B
25. B

EXAMINATION SECTION

TEST 1

DIRECTIONS: Each question or incomplete statement is followed by several suggested answers or completions. Select the one that BEST answers the question or completes the statement. *PRINT THE LETTER OF THE CORRECT ANSWER IN THE SPACE AT THE RIGHT.*

1. What is the BEST reason for not driving fast when there is a thin layer of water on the roadway?
   A. The water on the roadway is more slippery than wet pavement
   B. Your tires will tend to ride on top of the water
   C. Spray from other cars will make it hard to see clearly
   D. The spray may cause the engine to stop

   1._____

2. You are driving down an icy residential street with some dry patches. Suddenly there is trouble a block ahead and you have to stop. You are going 20 mph. What should you do?
   A. Take foot off accelerator and allow engine to slow the bus
   B. Apply the brakes and wait until you hit dry pavement
   C. Pump the brake hard several times
   D. Shift into low gear

   2._____

3. On a cold, wet day, the road is generally the most slippery
   A. on a curve
   B. on a hill
   C. in a tunnel
   D. on a bridge

   3._____

4. A little loose sand or gravel on dry pavement
   A. gives you better traction
   B. may lead to a skid
   C. is particularly dangerous when the road is wet
   D. means there is construction ahead

   4._____

5. If you suddenly lose your hydraulic brakes, going 35 mph, you should first pump your brakes, sound horn and flash your lights. Then:
   A. activate red flashing warning lamps
   B. drive off the road
   C. immediately downshift to 2nd gear
   D. try to shift to a lower gear

   5._____

6. The rear of your bus has skidded to the right. You have turned your wheel to the right and the bus is beginning to fishtail to the left. To get back on course, you should
   A. straighten the wheel
   B. brake
   C. counter-steer left
   D. counter-steer right

   6._____

7. You have just been forced to pull onto a firm shoulder to avoid an oncoming car. After the car passes, you see a highway sign directly in your path. You are going 30 mph. If you cannot stop in time, you should make sure the road is now clear and
    A. turn sharply back onto the roadway
    B. turn gradually back onto the roadway
    C. brake gently and turn sharply back onto the roadway
    D. brake gently and turn slowly back onto the roadway

7._____

8. As you come over the top of a hill at 40 mph, you see a car stalled in your lane right in front of you. You cannot stop in time. In the oncoming lane is a pickup truck. The shoulder is clear and wide enough for the bus. What should you do?
    A. Hit the brake hard and if you still cannot stop, take foot off brake and try to steer onto the shoulder
    B. Apply steady hard pressure to the brake and try to steer around the right of the car and onto the shoulder
    C. Pump the brake and try to steer left between the car and truck
    D. Leave your foot off the brake and try to steer right around the car onto the shoulder

8._____

9. You are driving at a high speed. Suddenly you hear a loud "pow" and the front of your bus begins to shake. You should
    A. brake hard
    B. brake gradually
    C. keep your foot off the brake
    D. turn off the road quickly

9._____

10. You are in the passing lane of a four-lane road with traffic on both sides. Suddenly an oncoming car crosses the centerline and heads right for you. You first try to get that driver's attention with horn, etc. Then:
    A. hit the brake and brace yourself for a head-on collision
    B. brake and steer right
    C. brake and steer left
    D. dodge oncoming car by crossing centerline, then steering back to your lane

10._____

11. Treating for shock, you should:
    A. place a coat, jacket, etc. under the victim
    B. put coat, jacket, etc. under and over sparingly according to temperature
    C. put coat, jacket, etc. under and over and apply external heat

11._____

12. If a car hits a power pole, what would you check for first?
    A. Hot wires
    B. Injuries
    C. Victims to be removed

12._____

13. If a victim is not breathing, you should:
    A. call a doctor and wait
    B. check airway, give artificial respiration
    C. take victim to hospital

13._____

14. If a victim has possible chest injuries and is not breathing, what method would you use?   14._____
    A. Back-pressure arm-lift
    B. Mouth-to-mouth
    C. Rush to hospital

15. When driving on a field trip, you may be expected to drive a(n) _____ route.   15._____
    A. hazardous
    B. longer than usual
    C. unfamiliar
    D. all of the above

16. It may be your responsibility to prepare a trip _____ report.   16._____
    A. accident
    B. evaluation
    C. chaperone
    D. authorization

17. If band instruments or other large items are to be transported on a field trip, they should be   17._____
    A. stored in a storage space under the bus
    B. kept behind stanchion bars if carried in passenger compartment
    C. kept out of the aisles and away from the emergency door(s)
    D. any of the above

18. You should check that no students board the bus at any time during the field trip unless authorized by you or by a(n)   18._____
    A. chaperone
    B. parent
    C. another bus driver
    D. none of the above

19. The final authority over student conduct while on the bus going on a field trip rests with   19._____
    A. parents
    B. you
    C. chaperones
    D. your supervisor

20. Students who are unfamiliar with the bus' rules of conduct may have to be given special   20._____
    A. consideration
    B. instructions
    C. privileges
    D. badges

21. The best way to learn an unfamiliar route is to   21._____
    A. use a map
    B. play it "by ear"
    C. travel the route in your car prior to field trip
    D. all of the above

22. A field trip to a destination which takes over an hour to reach may also have
    A. sightseeing
    B. overnight lodging requirements
    C. rest stops
    D. both b and c

22._____

23. Which of the following student behavior must NOT be permitted on a field trip?
    A. Leaning out windows
    B. Rocking the bus
    C. Both a and b
    D. Singing/cheering

23._____

24. Excesses in student behavior must be restrained because
    A. they're getting graded
    B. you must concentrate on your driving
    C. chaperones can't help with discipline
    D. all of the above

24._____

25. Accident fatalities and rear-end collisions can be expected to be high in _____ areas as a result of the increase of pedestrian and motor vehicle traffic.
    A. expressway
    B. rural
    C. urban
    D. all of the above

25._____

26. To detect hazards, you must be able to distinguish _____ within a complex, changing traffic situation.
    A. clues
    B. taillights
    C. accidents
    D. rules

26._____

27. You should develop a(n) _____ of the clues associated with each hazard.
    A. avoidance pattern
    B. "mental image"
    C. peripheral vision
    D. distraction habit

27._____

28. You should focus your eyes at farther distances ahead on the roadway as your speed
    A. decreases
    B. stabilizes
    C. increases
    D. none of the above

28._____

29. Many collisions occur at intersections where _____ is obstructed or limited by buildings, vegetation or parked cars.   29._____
    A. hearing
    B. stopping
    C. path
    D. vision

30. The more intently you fix your central vision on a particular object, the _____ aware you will be of clues from your larger field of indirect vision.   30._____
    A. less
    B. more
    C. better
    D. more directly

31. Driving alongside parked vehicles is potentially hazardous because your view is limited and hazards can appear when there is little time or space for   31._____
    A. accelerating quickly
    B. evasive action
    C. parking maneuvers
    D. both a and c

32. An example of a single vehicle hazard is   32._____
    A. an army convoy
    B. traffic at turnpike toll booths
    C. a slow moving tractor
    D. a car passing you when there is a vehicle in the oncoming lane

33. Multiple vehicle hazards include   33._____
    A. vehicles tailgating the bus
    B. a driver on an on-ramp entering the flow of traffic on a freeway
    C. vehicles that limit another vehicle's visibility
    D. all of the above

34. Any point in the roadway at which drivers are confronted with decisions are potential   34._____
    A. single vehicle hazards
    B. combination vehicle/roadway hazards
    C. off-road hazards
    D. none of the above

35. You should _____ the movement of other vehicles on and approaching the roadway so you can react safely.   35._____
    A. separate
    B. observe
    C. compete with
    D. avoid

36. You use the horn and directional signals to make sure that you are _____ by other drivers. 36._____
    A. not crowded
    B. overtaken
    C. being observed
    D. yielded to

37. Maintaining adequate separation means keeping a _____ between your bus and other vehicles. 37._____
    A. margin of safety
    B. margin of space
    C. extra space cushion
    D. all of the above

38. In addition to manipulative skills, you use your _____ skills in estimating the required space around the bus. 38._____
    A. psycho-motor
    B. driving
    C. perceptual
    D. unconscious

39. At *night*, the primary perceptual clue for judging your closing rate on the vehicle ahead is 39._____
    A. the distance between the lead vehicle's taillights
    B. the size of the lead vehicle's taillights
    C. the brightness of the lead vehicle's taillights
    D. none of the above

40. You use your _____ vision to observe vehicles not in your direct path of vision. 40._____
    A. depth
    B. night
    C. central
    D. peripheral

41. You should develop the habit of _____ 360 degrees around the bus. 41._____
    A. scanning
    B. screening
    C. driving
    D. separating

42. Which of the following circumstances call for a greater than normal following distance? When you are: 42._____
    A. behind an ambulance
    B. behind a motorcycle
    C. fatigued
    D. all of the above

43. You should maintain appropriate lateral separation when
    A. being passed
    B. being tailgated
    C. approaching a car stopped at a stop sign
    D. all of the above

43._____

44. Which of the following clues aid in maintaining longitudinal separation?
    A. Animals in the roadway
    B. Noise from traffic in cross streets
    C. Level of your gas gauge
    D. Your speedometer reading
    E. None of the above

44._____

45. Which of the following conditions would you treat first?
    A. No breathing
    B. Unconscious
    C. Bleeding heavily
    D. Dizzy

45._____

KEY (CORRECT ANSWERS)

1. B	11. B	21. C	31. B	41. A
2. A	12. A	22. D	32. C	42. D
3. D	13. B	23. C	33. D	43. A
4. B	14. B	24. B	34. B	44. D
5. D	15. D	25. C	35. B	45. C
6. C	16. D	26. A	36. C	
7. B	17. D	27. B	37. D	
8. A	18. A	28. C	38. C	
9. C	19. B	29. D	39. A	
10. B	20. B	30. A	40. D	

TEST 2

DIRECTIONS: Each question or incomplete statement is followed by several suggested answers or completions. Select the one that BEST answers the question or completes the statement. *PRINT THE LETTER OF THE CORRECT ANSWER IN THE SPACE AT THE RIGHT.*

Questions 1-10

Read each situation listed 1 through 10 and write the letter of the ACTION listed below (A-J) that you would take in the space at the right:

1. You are at the bottom of a snow-covered hill and you see cars stopped upon the hill

2. You notice wet leaves all across the street

3. You see a snowdrift in your lane (4-lane divided highway)

4. You are following another bus and the road begins to be icy

5. You are starting up at a traffic signal. There is freezing rain

6. You are approaching a long, snow-covered hill

7. You are on a highway in the rain, and your bus begins to hydroplane

8. You turn on your windshield washers and an ice glaze forms on your windshield, making it impossible to see

9. You are approaching a city intersection where you want to turn – it has just started to rain

10. You are on packed snow and an accident happens just ahead

A. Drive slower
B. Start up slowly
C. Speed up a little
D. Stop the bus
E. Increase following distance
F. Drive around it
G. Pump brakes rapidly
H. Turn more slowly
I. Ease up on the accelerator
J. Look out side windows to keep sight of road; gradually brake and Pull off

1._____
2._____
3._____
4._____
5._____
6._____
7._____
8._____
9._____
10._____

Questions 11-20

Read each statement numbered 11 through 20 and, in the space at the right, print the letter of the answer from the list below that best completes the statement:

11. A child whose actual age is 12 years old but whose mental age is 8 years is classified as _____

12. A child who must use a wheelchair is _____

13. A child whose learning disability is due to minimal brain injury is said to be _____

14. _____ patterns of each exceptional child are individual problems and should be handled accordingly

15. _____ are responsible for having the exceptional child ready to be transported to school each morning

16. Many buses used to transport exceptional children are equipped with _____ for the restraint and safety of the passengers

17. You must be able to operate the _____ on the bus during the loading and unloading procedure

18. Mentally retarded students and educationally handicapped students are likely to have a short _____

19. Exceptional students are likely to be upset by disturbances in the normal _____

20. Parents and doctors of exceptional children should provide you with information on any type of _____ the child may be taking

A. Bus attendants
B. Medication
C. Behavior
D. Seatbelts
E. Wheelchairs
F. Mentally retarded
G. Attention span
H. Educationally handicapped
I. Parents
J. Ramp
K. Accident
L. Physically handicapped
M. Routine
N. Bus driver

11._____
12._____
13._____
14._____
15._____
16._____
17._____
18._____
19._____
20._____

21. Before you can set priorities for treatment, you must evaluate: 21._____
    A. the scene for dangerous conditions
    B. types of injuries
    C. need for immediate treatment
    D. all of the above

22. Two types of injuries that require prompt treatment are: 22._____
    A. severe bleeding and blocked airways
    B. blocked airways and headache
    C. sprained ankle and leg cramps
    D. lightheadedness and nausea

23. When might you have to move an injured person BEFORE you administer   23._____
    first aid?
    A. When the injured person is not completely comfortable
    B. When the victim is in a spot that is not suitably lit for first aid administration
    C. When dangerous conditions (ex. fire) exist at the scene
    D. When the victim requests to be moved despite injuries

24. With any serious injury, you should also treat the person for   24._____
    A. dizziness
    B. neck injuries
    C. shock
    D. blood loss

Questions 25-50

Read statements 25 through 50 and, in the space at the right, mark "T" if the statement is true and "F" if it is false:

25. To minimize the effects of shock, keep the victim lying down and make   25._____
    him comfortable

26. The tourniquet should be used only for severe life-threatening   26._____
    hemorrhage that cannot be controlled by other means

27. Whenever possible, a person should be treated where he is found   27._____

28. If blood soaks through a dressing, remove dressing and apply another   28._____
    dressing

29. If you do not have a bus attendant, you must carry or guide each child   29._____
    onto the bus and fasten his seatbelt, if one is provided

30. Physically handicapped students have a lower mental age than non-   30._____
    handicapped students

31. If a child has a seizure, you should give him artificial respiration   31._____

32. When one child displays disruptive behavior, you must also be concerned   32._____
    about how the other passengers are affected

33. You should insist that no students soil themselves on your bus   33._____

34. Any point at which the roadway is compressed (ex. a four-lane road   34._____
    narrows into two lanes) represents a conflict point

35. Lack of communication by other drivers on the road is not a hazard to   35._____
    your safe driving

36. A driver frequently changing lanes is a potential hazard   36._____

37. Drivers who do not signal prior to a maneuver are potentially hazardous   37._____

38. There are certain locations on any route where you can anticipate that   38._____
    other vehicles will decelerate

39. The condition of the shoulder of the road shouldn't concern you if you   39._____
    don't intend to pull off the roadway

40. In urban areas, you have to be more alert for traffic lights because of   40._____
    neon lights and other lights on the street

41. The primary hazard around playgrounds, residential areas and schools is   41._____
    that other drivers tend to tailgate

42. You should depend on other drivers to signal their intentions as you do   42._____

43. You can use usual and unusual clues to assess how bad a hazard is   43._____
    before you take action

44. You should always swerve to avoid animals or pedestrians in the roadway   44._____

45. To maintain the appropriate lateral separation distance when changing   45._____
    lanes, you should position the bus in the center of the new lane

46. In general, pass on the right on a four-lane roadway   46._____

47. A "panic stop" is always better than no stop at all   47._____

48. When approaching a vehicle that is taking up two lanes, you should   48._____
    maintain longitudinal separation

49. When approaching an intersection with a car coming from the left cross   49._____
    street signaling his intention to turn right, it is all right to proceed into the
    intersection after the car has begun to turn

50. Since you drive a school bus, you have the right of way on a narrow   50._____
    bridge

KEY (CORRECT ANSWERS)

1. D	11. F	21. D	31. F	41. F
2. A	12. L	22. A	32. T	42. F
3. F	13. H	23. C	33. F	43. T
4. E	14. C	24. C	34. T	44. F
5. B	15. I	25. T	35. F	45. T
6. C	16. D	26. T	36. T	46. F
7. I	17. J	27. T	37. T	47. F
8. J	18. G	28. F	38. T	48. T
9. H	19. M	29. T	39. F	49. T
10. G	20. B	30. F	40. T	50. F

TEST 3

DIRECTIONS: Each question or incomplete statement is followed by several suggested answers or completions. Select the one that BEST answers the question or completes the statement. *PRINT THE LETTER OF THE CORRECT ANSWER IN THE SPACE AT THE RIGHT.*

Questions 1-44

Read statements 1 through 44 and, in the space at the right, mark "T" if the statement is true and "F" if it is false:

1. Two seconds is the minimum time interval to maintain behind a vehicle you are following   1._____

2. Drivers tend to underestimate bus lengths and distance measured in feet   2._____

3. You must know the approximate size of your bus so you can estimate whether your bus can safely clear structures with restricted lateral and overhead space   3._____

4. When driving on poor roads, a considerable part of your attention should be devoted to getting through with the greatest degree of comfort to the passengers and without damaging the bus   4._____

5. Probably the greatest danger on rural roads which are not hard-surfaced is the questionable condition of the outer edges of the grade   5._____

6. If your wheels run off the paved surface on a narrow road, you should slow down and turn your wheels gradually to cut back onto the pavement   6._____

7. Blind and uncontrolled intersections are often found on rural roads   7._____

8. One of the most common faults of school bus drivers in urban areas is that they do not stay in the proper lane of traffic   8._____

9. It's better to drive much slower than other urban traffic rather than much faster   9._____

10. You have more help in controlling the position of your bus at an intersection in an urban area than you do in any residential or rural intersection because at an urban intersection there are traffic lights, traffic officers, safety islands, etc.   10._____

11. Driving at twilight is more dangerous than driving during daylight   11._____

12. Distance and speed estimation for oncoming, standard-size vehicles at night is almost equal to that of daytime driving   12._____

13. If it's unexpectedly necessary to pull the bus off onto the shoulder of the road at night, you should activate the red flashing warning lights   13._____

14. A basic rule for driving in adverse weather is to shift to a lower gear   14._____

15. To avoid getting stuck or spinning the wheels when driving on ice, you should try to keep the bus moving slowly and steadily forward in gear   15._____

16. Accidents blamed on skidding or bad weather conditions are classed as preventable   16._____

17. When driving in snow and ice, you brake while negotiating turns   17._____

18. The problems of reduced visibility due to poor weather are similar to the reduced visibility due to darkness   18._____

19. When driving on an expressway, you should drive within a 25 percent range of the speed of traffic   19._____

20. When entering an expressway, you should stay in the acceleration lane until you are up to the speed of the traffic flow   20._____

21. If your wheels go off the pavement on an expressway, brake quickly to avoid collision   21._____

22. When you want to exit from an expressway, you should not activate your turn signal until you pull into the deceleration lane   22._____

23. You should enter the expressway by merging sharply into the flow of traffic, provided an acceptable gap of at least 8 seconds is permitted   23._____

24. You should not drive with your foot resting on the brake pedal   24._____

25. You should race the engine to warm it up because it's hard on the engine to drive it while it's cold   25._____

26. If you "lug" the engine when you go up hills (try to go up in too high a gear) you'll wear out the brake shoes   26._____

27. You should not drive the bus if oil pressure is low   27._____

28. You should *usually* avoid skipping gears when you upshift and downshift   28._____

29. Springs and shock absorbers are part of the suspension component   29._____

30. "Slipping the clutch" is the driving habit that wears out a clutch most quickly   30._____

31. The condition of the road (potholes, bumps) has the worst effect on the electrical system   31._____

32. If the ammeter indicates discharge, you should have your brakes checked immediately   32._____

33. Preventive maintenance consists of correctly diagnosing symptoms of component malfunctions   33._____

34. If your temperature gauge rises higher than normal, you should report it   34._____

35. If your bus swerves when you apply the brakes, it could mean that one or   35._____
    more wheels are not braking evenly

36. If your bus slips out of gear, you should shut off the engine immediately   36._____

37. If you hear a squealing sound when you depress the clutch pedal, it   37._____
    usually means your brake linings are worn

38. If the steering on your bus becomes very difficult, your wheels could be   38._____
    improperly aligned

39. If smoke appears around wires or switches, you should disconnect the   39._____
    battery immediately

40. If your lights are dim, you should go ahead and drive   40._____

41. If your bus bounces or rolls from side to side easily, you are just driving   41._____
    too fast for conditions

42. If you notice exhaust fumes, it is nothing to worry about unless your   42._____
    muffler is also excessively loud

43. If your engine "misses" at high speeds, you should shut off the engine   43._____
    immediately

44. A driver who frequently changes lanes should not be considered a   44._____
    potential hazard

45. What is your responsibility to parents when you know the bus will be late   45._____
    on the afternoon run due to a bad storm?
    A. Have the children call their parents and alert them of the situation
    B. Notify them of the delay and provide an estimated arrival time
    C. None; the parents should find out on their own
    D. Contact the school and have someone get the information out to
       all parents

46. What should you do if no one is home to receive the child in the   46._____
    afternoon?
    A. Let the child go to a friend's house
    B. Do not leave until a parent or guardian returns home, then
       continue with your run
    C. Take him to an alternate person (friend, neighbor, etc.) if someone
       else is designated on the child's information card
    D. Return the child to the school to wait for a parent or guardian

47. Who should you report to if you observe a child having an adverse reaction to medication?
    A. Parent
    B. Teacher
    C. Child's doctor
    D. All of the above

47._____

48. How would you explain to your passengers and their parents that the bus route is being changed to pick up a new student?
    A. New pick-up time should be specified, and passengers assured that the route will be different but nothing to worry about
    B. Apologize for the new student and continue without additional explanation
    C. Inform them of the new pick-up time only
    D. Provide information about the new student to all parents this way they can review the new situation themselves

48._____

49. Why must each exceptional child be treated individually?
    A. Their problems vary widely
    B. Each has their own level of comprehension, tolerance, adaptability, etc.
    C. Both A and B
    D. Neither A nor B

49._____

50. Suppose a child behaves in ways that aren't typical for him and that violently upset other bus passengers. What would you NOT do to try to resolve the problem?
    A. Pull off the road and stop the bus
    B. Try to eliminate the cause of the problem, if it is known
    C. Radio for help or stop a passing motorist if it gets beyond your control
    D. Yell at the child or children until they are no longer a distraction

50._____

KEY (CORRECT ANSWERS)

1. F	11. T	21. F	31. F	41. F
2. T	12. T	22. F	32. F	42. F
3. T	13. F	23. F	33. F	43. F
4. T	14. T	24. T	34. T	44. F
5. T	15. T	25. F	35. T	45. B
6. T	16. T	26. F	36. F	46. C
7. T	17. F	27. T	37. F	47. D
8. T	18. T	28. T	38. T	48. A
9. F	19. T	29. T	39. T	49. C
10. F	20. T	30. T	40. F	50. D

EXAMINATION SECTION
TEST 1

DIRECTIONS: Each question or incomplete statement is followed by several suggested answers or completions. Select the one that BEST answers the question or completes the statement. *PRINT THE LETTER OF THE CORRECT ANSWER IN THE SPACE AT THE RIGHT.*

Questions 1-10.

DIRECTIONS: Questions 1 through 10, inclusive, are based on the portion of a timetable shown below. Refer to this timetable in answering these questions.

TIMETABLE - RIVERVIEW LINE - WEEKDAYS

Bus No.	NORTHBOUND				SOUTHBOUND				
	Gold St.	New St.	Ace St.	Stone St.		Ace St.	New St.	Gold St.	
	Leave	Leave	Leave	Arrive	Leave	Leave	Leave	Arrive	Leave
8	7:30	7:45	8:00	8:10	8:15	8:25	8:40	8:55	9:00
9	7:45	8:00	8:15	8:25	8:30	8:40	8:55	9:10	9:15
10	8:00	8:15	8:30	8:40	8:45	8:55	9:10	9:25	9:30
11	8:15	8:30	8:45	8:55	9:00	9:10	9:25	9:40	9:45
12	8:25	8:40	8:55	9:05	9:10	9:20	9:35	9:50	9:55
13	8:35	8:50	9:05	9:15	9:20	9:30	9:45	10:00	10:05
14	8:45	9:00	9:15	9:25	9:30	9:40	9:55	10:10	10:15
15	8:55	9:10	9:25	9:35	9:40	9:50	10:05	10:20	10:25
8	9:00	9:15	9:30	9:40	9:45	9:55	10:10	10:25	LU*
16	9:05	9:20	9:35	9:45	9:50	10:00	10:15	10:30	10:35
17	9:10	9:25	9:40	9:50	9:55	10:05	10:20	10:35	LU*
9	9:15	9:30	9:45	9:55	10:00	10:10	10:25	10:40	10:45

*LU means that the bus is taken out of passenger service at the location where LU appears.

NOTE: Assume that the arrival times at New St. and Ace St. are the same as the leaving times.

1. The length of time required for a bus to make a southbound run from Stone St. to Gold St. is _____ minutes.

   A. 40 B. 45 C. 50 D. 80

   1.____

2. The length of time that buses are scheduled to remain at Gold St. is _____ minutes.

   A. always 5
   C. always 15
   B. always 10
   D. either 5 or 10

   2.____

3. The total length of time, including the five-minute layover at Stone St., required for one round trip from Gold St. to Stone St. and return is _____ minutes.

   A. 80 B. 85 C. 90 D. 125

4. The total number of different buses listed in the portion of the timetable shown is

   A. 9 B. 10 C. 11 D. 12

5. The number of buses for which two complete round trips are shown in the timetable is

   A. 1 B. 2 C. 3 D. 4

6. A person reaching New St. at 8:58 to board a southbound bus would have to wait until

   A. 9:00 B. 9:05 C. 9:10 D. 9:15

7. The average of the running times from Gold St. to New St., from New St. to Ace St., and from Ace St. to Stone St. is about _____ minutes.

   A. 12 B. 13 C. 14 D. 15

8. A passenger leaving Gold St. on the 7:30 bus is going to Stone St. to take care of some business. If his business takes a total of an hour and a half, he can be back at Gold St. by about

   A. 9:00 B. 9:30 C. 10:00 D. 10:30

9. From the entries in the timetable, you can infer that the location near which there is MOST likely to be a bus garage or storage yard is _____ St.

   A. Stone B. Ace C. New D. Gold

10. A person reaching New St. at 8:45 to leave on a northbound bus would expect to arrive at Stone St. at

    A. 8:50 B. 9:00 C. 9:15 D. 9:30

11. A crosstown bus operates between two terminals 22 blocks apart and makes 18 stops. It takes minute to travel each block and minute at each stop, and 5 minutes are lost at traffic lights.
    The total time required to go from one terminal to the other is_____ minutes.

    A. 15 B. 17 C. 20 D. 22

12. The operator is forbidden by the rules to converse unnecessarily with passengers while driving his bus.
    A logical reason for this rule is that such conversation

    A. takes the operator's attention off his driving
    B. makes a poor impression on the other passengers
    C. tends to block the entrance to the bus
    D. may lead to an argument with undesirable consequences

13. A bus operator would NOT be taking responsible care of his employer's property if he

    A. drove faster than 20 miles per hour in cold weather
    B. opened the front doors to let a passenger off at a bus stop

3 (#1)

   C. passed another bus while it was in a bus stop
   D. rubbed the wheels against the curb at a bus stop

14. If a bus operator has to call an ambulance for an injured person, the MOST important information he must transmit is

   A. where the ambulance is needed
   B. the name of the injured person
   C. how the accident occurred
   D. what part of the body has been injured

15. An operator entering a bus garage notices a lighting fixture that appears to be loose and in danger of falling from the ceiling.
    His BEST procedure would be to

   A. get a stepladder and tie the fixture up temporarily with cord
   B. find the switch and turn the light off
   C. tell his superior about the fixture
   D. forget it because the repairmen will find it

16. The Sunday bus timetable is generally operated in place of the regular weekday timetable when a legal holiday falls on a weekday.
    The logical reason is that passenger travel

   A. is never heavy on a holiday
   B. is heaviest on Sundays and holidays
   C. on weekdays is heavier than on holidays
   D. on holidays is generally similar to Sunday travel

17. When making change while standing at a bus stop, the bus operator should pay GREATEST attention to

   A. accuracy   B. courtesy   C. speed   D. safety

18. Courtesy to passengers is impressed on transit employees MAINLY to

   A. discourage vandalism
   B. assure passenger safety
   C. speed up bus operations
   D. maintain good public relations

19. It is reasonable to expect that a bus operator would be required to

   A. make minor repairs to his engine
   B. change burned out headlight lamps
   C. make written reports of his activities
   D. detain disorderly people

20. A passenger, who wishes to pay two 90-cent fares, hands the bus operator 2 dollar bills. If the fare box will take quarters, dimes, and nickels, the SMALLEST number of coins the passenger can be given is

   A. 10   B. 11   C. 12   D. 13

21. Employees MUST know the rules and regulations governing their jobs to

    A. please their supervisors
    B. foresee emergencies
    C. avoid accidents
    D. perform their duties properly

22. Bus operators are permitted to select their assignments in the order of seniority on the job.
    The MOST probable reason for using this method is to

    A. discourage absenteeism
    B. give every employee the assignment he desires
    C. give new employees preference in selection
    D. reward length of service

23. The total value of an operator's change fund consisting of 7 half-dollars, 19 quarters, 169 dimes, and 105 nickels is

    A. $28.40   B. $29.40   C. $30.40   D. $31.40

24. Standard forms frequently call for entries on them to be printed.
    This is done MAINLY because printing, as compared to writing, is generally

    A. more compact   B. more legal
    C. more legible   D. easier to do

25. If an angry passenger, boarding a bus at a busy stop, called the operator names because the bus was late, the operator would show BEST judgment by

    A. ignoring the name calling
    B. explaining the reason for the lateness to the passenger
    C. ejecting the passenger
    D. getting the passenger's name and address

26. On vehicles equipped with hydraulic braking, the MOST serious danger which may occur is

    A. unequal braking   B. high brake fluid pressure
    C. loss of the brake fluid D. freezing of the brake fluid

27. On vehicles equipped with manual shifting, the practice of coasting out of gear is UNDESIRABLE because

    A. it wastes gas
    B. the driver has less control of his vehicle
    C. it causes engine damage
    D. it generally causes rear axle damage

28. If a bus operator running his bus at 25 miles per hour notices that the reading of the engine oil pressure gauge has dropped to zero, he should

    A. stop the bus
    B. speed up to 30 miles per hour
    C. drive at speeds below 20 miles per hour
    D. shift to low gear

29. It would be CORRECT to state that

   A. it is impossible to slow down on ice
   B. rain on a road increases traction
   C. chains increase skidding in snow
   D. most car skids can be avoided

30. A man CANNOT drive safely if he is

   A. driving an old car
   B. unfamiliar with traffic laws
   C. under age 25
   D. over age 60

31. It is CORRECT to state that the greater the speed of a vehicle, the

   A. easier it is to stop
   B. easier it is to turn a corner
   C. longer the tire life
   D. harder it is to control the vehicle

32. If a vehicle swerves to one side whenever a sudden stop is made, the MOST likely cause would be

   A. a defective transmission
   B. a defective rear axle
   C. uneven brakes
   D. uneven steering radius

33. The very slow driver is considered a safety menace MAINLY because

   A. he never knows where he is going
   B. he is always driving a defective vehicle
   C. other cars are constantly cutting out to pass him
   D. he may back up at any moment

34. The SAFEST procedure to follow when another car is attempting to pass you on the road is to

   A. sound your horn
   B. be prepared to slow down
   C. speed up
   D. pay no attention to him

35. The BEST procedure for a bus operator to follow at an intersection where the traffic lights are stuck in the red position for all traffic is to

   A. wait for a traffic officer
   B. proceed cautiously across the intersection when traffic permits
   C. wait for a signal maintenance man
   D. have a passenger stop opposing traffic so you can cross

36. Night driving is more dangerous than daytime driving MAINLY because

   A. road vision is reduced
   B. more drivers ignore the traffic lights
   C. more people are shopping
   D. there are fewer police cars on duty

37. As a newly appointed bus operator, your supervisor would MOST likely expect you to

   A. pay close attention to instructions
   B. complete your runs ahead of schedule time
   C. make plenty of mistakes
   D. have arguments with passengers the first few days

38. When initially warming up a bus diesel engine which is cold, the engine should be

   A. raced violently
   B. run at slightly above idling speed
   C. raced rapidly in intermittent spurts
   D. run fast enough to keep engine oil pressure at maximum indication

39. Skidding of a vehicle on a dry road would be MOST likely to occur when

   A. braking slowly
   B. accelerating slowly
   C. entering a curve at high speed
   D. accelerating rapidly going down a hill

40. The equipment which requires the HEAVIEST current from the car battery is the

   A. generator
   B. starter motor
   C. horn
   D. ignition circuit

41. The weekly pay for 8 hours a day, 5 days a week, at $7.875 an hour can be calculated as

   A. 5 x 8 x 7.785
   B. 8 + 5 x 7.875
   C. 8 x 5 x 7.875
   D. 8 + 5 x 7.785

Questions 42-50.

   DIRECTIONS: Questions 42 through 50, inclusive, are based on the Bus Operator Instructions given below. Read these instructions carefully before answering these questions.

BUS OPERATOR INSTRUCTIONS

When running on public streets, operators must have all running lights on during hours of darkness. Practices such as having bus interior lights burning during daylight hours or operating after dark with only half the interior lights burning are forbidden. Tampering with the light circuits and removing fuses therefrom is forbidden. Poor driving practices such as sudden starts and stops, striking curbs, spinning wheels, sliding wheels, riding with handbrake on, or operating the bus with badly overheated or knocking engine must be avoided. Tires must be frequently inspected to detect improper inflation. When adjusting inside or outside rear-view mirrors, the use of force is prohibited, since only mild pressure is required. If adjustment cannot be made by use of mild pressure, report the assembly as defective.

42. Bus operators are forbidden to

   A. inspect tires
   B. remove light fuses
   C. adjust viewing mirrors
   D. stop close to curb

43. The MOST important reason for NOT operating a bus with the engine knocking is to prevent   43.____

    A. the noise   B. loss of power
    C. waste of gas   D. engine damage

44. A bus operator is required to make a report with respect to   44.____

    A. sliding wheels   B. striking curbs
    C. spinning wheels   D. stuck mirrors

45. Running lights on a bus operating on city streets would be required before 6 P.M. on every day in the month of   45.____

    A. December   B. April   C. June   D. August

46. All interior bus lights should be on when the bus   46.____

    A. is garaged for the night
    B. is being repaired
    C. is operating on public streets after dark
    D. fuses are all in place

47. Operating during daylight hours with bus interior lights on is forbidden in order to avoid   47.____

    A. a traffic violation   B. passenger complaints
    C. unsafe bus operation   D. unnecessary battery drain

48. Riding with the handbrake half on   48.____

    A. is a good safety practice
    B. is sometimes permissible
    C. does not cause brake wear
    D. is forbidden

49. The bus operator is required to   49.____

    A. repair tires
    B. repair defective mirror assemblies
    C. inspect tires
    D. make sudden starts

50. Making frequent sudden stops would be LEAST likely to cause   50.____

    A. improper tire inflation
    B. excessive brake wear
    C. passenger discomfort
    D. rear end collisions

KEY (CORRECT ANSWERS)

1. A	11. C	21. D	31. D	41. C
2. A	12. A	22. D	32. C	42. B
3. B	13. D	23. C	33. C	43. D
4. B	14. A	24. C	34. B	44. D
5. B	15. C	25. A	35. B	45. A
6. C	16. D	26. C	36. A	46. C
7. B	17. A	27. B	37. A	47. D
8. D	18. D	28. A	38. B	48. D
9. D	19. C	29. D	39. C	49. C
10. C	20. A	30. B	40. B	50. A

TEST 2

DIRECTIONS: Each question or incomplete statement is followed by several suggested answers or completions. Select the one that BEST answers the question or completes the statement. *PRINT THE LETTER OF THE CORRECT ANSWER IN THE SPACE AT THE RIGHT.*

Questions 1-9.

DIRECTIONS: Questions 1 through 9, inclusive, are based on the State Motor Vehicle Bureau's Point System given below. Read this point carefully before answering these questions.

<u>STATE MOTOR VEHICLE BUREAU'S POINT SYSTEM</u>
The newly revised point system was effective April 1. After that date, a driver having offenses resulting in an accumulation of eight points within two years, ten points within three years, or twelve points within four years, is to be summoned for a hearing which may result in the loss of his license. Under the point system, three points are charged for speeding, two points for passing a red light or crossing a double line or failing to stop at a stop sign, one and a half points for inoperative horn or insufficient lights, and one point for improper turn or failure to notify Bureau of change of address. The Commissioner of Motor Vehicles is required to revoke a driver's license if he has three speeding violations in a period of eighteen months, or drives while intoxicated or leaves the scene of an accident or makes a false statement in his application for a driver's license. This system is necessary because studies show violations of traffic laws cause four out of five fatal accidents in the state.

1. The traffic offense which calls for license revocation if repeated three times within a period of years is

    A. passing a red light B. passing a stop sign
    C. crossing a double line D. speeding

    1.____

2. The individual who has the power to revoke a driver's license is the

    A. traffic officer
    B. motor vehicle inspector
    C. Commissioner of Motor Vehicles
    D. Traffic Commissioner

    2.____

3. Crossing a double line has a penalty of twice as many points as for

    A. making an improper turn B. speeding
    C. passing a red light D. an inoperative horn

    3.____

4. Failure of a driver to properly notify the Bureau of Motor Vehicles of a change in his address carries a penalty of _____ point(s).

    A. $\frac{1}{2}$ B. 1   C. $1\frac{1}{2}$ D. 2

    4.____

5. The point system is specifically designed to penalize the driver who
   A. is inexperienced
   B. repeatedly violates traffic laws
   C. is overage
   D. ignores parking violations

6. A false statement on a driver's license application calls for a penalty of
   A. 10 points
   B. 8 points
   C. license suspension
   D. license revocation

7. Insufficient lights carries a penalty of _____ point(s).
   A. $\frac{1}{2}$
   B. 1
   C. $1\frac{1}{2}$
   D. 2

8. A driver is summoned for a hearing if, within a period of three years, he accumulates _____ points.
   A. 6
   B. 8
   C. 10
   D. 12

9. The percentage of fatal accidents caused by traffic violations is
   A. 80%
   B. 70%
   C. 60%
   D. 50%

Questions 10-18.

DIRECTIONS: Questions 10 through 18, inclusive, are based on the bus timetable shown below. Assume layover time at Prince St. and Duke St. is negligible. Refer to this timetable when answering these questions.

TIMETABLE - REGENT PARKWAY LINE - WEEKDAYS

	EASTBOUND					WESTBOUND		
Bus No.	King St. Leave	Prince St. Leave	Duke St. Leave	Queen St. Arrive	Queen St. Leave	Duke St. Leave	Prince St. Leave	King St. Arrive
20	7:15	7:20	7:30	7:45	7:50	8:05	8:15	8:20
21	7:25	7:30	7:40	7:55	8:00	8:15	8:25	8:30
22	7:35	7:40	7:50	8:05	8:10	8:25	8:35	8:40
23	7:45	7:50	8:00	8:15	8:20	8:35	8:45	8:50
24	7:55	8:00	8:10	8:25	8:30	8:45	8:55	9:00
25	8:05	8:10	8:20	8:35	8:40	8:55	9:05	9:10
26	8:10	8:15	8:25	8:40	8:43	8:58	9:08	9:13
27	8:15	8:20	8:30	8:45	8:48	9:03	9:13	9:18
28	8:20	8:25	8:35	8:50	8:53	9:08	9:18	9:23
20	8:30	8:35	8:45	9:00	9:05	9:20	9:30	9:35
21	8:40	8:45	8:55	9:10	9:15	9:30	9:40	9:45
22	8:50	8:55	9:05	9:20	9:25	9:40	9:50	9:55

10. The total running time (omit layover) for one round trip from King St. to Queen St. and back again is _____ minutes.
    A. 70
    B. 65
    C. 60
    D. 30

11. The LEAST time that any bus stops over at Queen St. is _____ minutes. 11._____
    A. 3　　　　B. 5　　　　C. 10　　　　D. 15

12. The time required for a bus to make the Eastbound run from King St. to Queen St. is_____minutes. 12._____
    A. 65　　　　B. 60　　　　C. 35　　　　D. 30

13. The total number of different buses shown in the time-table is 13._____
    A. 8　　　　B. 9　　　　C. 10　　　　D. 12

14. The timetable shows that the total number of buses which make two round trips is 14._____
    A. 1　　　　B. 2　　　　C. 3　　　　D. 4

15. A person reaching Duke St. at 8:28 to leave on a Westbound bus will have to wait _____ minutes. 15._____
    A. 2　　　　B. 5　　　　C. 7　　　　D. 10

16. The SHORTEST running time between any two bus stops is _____ minutes. 16._____
    A. 3　　　　B. 5　　　　C. 10　　　　D. 15

17. The bus which arrives at King St. three minutes after the preceding bus is bus No. 17._____
    A. 20　　　　B. 22　　　　C. 26　　　　D. 28

18. Bus No. 21 is scheduled to start its second round trip from King St. at 18._____
    A. 9:45　　　　B. 8:40　　　　C. 8:30　　　　D. 7:25

Questions 19-26.

DIRECTIONS:　Questions 19 through 26, inclusive, are based on the sketch below showing the routes of the Main St. (solid line) and the Bay St. (dotted line) buses. Refer to this sketch when answering these questions.

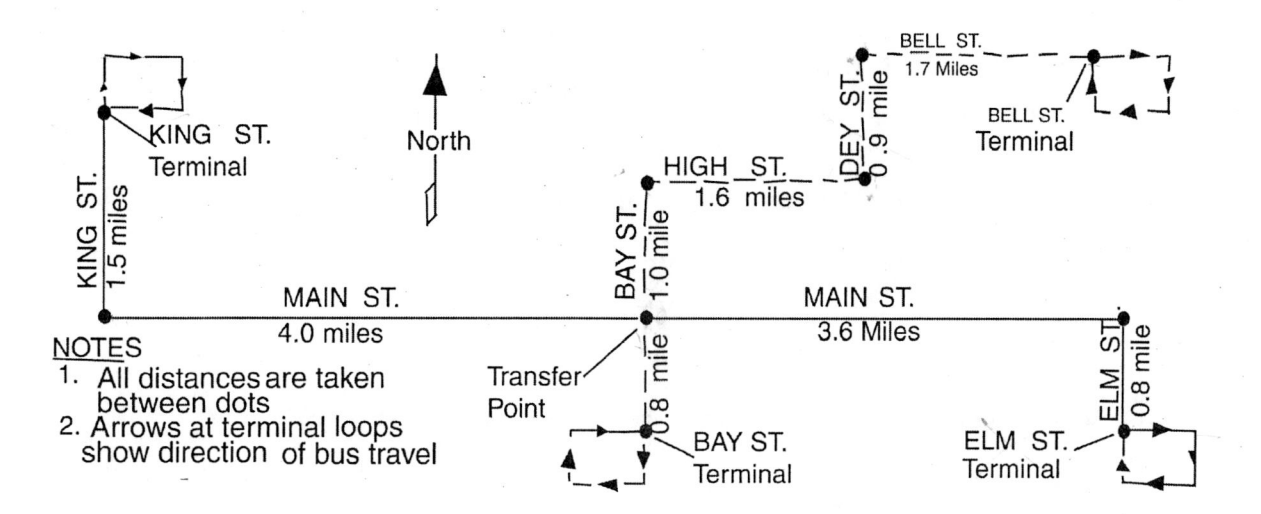

NOTES
1. All distances are taken between dots
2. Arrows at terminal loops show direction of bus travel

19. The distance from the King. St. Terminal to the Elm St. Terminal is ____ miles.   19.___

    A. 10   B. 9.9   C. 9.1   D. 7.6

20. A transfer is required for a passenger going from Bell St. Terminal to   20.___

    A. Bay St.   B. Dey St.   C. High St.   D. Elm St.

21. A bus running on Main St. and going from Bay St. to Elm St. is moving   21.___

    A. west   B. east   C. south   D. north

22. Buses are NOT required to make any left turns at the   22.___

    A. King St. Terminal   B. transfer point
    C. Bay St. Terminal   D. Bell St. Terminal

23. After discharging all passengers at Bell St. Terminal, the number of right turns required   23.___
    for the bus to reach Bay St. is

    A. 1   B. 2   C. 3   D. 4

24. If the average running speed of buses from King St. Terminal to the transfer point is 22   24.___
    miles an hour, and the time for stops totals 10 minutes, then this trip takes ___ minutes.

    A. 25   B. 20   C. 15   D. 12

25. A bus going from Bay St. Terminal to Bell St. Terminal travels in a northerly direction a   25.___
    total distance of _____ mile(s).

    A. 0.8   B. 1.8   C. 2.7   D. 4.3

26. The street having the SHORTEST bus mileage is   26.___

    A. Bay St.   B. Dey St.   C. Elm St.   D. King St.

27. The driver of a vehicle which injures a dog is required to report the accident to either the   27.___
    dog's owner or to

    A. a hospital   B. the S.P.C.A.
    C. the Sanitation Dept.   D. a police officer

28. Of the following, steering gear damage is MOST likely to result from   28.___

    A. sudden stops   B. fast acceleration
    C. excess lubrication   D. hitting curbs

29. At an intersection, the driver who has the preferred right of way is the one who is   29.___

    A. making a left turn
    B. making a right turn
    C. proceeding straight ahead
    D. making a U-turn

30. If a tire blows out, it is MOST important for the driver to   30.___

    A. hold the steering wheel tightly
    B. disengage the clutch immediately

C. shift to low gear
D. keep his foot on the gas

31. Driving through water puddles during a rainstorm should be avoided MAINLY because of the danger of

    A. the wheels rusting
    B. rotting the tires
    C. hitting deep holes
    D. splashing the headlights

31._____

32. Axle and spring damage is MOST likely to occur on a bus which is driven rapidly on a roadway which

    A. has wet leaves
    B. is oiled
    C. is rutted with ice
    D. is sanded

32._____

33. A bus operator should never shift gears while on a railroad crossing because it may cause engine

    A. stalling
    B. knocking
    C. overheating
    D. bearing failure

33._____

34. When the wheels of a bus are stuck in deep snow, the WORST thing for the bus operator to do is to

    A. back up
    B. try second gear
    C. accelerate rapidly
    D. start slowly

34._____

35. If a bus operator must leave his bus parked on a hilly street, he should park with

    A. rear wheels at least 3 inches from the curb
    B. front wheels parallel to the curb
    C. all wheels a few inches away from the curb
    D. front wheels cut into the curb

35._____

36. The MAJORITY of traffic accidents are MOST likely caused by

    A. negligence
    B. defective vehicles
    C. roadway conditions
    D. defective traffic

36._____

37. The MOST important reason for keeping traffic accident statistics is to

    A. justify law enforcement
    B. determine accident causes
    C. reduce speeding
    D. frighten pedestrians

37._____

38. Pedestrian fatalities are MOST likely to occur at

    A. crossings having traffic lights
    B. other than designated crossings
    C. railroad crossings
    D. full-stop crossings

38._____

39. Skidding on a slippery road is MOST likely to occur if the tires are

    A. new
    B. under-inflated
    C. of the cushion type
    D. over-inflated

39._____

40. Certain traffic regulations are designed to specifically protect school buses. This is MAINLY because

    A. these buses make frequent stops
    B. school children are careless pedestrians
    C. these buses travel slowly
    D. children must reach school on time

41. The driver of a truck cuts over in front of a bus, blocking further movement of the bus. He gets out of his truck and complains violently to the bus operator that the bus cut him off some distance back, forcing him to stop suddenly to avoid a collision with the bus.
    In this case, it would be BEST for the bus operator to

    A. cut the argument short by moving the obstructing truck out of the way
    B. avoid argument by saying it was unavoidable if it occurred and request the truck driver to move his truck
    C. send a passenger to look for a traffic officer
    D. request the passengers to verify the fact that the bus driver was not guilty of this accusation

42. A rule of the transit authority is that operators of buses must never accept cash fares by hand, but must request passengers to deposit their own fares in the fare box. The MOST likely reason for this rule is to

    A. reduce the chance of money dropping to the floor of the bus
    B. register every fare through the box
    C. permit the passenger to count his change
    D. prevent distraction of the operator while he is driving the bus

43. At an intersection having no traffic light or other protection, the right of way belongs to

    A. the avenue traffic
    B. pedestrians attempting to cross
    C. cars attempting to turn
    D. buses crossing the intersection to make a passenger stop

44. When a bus operator sees a ball roll out into the roadway, it is MOST important for the operator to

    A. swerve the bus to avoid the ball
    B. avoid the ball by straddling the bus over it
    C. stop the bus to avoid the ball
    D. be prepared to stop

45. If a bus operator notices a vehicle which is moving erratically in the traffic ahead of his bus, then it would be BEST for the bus operator to

    A. stay behind this vehicle
    B. ask the driver to pull over to the curb
    C. be especially careful if it is necessary to pass this vehicle
    D. determine if the driver is ill

46. High school children are given special cards for reduced fare transportation on city buses when travelling to and from school.
In view of this, it is likely that

    A. these cards would be valid for use on the first day of January
    B. these cards would never be honored after 3 P.M.
    C. the card holders deposit money in the fare box
    D. these cards would not be honored before 9 A.M.

47. The right of way in proceeding across an intersection against a red light is NOT given to a

    A. private passenger car taking a patient from a hospital
    B. fire engine truck returning to the fire house after a fire
    C. vehicle instructed to pass the red light by the traffic officer on duty at the intersection
    D. pedestrian guided by a seeing-eye dog

48. Operators of buses are instructed to adjust ventilators and windows to conform with weather conditions and passenger loads.
This MOST likely means that

    A. open windows are not necessary if the bus has only a few passengers
    B. for the same kind of weather, fewer windows should be opened if the bus is full
    C. all ventilators and all windows must be closed in months like September, regardless of the number of passengers
    D. for the same kind of weather, more open windows may be required when the bus is crowded

49. One of the duties of a bus operator is to issue and accept transfers for passengers using intersecting or connecting routes.
To perform this duty properly, the operator is NOT required to

    A. check the date on the transfers he accepts
    B. know the specific privileges on the transfers he issues
    C. know the specific privileges on the transfers he accepts
    D. question each passenger to whom he issues a transfer

50. The transit authority has specifically called to the attention of its bus operators that driving an uninsured motor vehicle results in certain penalties.
The MOST probable reason for this is to

    A. make certain a bus operator does not lose his driving license
    B. warn the operators to check the liability insurance windshield sticker required on all vehicles
    C. warn the operators who never drive a private vehicle to carry personal insurance
    D. inform the operators they should never drive a car they do not own

KEY (CORRECT ANSWERS)

1. D	11. A	21. B	31. C	41. B
2. C	12. D	22. B	32. C	42. B
3. A	13. B	23. D	33. A	43. B
4. B	14. C	24. A	34. C	44. D
5. B	15. C	25. C	35. D	45. C
6. D	16. B	26. C	36. A	46. C
7. C	17. C	27. D	37. B	47. A
8. C	18. B	28. D	38. B	48. D
9. A	19. B	29. C	39. D	49. D
10. C	20. D	30. A	40. B	50. A

TEST 3

DIRECTIONS: Each question or incomplete statement is followed by several suggested answers or completions. Select the one that BEST answers the question or completes the statement. *PRINT THE LETTER OF THE CORRECT ANSWER IN THE SPACE AT THE RIGHT.*

Questions 1-10.

DIRECTIONS: Questions 1 through 10, inclusive, are based on the sketch shown below. Refer to this sketch when answering these questions.

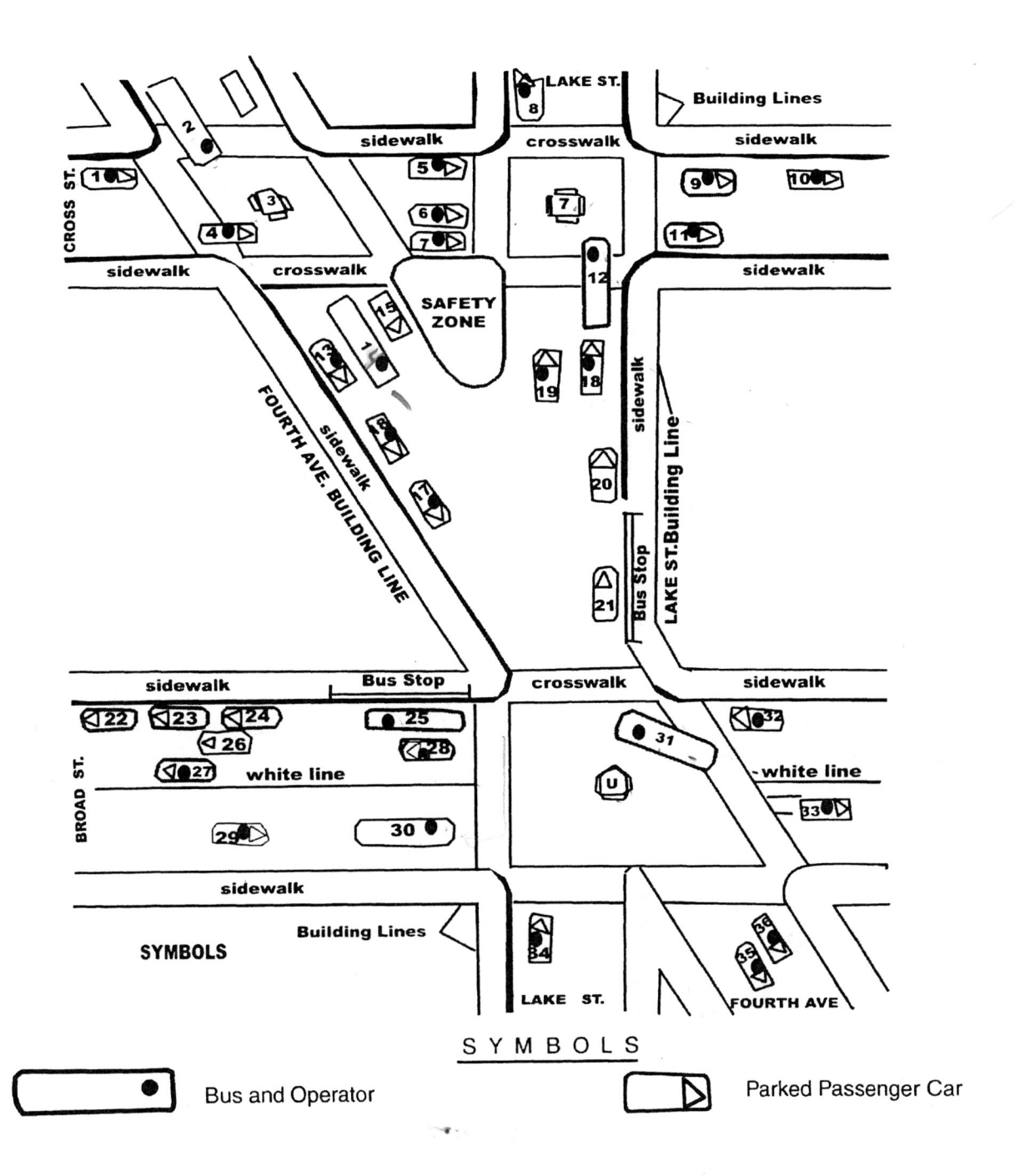

SYMBOLS

● Bus and Operator ▷ Parked Passenger Car

1. A car which is definitely violating a parking law is

   A. No. 15   B. No. 22   C. No. 24   D. No. 32

2. If traffic light T turns from green to yellow for Lake St. traffic when bus No. 12 is traveling as shown, it would be BEST for the bus operator to

   A. stop where he is
   B. continue past the light
   C. back up
   D. turn left

3. If car No. 21 displaying a flashing red light is a vacant police patrol car parked in the Lake St. bus stop, then the operator of bus No. 31 normally making this stop should open his door for passengers

   A. at the bus stop, waiting until the police car moves out
   B. after pulling up past car No. 21 until rear door clears
   C. directly behind the police car
   D. right where he is

4. If traffic light S is green for Fourth Avenue traffic when bus No. 2 and car No. 4 are traveling as shown, it would be BEST for the bus operator to

   A. speed up
   B. start backing up
   C. cut in front of car No. 4
   D. slow down

5. In making the wide right turn into Lake St., the operator of bus No. 31 should

   A. consider the possibility of a car trying to pass him on his right
   B. intermittently work the directional indicator switch on and off
   C. be careful of cars making a right turn from Lake St. to Fourth Ave.
   D. have gone to the left of the light before turning

6. For bus No. 30 to make a right turn from Broad St. into Fourth Ave., traffic light U would MOST likely be

   A. green for Lake St.
   B. red for Lake St.
   C. green for Fourth Ave.
   D. red for Cross St.

7. When traffic light T turns green for Cross St., the vehicle which is in the proper position for a left turn from Cross St. to Lake St. is

   A. No. 11   B. No. 7   C. No. 6   D. No. 5

8. If an ambulance with its warning signal sounding is coming into Fourth Ave. from Cross St., then bus No.

   A. 14 should stop where it is
   B. 2 should turn right
   C. 2 should speed up
   D. 14 should pull in front of car No. 15 and stop

9. The total number of two-way thoroughfares shown in the sketch is

   A. 1   B. 2   C. 3   D. 4

10. If the operator of bus No. 25 on Broad St. is ready to start moving, he should wait 10._____

   A. until car No. 27 pulls in front of car No. 26
   B. for car No. 26 to move out of the way
   C. for car No. 28 to pass
   D. for traffic light U to turn green

11. When a person carrying a large package is permitted to ride a bus, it is MOST important for the bus operator to make certain that the 11._____

   A. package is not placed on an unoccupied seat
   B. passenger does not forget his package
   C. aisles and doorways are not obstructed
   D. package is securely tied and will not come apart

12. A bus operator starts out with $10.00 in change, and his fare box indicates he collects $85.50 in passenger fares. On counting his money, he finds he has 75 one dollar bills, 10 fifty-cent pieces, 22 quarters, and 70 dimes. 12._____
    To have the CORRECT amount, the number of nickels he should have is

   A. 45   B. 50   C. 55   D. 60

13. Bus operators are required to turn in all unused transfers after completing their tour of duty. 13._____
    The MOST important reason for this rule is to

   A. provide a means for checking the bus fare totals
   B. determine if it is necessary to discontinue transfer privileges from one bus route to another
   C. prevent misuse of transfers if discarded
   D. determine if the bus operator is issuing transfers properly

14. If the operator of a bus hears two of his passengers arguing over the right to occupy a certain seat, it is BEST for the operator to 14._____

   A. decide which passenger is entitled to the seat
   B. ask both passengers to leave the bus
   C. ignore the situation unless they resort to force
   D. ask an impartial observer to settle the dispute

15. If traffic conditions permit, when passing a line of cars parked at the curb, the BEST driving procedure would be for the bus operator to drive his bus 15._____

   A. about 3 feet away from the parked cars
   B. within a few inches of the parked cars
   C. at least a car width away from these cars
   D. close to unoccupied cars and six feet away from occupied cars

16. If a bus operator is within a few bus stops from his terminal point, he would MOST likely have to request his passengers to take another bus if the 16._____

   A. rear exit door should jam in the closed position
   B. rear exit door should jam in the open position

C. fare box should become inoperative
D. buzzer signal system goes out of order

17. A passenger has a bus operator change a ten dollar bill, pays his fare, and seats himself. A few minutes later, he returns to the bus operator and claims his change was short by a dollar.
The FIRST thing the bus operator should do is

A. ask the passenger to search the floor for the missing change
B. remind the passenger he deposited his fare in the fare box
C. give the passenger the dollar without discussing it
D. ask the passenger if he has a hole in his pocket

18. If two men ignore the bus operator's warning to stop vandalism while riding in his bus, it would be BEST for the bus operator to

A. attract the attention of a patrolman as soon as possible
B. ask the other passengers to leave the bus
C. forcibly eject the trouble-makers
D. take the names and addresses of the trouble-makers

19. It would be LEAST desirable for a bus operator whose bus is in motion to tell a passenger

A. the location of a bus transfer point
B. the length of time required to reach his destination
C. to move away from the front doors
D. why his complaint of poor service is not justified

20. When driving up a hill on a narrow roadway, passing another car is dangerous because

A. it is difficult to make a quick stop
B. the engine will overheat
C. steering control is lost
D. vision is limited

21. Grease on brake lining

A. is necessary for long brake life
B. is necessary for quiet braking
C. results in unsafe brakes
D. results in safer braking

22. Official regulations prescribe that an operator's uniform should always appear neat.
The MOST probable reason for this requirement is that a neat uniform

A. is easier to keep clean
B. makes a good impression on the public
C. attracts attention
D. makes a better bus operator

23. Under certain roadway conditions, it is advisable to come to a stop by *pumping* the brake pedal several times instead of making a single brake application and holding it.
Such handling of the brake is necessary when the roadway is

A. banked   B. dark   C. bumpy   D. slippery

24. The battery in a car furnishes the energy to operate the   24.____

   A. starter
   B. distributor
   C. fuel pump
   D. radiator fan

25. Antifreeze is used in automobiles to   25.____

   A. heat the interior
   B. keep the windshield free of ice
   C. prevent freezing of the fuel supply
   D. keep the cooling water from freezing

26. In the average passenger car that is not over five years old, the battery is located under the   26.____

   A. driver's seat
   B. dashboard
   C. hood
   D. chassis

27. The *stock-car* taxicab as compared with the older type of taxicab is definitely   27.____

   A. safer
   B. shorter
   C. more comfortable
   D. more expensive

28. The shape of traffic sign which means STOP is   28.____

   A. ○   B. ⬡   C. ◇   D. □

29. If the first day of a 30-day month falls on a Saturday, the last day of the month will fall on a   29.____

   A. Friday   B. Saturday   C. Sunday   D. Monday

Questions 30-36.

DIRECTIONS: Questions 30 through 36, inclusive, are based on the Extract of Rules for System Pick for Bus Operators given below. Read this extract carefully before answering these questions.

EXTRACT OF RULES FOR SYSTEM PICK FOR BUS OPERATORS

Operators picking an early run (one ending before 9:00 P.M. including all time allowances) on weekdays must pick an early run on Saturday and Sunday.

No operator will be allowed to pick on the extra list unless Trie desires to transfer to a depot where all runs, tricks, etc., have been picked.

After an operator finishes picking and the monitor has entered the operator's name for the run on the picking board, no change of run will be permitted. Erasures and other signs of mutilation will not be permitted on the picking board.

It is planned to permit about 100 men in the picking room at one time, but the time allowed for any one man to pick will not exceed five minutes. If, for any reason, you cannot attend, you may submit a preference slip or be represented by proxy.

An operator inactive because of sickness, injury, etc. for sixty days prior to his pick assignment must present a certificate from a doctor stating he may return to duty not later than two weeks after date of pick.

Your cooperation is requested. Please be on hand to pick at your designated time and leave picking room promptly when you have finished picking.

30. The rules apply to a _____ pick.

   A. Saturday and Sunday
   B. depot extra
   C. weekday
   D. system

31. An operator picking an early run on weekdays

   A. cannot be off on Saturdays or Sundays
   B. must submit a preference slip
   C. will be assigned to the extra list on other days
   D. must pick an early run on Saturday and Sunday

32. According to these rules, an operator

   A. will be in the picking room alone while designating his choice
   B. must wait in the picking room after making his choice until all the runs have been chosen
   C. is informed that he may pick his run at any time he wishes to on pick day
   D. may have someone else pick for him if he cannot be present on the day of the pick

33. In order to pick on the extra list, an operator must

   A. present a doctor's certificate
   B. have been inactive for sixty days
   C. appear at the picking room in person
   D. be willing to transfer to a terminal where all the runs have been picked

34. Once a bus operator picks a run and his name has been entered by the monitor, he

   A. must accept the run picked as no changes will be permitted
   B. can change his mind if the choice was made by proxy
   C. may ask the monitor to erase his pick if the next man has not yet picked
   D. can swap runs with another operator but only after sixty days

35. An operator making his pick after having been out sick for three months must

   A. pick on the extra list
   B. present a doctor's certificate to the monitor
   C. wait two weeks before returning to duty
   D. pick an early run or trick

36. The rules state that

   A. only 100 men can pick in any one day
   B. cooperation is demanded and a penalty will be imposed on any operator who is uncooperative
   C. a preference slip must be signed by the monitor
   D. an operator must make his pick within 5 minutes time

Questions 37-42.

DIRECTIONS: Questions 37 through 42, inclusive, are based on the Information for Operators given below. Read this information carefully before answering these questions.

INFORMATION FOR OPERATORS

In spite of caution signs and signal lights, more than 42% of all automobile accidents occur at intersections. In narrow city streets with narrow sidewalks and heavy traffic, you should approach intersections at 15 miles per hour with your foot just touching the brake pedal, in wet weather, 10 miles per hour. At rural intersections, be sure you have a clear view of the intersecting road to the right and left at least 300 feet before you reach the intersection, otherwise slow down.

At an intersection, the vehicle on your right has the right of way if both of you reach the intersection at the same time. You have the right of way over the vehicle at your left under the same condition, but must not insist upon it if there is risk of a collision.

Do not pass another vehicle at an intersection. Stop your vehicle to allow pedestrians to cross in front of you at intersections if they have stepped off the curb. Operators must use extreme caution when approaching or turning at intersections not controlled by a signal light.

37. One of the facts given is that 37.____
    A. nearly all accidents occur at country crossroads
    B. nearly half of all accidents occur at traffic lights in cities
    C. approximately two-fifths of all accidents occur where roads or streets cross one another
    D. 42% of all accidents occur on narrow city streets

38. According to this information, if you are approaching an intersection at which there is no 38.____
    traffic light and a man has started to cross the street in front of you, you must
    A. reduce your speed to 15 miles per hour
    B. blow your horn lightly
    C. stop to allow him to cross
    D. place your foot so it just touches the brake pedal

39. At an intersection not protected by a traffic light, you should grant the right of way to the 39.____
    vehicle approaching from the
    A. right if it is 300 feet from the intersection
    B. left if it is 300 feet from the intersection
    C. opposite direction if its right turn indicator is flashing
    D. left or the right if there is danger of a collision

40. In the information, it is clearly stated that an intersection should be approached at 15 40.____
    miles per hour if you
    A. are driving on a narrow city street in heavy traffic
    B. do not see a warning sign 300 feet from the intersection
    C. do not intend to pass the vehicle ahead
    D. see a car stopped on the intersecting street waiting to cross

41. The information clearly states 41.___

    A. most city streets are narrow
    B. all city intersections should be approached at 10 miles per hour
    C. passing another vehicle at an intersection is forbidden
    D. there is a clear view of rural intersections from a distance of 300 feet

42. The type of accident referred to probably does NOT include the striking of a 42.___

    A. pedestrian by a railroad train
    B. pedestrian by a passenger car
    C. bus by a taxicab
    D. bus by a truck

43. The register on the fare box of a certain bus has five dials and shows the total number of 43.___
    cents collected. When a particular bus operator starts his tour of duty, the register reading is 08980, and at the conclusion of his tour of duty, the reading is 14560. The total number of 90-cent fares collected during this operator's tour was

    A. 62   B. 68   C. 73   D. 77

44. Increasing use is being made today of unmarked police cars. 44.___
    The PRINCIPAL reason for the use of such cars is to

    A. increase the city's revenue from traffic tickets
    B. enforce the regulation against hitch-hikers
    C. prevent accidents by stopping traffic violators
    D. man them with detectives instead of uniformed policemen

45. The operator of the car ahead going at about the speed limit extends his hand and arm in 45.___
    a straight line at about 45 degrees upward.
    Since this is NOT one of the standard hand signals, your SAFEST move is to

    A. swing out and pass him immediately to avoid any more confusion
    B. remain behind prepared for any move on his part until the situation is clarified
    C. pull up alongside and tell him to signal properly
    D. blow your horn until he gives a correct signal

46. Colored lights in the shape of arrows are used to help control traffic at certain intersections. 46.___
    When a driver approaches a signal consisting of a green light, a green arrow pointing to the right, and a red arrow pointing to the left, he knows that he is permitted to go straight ahead

    A. if in the right hand lane only
    B. or make a right turn, but not a left turn
    C. only if there is no cross traffic from the right
    D. but watch out for merging traffic from the left

47. The meaning conveyed by a *Yield Right of Way* sign is that drivers must 47.___

    A. come to a complete stop before passing the sign
    B. grant the right of way to oncoming traffic making a left turn

C. grant the right of way to cars on the intersecting street
D. grant the right of way to pedestrians

48. The law requires that cars having four-wheel brakes must be able to stop in 30 feet from a speed of 20 miles per hour, and in 120 feet from 40 miles per hour.
From these requirements and your own knowledge of automobiles in motion, it is MOST logical to conclude that

   A. the law is more lenient in regard to fast cars than slow ones
   B. when speed is doubled, the needed braking distance is multiplied by four
   C. drivers' reactions slow down greatly as speed increases
   D. any 20 mile per hour increase in speed will require 90 feet more of braking distance

48.____

49. One of the rules governing bus operators states that *They must not use omnibuses to push other omnibuses or vehicles unless ordered by a member of the supervisory force.*
According to this rule, if a taxicab driver asks the operator of an empty bus to give him a push to get started, the operator should

   A. tell the taxicab driver it is against the rules, and go on
   B. do so if there is a patrolman nearby
   C. telephone headquarters to get permission
   D. tell the taxicab driver to ask the operator of a private car

49.____

50. A particular bus has twelve cross seats holding two passengers each, plus rear and longitudinal seats holding a total of 14 additional passengers.
If the number of standees permitted on a bus is one-half the number of seated passengers, the total passenger capacity of this bus is

   A. 26   B. 38   C. 39   D. 57

50.____

KEY (CORRECT ANSWERS)

1. A	11. C	21. C	31. D	41. C
2. B	12. D	22. B	32. D	42. A
3. B	13. C	23. D	33. D	43. A
4. D	14. C	24. A	34. A	44. C
5. A	15. A	25. D	35. B	45. B
6. B	16. B	26. C	36. D	46. B
7. D	17. B	27. B	37. C	47. C
8. D	18. A	28. B	38. C	48. B
9. A	19. D	29. C	39. D	49. A
10. C	20. D	30. D	40. A	50. D

EXAMINATION SECTION
TEST 1

DIRECTIONS: Each question or incomplete statement is followed by several suggested answers or completions. Select the one that BEST answers the question or completes the statement. *PRINT THE LETTER OF THE CORRECT ANSWER IN THE SPACE AT THE RIGHT.*

1. A certain bus operator reports for work on Monday at 9:00 A.M. and normally clears at 4:30 P.M. He is paid at the hourly rate of $12.80.
   What should his GROSS pay be for this day if due to unusually heavy traffic conditions he gets only 10 minutes for lunch?

   A. $114.00　　B. $109.80　　C. $108.80　　D. $102.40

   1._____

2. On the dispatcher's daily report of intervals operated and passenger traffic checks, there are column headings for recording each of the following EXCEPT

   A. run numbers　　　　　　B. route numbers
   C. passenger counts　　　　D. names of bus operators

   2._____

3. On the daily trip report, the code letter *A* is used to indicate

   A. extra trips (scheduled or unscheduled)
   B. late pull-in
   C. turned short of scheduled destination
   D. scheduled one-way trips lost

   3._____

4. When a bus operator is required to report to the medical staff for a physical examination outside his tour of duty, he will be paid at his regular rate for _____ hour(s).

   A. 1　　B. 2　　C. 3　　D. 4

   4._____

5. Following are four statements concerning the operation of buses which might be correct:
   I. Operators of buses must exercise such control as to preclude the possibility of more than two buses entering or standing in a bus stop simultaneous
   II. Where flood conditions exist, bus operators must not operate through the water even at a slow rate of speed
   III. Bus operators must operate their buses in accordance with their schedule at all times
   IV. In no case should a bus operator use a bus to push other buses or vehicles

   Which of the following choices lists all of the above statements that are correct and none that is incorrect?

   A. I　　B. I, II　　C. III　　D. III, IV

   5._____

Questions 6-9.

DIRECTIONS: Questions 6 through 9 are based on the bulletin order shown below titled TRESPASSERS ON TRANSIT AUTHORITY SURFACE PROPERTIES. Refer to this bulletin order when answering these questions.

TRESPASSERS ON TRANSIT AUTHORITY SURFACE PROPERTIES

Your attention is again directed to the need for rigid controls . to prevent unauthorized persons from entering Transit Authority property.

All strangers or persons who are not recognized as having official business on the property will be questioned by the first member of supervision who encounters them and such persons will be ejected immediately upon failure to present authorization or valid reason for being on the property.

In all cases where trespassers refuse to leave the property, or offer physical resistance to ejection, the Transit Authority police will be promptly notified for assistance and all members of supervision present will assist in the immediate identification and ejection of the trespassers.
Where property protection employees are assigned, they too will be notified.

Immediately following the call for Transit police assistance, notice of the circumstances will be given to surface control on Extension B6-504.

All surface transportation employees must be advised that entrance and exit from surface properties must be through authorized locations only, and failure to comply will be considered a flagrant disregard for outstanding regulations.

Finally, a complete written report is to be forwarded to the Assistant General Superintendent, Operations, of all instances dealing with the above.

6. The following are four possible cases that might be correct in which a supervisor may eject a person whom he does not recognize from Transit Authority property: The person
    I. has a legitimate reason for being on Transit Authority property
    II. presents authorization for being on Transit Authority property
    III. has accidently wandered onto Transit Authority property
    IV. has no proof of his identity

    Which of the following choices lists all of the above cases that are CORRECT?

    A. I, II B. I, III C. II, IV D. III, IV

7. If a supervisor is uncertain that a person who he does NOT know has official business on Transit Authority property, the FIRST action that the supervisor should take is to

    A. eject the person
    B. call the Transit Authority police
    C. call other members of supervision for assistance
    D. question the person

8. When an unauthorized person has been ejected from Transit Authority property, a written report of the incident must be forwarded to

    A. the Superintendent of Operations
    B. Surface Control
    C. the Assistant General Superintendent, Operations
    D. the location chief

3 (#1)

9. The following are four possible situations that might be correct in which the Transit Authority police should be notified for assistance:
    I. A trespasser refuses to leave Transit Authority property
    II. A trespasser is encountered on Transit Authority property
    III. A stranger enters Transit Authority property through an unauthorized entrance
    IV. A trespasser physically resists ejection
   Which of the following choices lists all of the above situations that are CORRECT?

   A. I, III B. I, IV C. II, III D. III, IV

10. When a general dispatcher assigns a code classification of C for an accident, it indicates that the degree of responsibility for the bus operator involved in the accident is

    A. 25% B. 50% C. 75% D. 100%

11. When a special inspector requests information from a bus operator, the inspector is required to identify himself by showing the operator

    A. a special identification card
    B. his badge
    C. both a special identification card and his badge
    D. a letter authorizing his request for information

12. A situation arises and you find that you must criticize a bus operator for poor work performance.
    Of the following, it is MOST important for you to

    A. inform the operator about his grievance rights
    B. obtain approval of your action from your supervisor
    C. keep a record of what you say to the operator
    D. be specific about your criticism and not to use generalities

13. When two bus operators want to exchange runs permanently after schedules are picked, the exchange must be approved by the

    A. assistant general superintendent
    B. superintendent of operations
    C. location chief
    D. crew dispatcher

14. A bus operator reports on a Monday at 2:09 A.M., swings from 5:32 A.M. to 6:16 A.M., and clears at 10:21 A.M.
    The night differential for this run, in hours and minutes, is ____ hours and ____ minutes.

    A. 8; 12 B. 3; 50 C. 3; 23 D. 0; 0

15. The run pay, in hours and minutes, for a bus operator who reports on a weekday at 11:42 M., swings from 3:29 P.M. to 4:17 P.M., and clears at 9:08 P.M. is ____ hours and ____ minutes.

    A. 10; 9 B. 9; 45 C. 9; 23 D. 8; 0

16. The code that is used over the two-way radio for messages pertaining to winter operations, such as reporting snow drifts, is code   16.___

    A. 9   B. 10   C. 11   D. 12

17. Bus operators who qualify to receive 60% sick pay may receive this benefit if they are out sick for a MINIMUM of _____ or more consecutive working days.   17.___

    A. 5   B. 9   C. 14   D. 21

18. When a dispatcher makes it a practice to be fair and firm in disciplining bus operators in all cases of rule violations, including those of a minor nature, it is considered a   18.___

    A. *good* practice, because it makes it easier for the dispatcher to administer discipline on this basis
    B. *bad* practice, because employees do not want to be disciplined for minor violations
    C. *good* practice, because not administering discipline for minor violations can lead to a more serious erosion of discipline
    D. *bad* practice, since administering discipline for minor violations leads to union complaints

19. After the commencement of operations of a new line, all runs on the new line must be put up for a depot pick WITHIN   19.___

    A. 48 hours   B. 3 days   C. 5 days   D. 2 weeks

20. Of the following, the BEST course of action for a dispatcher to follow when he observes for the first time a bus operator scraping the tires of his bus against the curb is to   20.___

    A. observe the operator to see whether he commits other driving mistakes
    B. inform the operator of the mistake he made and observe whether he makes this same driving mistake in the future
    C. reprimand the operator and warn him that you will be watching him closely
    D. make a record of the occurrence and bring it to the attention of the location chief

KEY (CORRECT ANSWERS)

1.	C	11.	A
2.	D	12.	D
3.	D	13.	A
4.	C	14.	B
5.	A	15.	B
6.	D	16.	C
7.	D	17.	B
8.	C	18.	C
9.	B	19.	A
10.	B	20.	B

TEST 2

DIRECTIONS: Each question or incomplete statement is followed by several suggested answers or completions. Select the one that BEST answers the question or completes the statement. *PRINT THE LETTER OF THE CORRECT ANSWER IN THE SPACE AT THE RIGHT.*

Questions 1-12.

DIRECTIONS: Questions 1 through 12 are based on the partly filled-in schedule shown on the next page..

1. The TOTAL PAY for Run No. 27, in hours and minutes, is 1.____
   A. 8:00 B. 8:53 C. 8:55 D. 9:20

2. Of the following runs, the one which has the most TRAVEL time is Run No. 2.____
   A. 26 B. 29 C. 30 D. 31

3. The paid SWING for Run No. 28, in minutes, is 3.____
   A. 0 B. 52 C. 56 D. 60

4. The total TRAVEL time for Run No. 27, in minutes, is 4.____
   A. 5 B. 10 C. 15 D. 20

5. The overtime ALLOWANCE for Run No. 28, in minutes, is 5.____
   A. 0 B. 5 C. 9 D. 14

6. The TOTAL PAY for Run No. 30, in hours and minutes, is 6.____
   A. 7:14 B. 8:00 C. 8:02 D. 8:03

7. For Run No. 29, the total number of TRIPS, including any trips made going to and from the depot, for both halves of the run is 7.____
   A. 4 B. 7 C. 8 D. 9

8. The SPREAD for Run No. 29, in hours and minutes, is 8.____
   A. 7:07 B. 7:18 C. 7:23 D. 7:43

9. The total MILEAGE accumulated for all six runs shown on the schedule is 9.____
   A. 330 B. 339 C. 340 D. 350

10. The VEHICLE time for Run No. 30, in hours and minutes, is 10.____
    A. 6:49 B. 7:14 C. 7:19 D. 7:37

11. The BOOST time for Run No. 26, in minutes, is 11.____
    A. 0 B. 7 C. 17 D. 59

12. For Run No. 27, the total number of TRIPS, including any trips made going to and from the depot, for the first half of the run is 12.____
    A. 4 B. 5 C. 6 D. 7

USE THIS SCHEDULE FOR ANSWERING QUESTIONS 1 TO 12

ROUTE: B - 909 - APPLE ST.　　BROOKLYN DIVISION

WEEKDAY SCHEDULE MO. S - 305

EFFECTIVE: APRIL 26　　EAST NEW TOW1 DEPOT

Run	Re-port	A.M.											Mileage	Clear	TIME-HOURS & MINUTES PAY TIME: STR/PRE/SRI-P/WAL-D/HAC/LVE/A-LONG/SIN-WIG/TDI-OG/TPG/AAF/LYY
26	A.M. 916	P.O. 926	936 1041	1142 1247	158 —	207 R-22		W 259 R-7	— 359	454 R-40			39 19	509	
27	A.M. 921		R-7	936	955 1102	1214 119	T 222 —	227 R-44			322 R-21	T 334 429	550 —	559 R-47	38 24	614
28	A.M. 928		R-4	943	1006 1111	1214 119	230 —	239 R-35			335 R-14	— 431	552 R-43		39 18	537
29	A.M. 930	P.O. 940	T 945 1052	1206	1215 R-18			W 1251 R-3	— 151	302 407	458 R-41				23 35	513
30	A.M. 936	P.O. 946	956 1101	T 1206 111	222 —	231 R-23			319 R-8	— 415	518	T 523 R-66			39 20	538
31	A.M. 1008	R-10	1023	— 1119	1222 127	222 R-25			W 315 R-33	— 415	526 —	535 R-67			34 22	550

SYMBOLS:
PLAIN TRIPS - Lemon St. and Orange St. to Apple St. and Oak St.
T TRIPS - Peach St. and Apple St. to Elm St.
W TRIPS - Lemon St. and Orange St. to 11m St.

NOTES:
FROM: Lemon St. and Orange St. via Orange St. and Apple St. to Oak St.
RETURN: Via Apple St. and Orange St. to Lemon St.
RELIEFS MADE AT CHERRY ST. AND APPLE ST. 3 5 MINUTE
TRAVEL ALLOWANCE, VIA ROUTE B-816

13. Supervisors should see to it that personal calls made by employees over the transit authority telephone system are reduced to the barest minimum PRIMARILY because

    A. these calls interfere with essential transit authority business
    B. allowing employees to make too many personal calls may cause a reduction in morale
    C. these calls usually involve emergencies which can affect an employee's performance
    D. these calls deprive the telephone company of revenue in their public telephones on transit authority property

14. When a dispatcher gives instructions to a bus operator, the dispatcher will MOST likely avoid confusing the operator if

    A. he gives the instructions to the operator as quickly as possible
    B. he repeats the instructions to the operator several times using different words each time
    C. his instructions are clear and concise
    D. his instructions contain as many details as possible

15. A recent bulletin order cautions bus operators NOT to operate close to burning flares marking traffic hazards. Following are four possible reasons for this caution which may be correct:
    I. The transit authority must pay for the cost of replacing damaged flares
    II. The bus equipment can be damaged
    III. The effectiveness of these flares may be impaired
    IV. Operating closer than 10 feet from a burning flare constitutes a traffic violation

    Which of the following choices lists all of the above reasons that are CORRECT according to the bulletin order?

    A. I, II   B. I, III   C. II, III   D. III, IV

16. The patrol car log is used by patrol car dispatchers to keep a record of

    A. violations issued
    B. schedule changes
    C. maintenance performed on the patrol car
    D. radio messages received in the patrol car

17. A bus operator finishes his regular run and is then assigned a second piece of work. He will be paid time and one-half for reserve time, provided the difference between the clearing time of the first piece and the reporting time of the second piece of work does NOT exceed

    A. 30 minutes   B. 45 minutes
    C. 59 minutes   D. 2 hours

18. On a particular bus line, 10 buses per hour are scheduled to leave a terminal between the hours of 4:00 P.M. and 6:00 P.M., while 6 buses per hour are scheduled to leave between 6:00 P.M. and 8:00 P.M.
    The increase in headway after 6:00 P.M. is CLOSEST to _____ minutes.

    A. 10　　B. 8　　C. 6　　D. 4

19. According to step 1 of the grievance procedure, a bus operator may present a grievance to his immediate superior

    A. in writing personally only
    B. orally only
    C. orally, or in writing personally only
    D. orally, or in writing personally, or through the union

20. According to the grievance procedure, after an aggrieved bus operator has received an unfavorable step 2 decision, he nay appeal this decision, but must do so within _____ days.

    A. 2　　B. 3　　C. 4　　D. 5

KEY (CORRECT ANSWERS)

1.	B	11.	B
2.	D	12.	C
3.	C	13.	A
4.	B	14.	C
5.	A	15.	C
6.	C	16.	D
7.	C	17.	C
8.	D	18.	D
9.	D	19.	D
10.	A	20.	B

EXAMINATION SECTION
TEST 1

DIRECTIONS: Each question or incomplete statement is followed by several suggested answers or completions. Select the one that BEST answers the question or completes the statement. *PRINT THE LETTER OF THE CORRECT ANSWER IN THE SPACE AT THE RIGHT.*

1. An employee under your supervision complains that he is assigned to work late more often than any of the other employees in the garage. You check the records and find that this isn't so.
   You should

   A. advise this employee not to worry about what the other employees do but to see that he puts in a full day's work himself
   B. explain to this employee that you get the same complaint from all the other employees
   C. inform this employee that you have checked the records and the complaint is not justified
   D. not assign this employee to work late for a few days in order to keep him satisfied

   1._____

2. A garage employee has reported late for work several times.
   His supervisor should

   A. give this employee less desirable assignments
   B. overlook the lateness if the employee's work is otherwise exceptional
   C. recommend disciplinary action for habitual lateness
   D. talk the matter over with the employee before doing anything further

   2._____

3. In choosing a man to be in charge in his absence, the supervisor should select first the employee who

   A. has ability to supervise others
   B. has been longest with the organization
   C. has the nicest appearance and manner
   D. is most skilled in his assigned duties

   3._____

4. An employee under your supervision comes to you to complain about a decision you have made in assigning the men. He is excited and angry. You think what he is complaining about is not important, but it seems very important to him.
   The BEST way for you to handle this is to

   A. let him talk until *he gets it off his chest* and then explain the reasons for your decision
   B. refuse to talk to him until he has cooled off
   C. show him at once how unimportant the matter is and how ridiculous his arguments are
   D. tell him to take it up with your superior if he disagrees with your decision

   4._____

5. Suppose that a new employee has been appointed and assigned to your supervision. When this man reports for work, it would be BEST for you to

   5._____

A. ask him questions about different problems connected with a motor vehicle and see if he answers them correctly
B. check him carefully while he carries out some routine assignment that you give him
C. explain to him the general nature of the work he will be required to do
D. make a careful study of his previous work record before coming to the Department

6. The competent supervisor will be friendly with the employees under his supervision but will avoid close familiarity.
This statement is justified MAINLY because

    A. a friendly attitude on the part of the supervisor toward the employee is likely to cause suspicion on the part of the employee
    B. a supervisor can handle his employees better if he doesn't know their personal problems
    C. close familiarity may interfere with the discipline needed for good supervisor-subordinate relationships
    D. familiarity with the employees may be a sign of lack of ability on the part of the supervisor

7. An employee disagrees with the instructions that you, his supervisor, have given him for carrying out a certain assignment.
The BEST action for you to take is to tell this employee that

    A. he can do what he wants but you will hold him responsible for failure
    B. orders must be carried out or morale will fall apart
    C. this job has been done in this way for many years with great success
    D. you will be glad to listen to his objections and to his suggestions for improvement

8. As a supervisor, it is LEAST important for you to use a new employee's probationary period for the purpose of

    A. carefully checking how he performs the work you assign him
    B. determining whether he can perform the duties of his job efficiently
    C. preparing him for promotion to a higher position
    D. showing him how to carry out his assigned duties properly

9. Suppose you have just given an employee under your supervision instructions on how to carry out a certain assignment.
The BEST way to check that he has understood your instructions is to

    A. ask him to repeat your instructions word for word
    B. check the progress of his work the first chance you get
    C. invite him to ask questions if he has any doubts
    D. question him briefly about the main points of the assignment

10. Suppose you find it necessary to change a procedure that the men under your supervision have been following for a long time.
A good way to get their cooperation for this change would be to

    A. bring them together to talk over the new procedure and explain the reasons for its adoption
    B. explain to the men that if most of them still don't approve of the change after giving it a fair try, you will consider giving it up

C. give them a few weeks' notice of the proposed change in procedure
D. not enforce the new procedure strictly at the beginning

11. An order can be given by a supervisor in such a way as to make the employee want to obey it.
According to this statement, it is MOST reasonable to suppose that

    A. a person will be glad to obey an order if he realizes that he must
    B. if an order is given properly, it will be obeyed more willingly
    C. it is easier to obey an order than to give one correctly
    D. supervisors should inspire confidence by their actions as well as by their words

12. If one of the men you supervise disagrees with how you rate his work, the BEST way for you to handle this is to

    A. advise him to appeal to your superior about it
    B. decline to discuss the matter with him in order to keep discipline
    C. explain why you rate him the way you do and talk it over with him
    D. tell him that you are better qualified to rate his work than he is

13. A supervisor should be familiar with the experience and abilities of the employees under his supervision MAINLY because

    A. each employee's work is highly important and requires a person of outstanding ability
    B. it will help him to know which employees are best fitted for certain assignments
    C. nearly all men have the same basic ability to do any job equally well
    D. superior background shortly shows itself in superior work quality, regardless of assignment

14. The competent supervisor will try to develop respect rather than fear in his subordinates.
This statement is justified MAINLY because

    A. fear is always present and, for best results, respect must be developed to offset it
    B. it is generally easier to develop respect in the men than it is to develop fear
    C. men who respect their supervisor are more likely to give more than the required minimum amount and quality of work
    D. respect is based on the individual and fear is based on the organization as a whole

15. If one of the employees you supervise does outstanding work, you should

    A. explain to him how his work can still be improved so that he will not become self-satisfied
    B. mildly criticize the other men for not doing as good a job as this man
    C. praise him for his work so that he will know it is appreciated
    D. say nothing or he might become conceited

16. A supervisor can BEST help establish good morale among his employees if he

    A. confides in them about his personal problems in order to encourage them to confide in him
    B. encourages them to become friendly with him but discourages social engagements with them

C. points out to them the advantages of having a cooperative spirit in the department
D. sticks to the same rules that he expects them to follow

17. The one of the following situations which would seem to indicate poor scheduling of work by the supervisor in a garage is 17.___

    A. everybody in the garage seeming to be very busy at the same time
    B. re-assignment of a man to other work because of breakdown of a piece of equipment
    C. two employees on vacation at the same time
    D. two operators waiting to have their vehicles greased and the oil changed

Questions 18-20.

DIRECTIONS: Questions 18 through 20 are to be answered ONLY on the basis of the information given in the following paragraph.

The supervisor will gain the respect of the members of his staff and increase his influence over them by controlling his temper and avoiding criticizing anyone publicly. When a mistake is made, the good supervisor will talk it over with the employee quietly and privately. The supervisor will listen to the employee's story, suggest the better way of doing the job, and offer help so the mistake won't happen again. Before closing the discussion, the supervisor should try to find something good to say about other parts of the employee's work. Some praise and appreciation, along with instruction, is more likely to encourage an employee to improve in those areas where he is weakest.

18. A good title that would show the meaning of this entire paragraph would be 18.___

    A. How to Correct Employee Errors
    B. How to Praise Employees
    C. Mistakes are Preventable
    D. The Weak Employe

19. According to the above paragraph, the work of an employee who has made a mistake is more likely to improve if the supervisor 19.___

    A. avoids criticizing him
    B. gives him a chance to suggest a better way of doing the work
    C. listens to the employee's excuses to see if he is right
    D. praises good work at the same time he corrects the mistake

20. According to the above paragraph, when a supervisor needs to correct an employee's mistake, it is important that he 20.___

    A. allow some time to go by after the mistake is made
    B. do so when other employees are not present
    C. show his influence with his tone of voice
    D. tell other employees to avoid the same mistake

Questions 21-24.

DIRECTIONS: Questions 21 through 24 are to be answered ONLY on the basis of the information given in the following paragraph.

All automotive accidents, no matter how slight, are to be reported to the Safety Division by the employee involved on Accident Report Form S-23 in duplicate. When the accident is of such a nature that it requires the filling out of the State Motor Vehicle Report Form MV-104, this form is also prepared by the employee in duplicate and sent to the Safety Division for comparison with the Form S-23. The Safety Division forwards both copies of Form MV-104 to the Corporation Counsel, who sends one copy to the State Bureau of Motor Vehicles. When the information on the Form S-23 indicates that the employee may be at fault, an investigation is made by the Safety Division. If this investigation shows that the employee was at fault, the employee's dispatcher is asked to file a complaint on Form D-11. The foreman of mechanics prepares a damage report on Form D-8 and an estimate of the cost of repairs on Form D-9. The dispatcher's complaint, the damage report, the repair estimate, and the employee's previous accident record are sent to the Safety Division where they are studied together with the accident report. The Safety Division then recommends whether or not disciplinary action should be taken against the employee.

21. According to the above paragraph, the Safety Division should be notified whenever an automotive accident has occurred by means of

    A. Form S-23
    B. Forms S-23 and MV-104
    C. Forms S-23, MV-104, D-8, D-9, and D-11
    D. Forms S-23, MV-104, D-8, D-9, and D-11 and employee's accident report

21.____

22. According to the above paragraph, the forwarding of the Form MV-104 to the State Bureau of Motor Vehicles is done by the

    A. Corporation Counsel
    B. dispatcher
    C. employee involved in the accident
    D. Safety Division

22.____

23. According to the above paragraph, the Safety Division investigates an automotive accident if the

    A. accident is serious enough to be reported to the State Bureau of Motor Vehicles
    B. dispatcher files a complaint
    C. employee appears to have been at fault
    D. employee's previous accident report is poor

23.____

24. Of the forms mentioned in the above paragraph, the dispatcher is responsible for preparing the

    A. accident report form
    B. complaint form
    C. damage report
    D. estimate of cost of repairs

24.____

Questions 25-27.

DIRECTIONS: Questions 25 through 27 are to be answered ONLY on the basis of the information given in the following paragraph.

One of the major problems in the control of city motor equipment, and especially passenger equipment, is keeping the equipment working for the city and for the city alone for as many hours of the day as is practical. Even when most city employees try to get the most out of the cars, a poor system of control will result in wasted car hours. Some city employees have a legitimate use for a car all day long while others use a car only a small part of the day and then let it stand. As a rule, trucks are easier to control than passenger cars because they are usually assigned to a specific job where a foreman continually oversees them. Even though trucks are usually fully utilized, there are times when the normal work assignment cannot be carried out because of weather conditions or seasonal changes. At such times, a control system could plan to make the trucks available for other uses.

25. According to the above paragraph, a problem connected with controlling the use of city motor equipment is

    A. increasing the life span of the equipment
    B. keeping the equipment working all hours of the day
    C. preventing the over-use of the equipment to avoid breakdowns
    D. preventing the private use of the equipment

26. According to the above paragraph, a good control system for passenger equipment will MOST likely lead to

    A. better employees being assigned to operate the cars
    B. fewer city employees using city cars
    C. fewer wasted car hours for city cars
    D. insuring that city cars are used for legitimate purposes

27. According to the above paragraph, a control system for trucks is useful because

    A. a foreman usually supervises each job
    B. special conditions sometimes prevent the planned use of a truck
    C. trucks are easier to control than passenger cars
    D. trucks are usually assigned to specific jobs where they cannot be fully utilized

Questions 28-33.

DIRECTIONS: In the paragraph below, some of the underlined words have been purposely changed and spoil the meaning that the rest of the paragraph is meant to give. Read the paragraph carefully, then answer Questions 28 through 33.

The motor vehicle supervisor who is <u>responsible</u> for training drivers in the operation of <u>special</u> equipment cannot expect a man to carry out all of his duties <u>poorly</u> <u>immediately</u> after receiving instruction. The employee may be <u>overwhelmed</u> by all of the details he must master, <u>happy</u> because he is <u>associated</u> with new fellow workers, or fearful that he may not <u>succeed</u> on the job. It is the supervisor's <u>job</u> to make the <u>operator</u> feel at ease and <u>discourage</u> his self-confidence. The supervisor must also vary the speed of the <u>driving</u> according to the operator's <u>capacity</u> to <u>absorb</u> the instruction without undue <u>pressure</u> or confusion. All learners <u>progress</u> through <u>several</u> stages of <u>development</u> <u>unless</u> they become expert in their duties. As the operator's skills <u>increase</u>, he will require <u>more</u> instruction but the supervisor should be available to correct <u>mistakes</u> promptly to prevent wrong <u>habits</u> being formed.

28. Of the following words underlined in the above paragraph, the one that does NOT give the real meaning that the rest of the paragraph is meant to give is

    A. responsible B. special
    C. happy   D. immediately

29. Of the following words underlined in the above paragraph, the one that does NOT give the real meaning that the rest of the paragraph is meant to give is

    A. overwhelmed B. happy
    C. associated   D. succeed

30. Of the following words underlined in the above paragraph, the one that does NOT give the real meaning that the rest of the paragraph is meant to give is

    A. job   B. operator
    C. discourage   D. self-confidence

31. Of the following words underlined in the above paragraph, the one that does NOT give the real meaning that the rest of the paragraph is meant to give is

    A. driving   B. capacity   C. absorb   D. pressure

32. Of the following words underlined in the above paragraph, the one that does NOT give the real meaning that the rest of the paragraph is meant to give is

    A. progress   B. several
    C. development D. unless

33. Of the following words underlined in the above paragraph, the one that does NOT give the real meaning that the rest of the paragraph is meant to give is

    A. increase B. more   C. mistakes   D. habits

Questions 34-40.

DIRECTIONS: Each of Questions 34 through 40 consists of a word in capital letters followed by four suggested meanings of the word. Select the word or phrase which means MOST NEARLY the same as the word in capital letters.

34. ACCELERATE

    A. adjust   B. press   C. quicken   D. strip

35. ALIGN

    A. bring into line   B. carry out
    C. happen by chance   D. join together

36. CONTRACTION

    A. agreement   B. denial
    C. presentation D. shrinkage

37. INTERVAL

    A. ending   B. mixing together of
    C. space of time D. weaken

38. LUBRICATE 38.____
   A. bend back   B. make slippery
   C. rub out   D. soften

39. OBSOLETE 39.____
   A. broken-down   B. hard to find
   C. high-priced   D. out of date

40. RETARD 40.____
   A. delay   B. flatten   C. rest   D. tally

KEY (CORRECT ANSWERS)

1. C	11. B	21. A	31. A
2. D	12. C	22. A	32. D
3. A	13. B	23. C	33. B
4. A	14. C	24. B	34. C
5. C	15. C	25. D	35. A
6. C	16. D	26. C	36. D
7. D	17. D	27. B	37. C
8. C	18. A	28. C	38. B
9. D	19. D	29. B	39. D
10. A	20. B	30. C	40. A

TEST 2

DIRECTIONS: Each question or incomplete statement is followed by several suggested answers or completions. Select the one that BEST answers the question or completes the statement. *PRINT THE LETTER OF THE CORRECT ANSWER IN THE SPACE AT THE RIGHT.*

Questions 1-3.

DIRECTIONS: Questions 1 through 3 consist of a word in capital letters followed by four suggested meanings of the word. Select the word or phrase which means MOST NEARLY the same as the word in capital letters.

1. SYNCHRONIZE
   A. draw out
   B. happen at the same time
   C. move at a steady rate
   D. turn smoothly

2. OSCILLATE
   A. attract   B. echo   C. roll   D. swing

3. TERMINAL
   A. last   B. moldy   C. named   D. spoken

4. In a certain garage, when the dispatcher issues gas and oil to a vehicle, he notes on his record the mileage reading of the vehicle.
   This is probably done MAINLY in order to
   A. check gas consumption against distance traveled
   B. compare age of vehicle with economy of operation
   C. decide when the vehicle should be scheduled for a grease job
   D. estimate future life expectancy of the vehicle

5. A supervisor of motor vehicle equipment was asked by the head of the bureau to investigate a certain procedure used in the garage and write a report with a recommendation whether the procedure should be changed. The supervisor, after he finished his investigation, made his report in which he said: *I recommend that you base your decision* to change the present procedure on whether or not the new procedure will improve operations.
   In this case, the supervisor carried out his assignment
   A. *poorly,* because he should have given his recommendation right at the beginning of the report
   B. *poorly,* because his investigation should have brought out whether the new procedure would improve operations
   C. *well,* because he left the final decision about changing the procedure up to the head of the bureau
   D. *well,* because he made an investigation and turned in a report as required

6. When a supervisor writes a report, it is LEAST important that 6.____

    A. all paragraphs in the report be of the same length
    B. a summary or list of the recommendations be given at the beginning of the report if the report is long
    C. independent ideas be taken up in separate paragraphs of the report
    D. the report give all the evidence on which the conclusions are based

7. The supervisor who makes a special point of using long words in preparing written reports is, in general, PROBABLY being 7.____

    A. *unwise,* because a written report should be factual and accurate
    B. *unwise,* because simplicity in a report is usually desirable
    C. *wise,* because the written report will become a permanent record
    D. *wise,* because with long words he can use the right emphasis in his report

8. The most thorough investigation is of no value if the report written by the person who made the investigation does not help his superior to decide what action to take. According to this statement, it is LEAST correct to suppose that 8.____

    A. an investigation is of no value unless it is thorough
    B. a purpose of the report turned in after an investigation is to help supervisors decide what action to take
    C. the report on an investigation is usually written by the person who made the investigation
    D. the value of an investigation depends in part on the report turned in

9. Before you turn in a report you have written of an investigation that you made, you discover some additional information that you didn't know about before.
Whether or not you rewrite your report to include this additional information should depend MAINLY on the 9.____

    A. amount of time left in which to submit the report
    B. effect this information will have on the conclusions of the report
    C. number of changes that you will have to make in your original report
    D. possibility of turning in a supplementary report later

10. The advantage of using an *inspection check sheet* when making inspections of premises or equipment is that 10.____

    A. fewer inspections are required
    B. the inspection becomes easy and can be done by a subordinate
    C. there is less chance of forgetting some important point of the inspection
    D. there is less paper work

11. Of the following methods for keeping supplies and records of supplies, the one that will MOST quickly tell you at any time how many pieces of any item are on hand in the supply room is 11.____

    A. keeping a minimum number of each item on hand
    B. recording each item when it is added to or removed from stock
    C. stocking the same number of pieces of each item and reordering weekly to keep the count even
    D. taking a daily count

12. When a supervisor submits a report on a motor vehicle accident, it is LEAST important for him to include in his report the

    A. addresses of the witnesses to the accident
    B. number of the police precinct where the accident happened
    C. probable cause of the accident
    D. time of the accident

13. The MAIN reason a supervisor in charge of motor vehicle equipment or personnel should make sure that his men obey the safety rules is that

    A. accident prevention is a new program and should be tried out
    B. every accident can be prevented
    C. other safety measures are not needed where safety rules are obeyed
    D. safety rules are based on proven methods of accident prevention

14. When he investigates an accident in which a city vehicle was involved, the MAIN object of the supervisor should be to

    A. complete the investigation as fast as possible
    B. determine if the city operator's record is so bad that he should be fired
    C. get all the facts to establish the cause of the accident
    D. try to establish that the other driver was at least equally to blame

15. If witnesses to an automobile accident are interviewed separately, they are more likely to give different versions of the circumstances of the accident than if they are interviewed together.
    According to this statement, it is MOST probable that

    A. a truer picture of the circumstances of an accident can be gotten by interviewing the witnesses together rather than separately
    B. a witness's impression of what he saw is influenced by the statement of the other witnesses as to what they saw
    C. people who see an accident as a group will agree about the details of the accident more than people who are not together when they see the accident
    D. witnesses are less likely to tell the truth when interviewed privately than when interviewed as a group

16. A thorough investigation should always be made of an accident in which a city vehicle is involved.
    The MAIN value of such an investigation is to

    A. discover any factors that contributed to the accident which may be corrected
    B. keep compensation claims down
    C. provide good records from which statistics can be developed
    D. show the operators that accidents are taken seriously, no matter how small

17. An accident has been described as *an unplanned event caused by an unsafe act or condition.*
    An example of an unsafe act, rather than of an unsafe condition, in a garage is

    A. blocked fire exits   B. defective tools or equipment
    C. horseplay or teasing   D. oil and grease on floors

18. Of the following rules, the one that is LEAST directly concerned with the prevention of accidents is:

    A. Check brake fluid before leaving garage
    B. Do not use garage equipment if safety devices do not work
    C. No smoking in garage
    D. Reports of time lost due to accident must be submitted in 5 days

19. Which of the following entries on a Department Accident Report Form is MAINLY for the purpose of showing what is being done so that this type of accident will not happen again?

    A. Describe accident, including vehicle or vehicles involved
    B. What are you doing to prevent similar accidents?
    C. Why did the unsafe condition exist?
    D. Why was the unsafe act committed?

20. With respect to motor vehicle accidents, it is necessary to report in duplicate to the Bureau of Motor Vehicles on its printed forms

    A. all accidents
    B. only those accidents in which someone is killed or injured
    C. only those accidents in which someone is killed or injured or there is property damage of more than $50
    D. only those accidents in which someone is killed or injured or there is property damage of more than $100

21. A section of a garage used for parking vehicle measures 162 1/2' x 25 3/4'.
    If each vehicle to be parked in this section requires, on the average, 84 sq.ft. of parking space, the MAXIMUM number of vehicles that can be parked in this section is CLOSEST to

    A. 50   B. 45   C. 40   D. 35

22. Each of the 23 vehicles in a garage uses an average of 114 gallons of gas every 4 weeks.
    If the motor vehicle dispatcher is required to re-order gas when the gas tank in the garage shows no more than a one week supply, he MUST re-order when the gas tank shows _____ gallons.

    A. 655   B. 705   C. 830   D. 960

23. An employee's annual salary is $45,800. His total and annual deductions are 22% for withholding tax, 8 1/2% for pension and social security, and $1,820 for health insurance. The take-home pay that this employee would get on the check he receives every other week is MOST NEARLY

    A. $577.10   B. $845.00   C. $1,154.20   D. $1,220.40

24. A vehicle which averages 14 1/2 miles to a gallon of gas uses a quart of oil for every 21 1/2 gallons of gas.
    If the vehicle traveled 19,952 miles in a year, its oil consumption for the year would be _____ quarts.

    A. 52   B. 56   C. 60   D. 64

25. Thirteen percent of all the vehicles in a certain garage are trucks.
If there are 26 trucks, then the number of vehicles of other types in this garage is

   A. 174   B. 200   C. 260   D. 338

26. Of 12 employees in a garage, four earn $3,500 a year, two earn $3,150 a year, one earns $4,550 a year, and the rest each earn $3,800 a year.
The average yearly salary of these employees is CLOSEST to

   A. $3,550   B. $3,650   C. $3,750   D. $3,850

27. A garage bin used for storing supplies and parts measures 1 yard x 2 yards x 7 feet.
The cubic volume of this bin is

   A. 5 1/3 cubic yards   B. 16 cubic feet
   C. 63 cubic feet   D. 126 cubic feet

28. A garage has a gas tank with a capacity of 1,300 gallons. If there are only 520 gallons of gas in the tank, then the tank is _____ full.

   A. 40%   B. 33 1/3%   C. 25%   D. 16 3/4%

29. Of a specially selected group of vehicles, 1/5 are 6 months old, 2/5 are 12 months old, and 2/5 are 15 months old.
The average age of this group of vehicles is _____ months.

   A. 9   B. 10   C. 11   D. 12

30. A suggestion has been made that every vehicle have its gas tank filled and oil and water checked when it returns to the garage at the end of the day.
This suggestion is

   A. *good*, mainly because the gas pump can be kept locked the rest of the day
   B. *good*, mainly because vehicles will be ready to go out promptly the next day
   C. *poor*, mainly because it would take too long to fill each vehicle
   D. *poor*, mainly because not every vehicle will need gas, oil, and water

31. Brakes do not generally have to be adjusted until the clearance between the bottom of the brake pedal and the floorboard goes below _____ inch(es).

   A. 2-2 1/2   B. 1 1/2-2   C. 1-1 1/2   D. 1/2-1

32. *Play* in the steering wheel is generally NOT considered to be excessive until it reaches about _____ inch(es).

   A. 1/2   B. 1   C. 1 1/2   D. 2

33. If the oil pressure gauge in a sedan reads unduly high even after the engine is warmed up, the MOST probable reason is

   A. a low oil level in the crankcase
   B. an internal leak in the oil system
   C. an obstruction in the oil line
   D. too light an oil being used

34. In order to keep tire pressure at the level recommended by the manufacturer, the air pressure in the tires should be

   A. checked at the end of the day's driving
   B. checked in the morning, before the vehicle is driven
   C. lower in summer than in winter
   D. reduced before a long trip to leave room for expansion

35. When inspecting one of your vehicles, you notice excessive wear on the center of the tread of both front tires.
This unusual wear is MOST likely caused by

   A. excessive toe-in of the front wheels
   B. over-inflation of the front tires
   C. too much camber of the front wheels
   D. under-inflation of the front tires

36. The level of the fluid in the battery should be _____ the top of the plates.

   A. barely covering
   B. exactly even with
   C. well below
   D. well over

37. A heavy layer of oil on the water in the radiator would MOST probably indicate a

   A. cracked block
   B. dirty air cleaner
   C. loose hose connection
   D. water pump leak

38. If a five gallon can of gasoline is spilled on the garage floor, the BEST action to take is to

   A. let the gasoline evaporate
   B. pour sand over the puddle of gasoline
   C. squirt a foam-producing fire extinguisher on the puddle
   D. use a hose to flush the gasoline away

39. Greasy rags and waste in a garage should be

   A. hung up on a line to air out
   B. put in boxes that will be emptied daily
   C. put in covered metal cans or barrels
   D. put in wire baskets outside the garage

40. Adjusting the carburetor to give a mixture that is richer in fuel is

   A. *good* practice in cold weather as it improves engine operation
   B. *good* practice in very hot weather as it prevents stalling
   C. *poor* practice as it increases the chance of vapor lock
   D. *poor* practice in stop-and-go city driving as it greatly increases gas consumption

KEY (CORRECT ANSWERS)

1.	B	11.	B	21.	A	31.	C
2.	D	12.	B	22.	A	32.	D
3.	A	13.	D	23.	C	33.	C
4.	A	14.	C	24.	D	34.	B
5.	B	15.	B	25.	A	35.	B
6.	A	16.	A	26.	B	36.	D
7.	B	17.	C	27.	D	37.	A
8.	A	18.	D	28.	A	38.	D
9.	B	19.	B	29.	D	39.	C
10.	C	20.	D	30.	B	40.	A

TEST 3

DIRECTIONS: Each question or incomplete statement is followed by several suggested answers or completions. Select the one that BEST answers the question or completes the statement. *PRINT THE LETTER OF THE CORRECT ANSWER IN THE SPACE AT THE RIGHT.*

Questions 1-10.

DIRECTIONS: Questions 1 through 10 are based on the information given in the map on page 2.

1. On pay day, you assign an operator to deliver paychecks by car to the four work crews assigned to street jobs in the area. He starts from the garage and is to return there when finished.
   The order of delivery that would take the operator over the shortest allowable route would be crew

   A. 1, 2, 3, 4
   B. 2, 1, 4, 3
   C. 3, 2, 1, 4
   D. 4, 3, 2, 1

   1.____

2. Work crew 4 will be finished with its job at 1 P.M. and has to be moved to a new work location at Fir Ave. and 5th St. Work crew 3 will be finished with its job at the same time and has to be moved to begin work on a new job at 6th St. and Elm Ave. The operator assigned to the truck is to start from and return to the garage.
   In order to get each of these crews to their new locations as soon as possible, the dispatcher should instruct the operator assigned to pick up crew

   A. 3 and drop them at their new location; then pick up crew 4 and drop them at their new location
   B. 4 and drop them at their new location; pick up crew 3 and drop them at their new location
   C. 3; pick up crew 4; drop off crew 3; drop off crew 4
   D. 4; pick up crew 3; drop off crew 3; drop off crew 4

   2.____

3. The shortest allowable route for driving from the repair shop to the garage is 2nd Street and

   A. Fir Ave.
   B. Gladiola Ave.
   C. Gladiola Ave., 3rd St., Fir Ave.
   D. Holly Ave., 1st St., Gladiola Ave.

   3.____

4. You have requests for the following pick-ups and deliveries: a record player and loudspeaker to be moved from the playground to the skating rink, a case of pictures to be taken from the museum to the high school, and a ticket box to be moved from the stadium to the skating rink.
   Using the shortest allowable route from the garage and back, the order in which these pick-ups and deliveries should be made with the LEAST number of stops is

   A. museum, high school, playground, skating rink, stadium
   B. museum, playground, high school, stadium, skating rink
   C. playground, skating rink, museum, high school, stadium
   D. stadium, skating rink, museum, high school, playground

   4.____

2 (#3)

A ◯ indicates a street work crew.

A ✗ indicates a an entrance.

Arrows on streets indicate one-way and two-way streets.
No U turns are permitted.

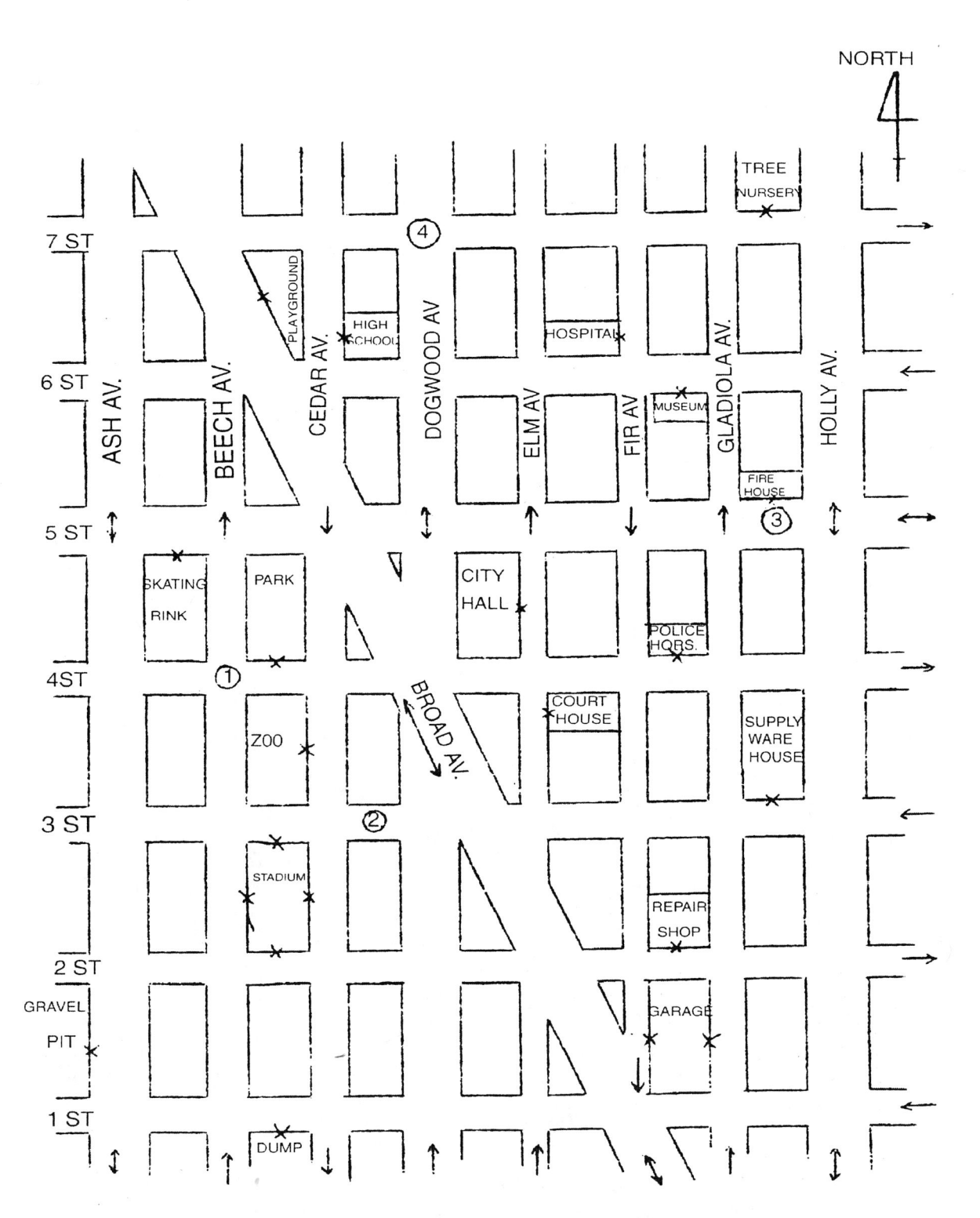

NORTH

5. To help a newly assigned motor vehicle operator learn this area, you might ask him to study the direction of traffic patterns on the map.
It would be MOST helpful if you pointed out to him that two-way traffic is permitted on

   A. all but one of the numbered streets
   B. all but three of the named avenues
   C. only one of the numbered streets
   D. only three of the named avenues

6. In routing motor equipment to the northwestern part of the mapped area, the dispatcher would be wise to use Broad Avenue MAINLY because it is

   A. a two-way street
   B. a wide street
   C. near the garage
   D. the most direct route

7. A disadvantage of the construction and location of the repair shop, according to the map, is that

   A. it has only one entrance on 2nd St.
   B. it is located too close to the garage as equipment breakdowns would happen in the field
   C. motor equipment leaving the garage must go around the block to enter the shop
   D. the shop is too small in comparison to the size of the garage

8. Two factors about the construction and location of the garage that are of special advantage to the dispatcher are that it

   A. has two entrances and is near the repair shop
   B. has two entrances and one-way streets on all sides
   C. is near the repair shop and occupies a whole block
   D. occupies a whole block and has one-way streets on all sides

9. When dispatching equipment from the garage to the hospital, the dispatcher should use the entrance on

   A. either Gladiola Ave. or Fir Ave.
   B. Fir Ave.
   C. Gladiola Ave.
   D. 2nd St.

10. You have requests to pick up some small trees at the tree nursery to be delivered to the park, to pick up gravel at the gravel pit and deliver the load to the zoo, to take some broken benches from the park to the repair shop, to pick up supplies at the warehouse for delivery to City Hall and the court house.
The order in which a truck should do these jobs, starting from the garage and using the shortest allowable route is

    A. gravel pit, zoo; park, repair shop; warehouse, court house, City Hall; tree nursery, park, garage
    B. gravel pit, zoo; warehouse, court house, City Hall; tree nursery, park; park, repair shop; repair shop, garage
    C. tree nursery, park; park, repair shop; zoo, gravel pit; warehouse, court house, City Hall, garage
    D. warehouse, court house, City Hall; tree nursery, park; park, repair shop; gravel pit, zoo; zoo, garage

Questions 11-20.

DIRECTIONS: Answer Questions 11 through 20 ONLY on the basis of the information given below in the two charts and the Rules of the Department. You are to assume that you are the dispatcher in the garage where these charts are kept and where they are used in making daily assignments of operators and vehicles.

SECOND AVE. GARAGE MOTOR VEHICLE OPERATOR CONTROL SHEET Date: May 25, 19 __				SECOND AVE. GARAGE MOTOR VEHICLE OPERATOR CONTROL SHEET Date: May 25, 19 __			
Name of Operator	Cleared on	Hours of Overtime Credit as of May 25	On Vacation	Vehicle Number and Type	In Repair Shop as of May 25	Date Due in Shop for Preventive Maintenance Inspection	Date Last In Repair
Allen	P T	74		20-P		7/13	3/2
Boyd	P W	31	5/18-30	21-P		6/15	2/16
Cohen	P T	129		22-T		5/26	1/19
Diggs	P	15		23-P		6/1	5/8
Egan	P T	92	6/1-13	24-P		6/8	2/2
First	P T W	49		25-P		7/6	2/24
Gordon	P	57		26-W		6/1	1/21
Hanson	P T	143	6/15-27	27-T		7/20	4/6
				28-T	X	7/27	3/16
				29-P	X	5/18	1/12

Symbols: P - Passenger Car
T - Truck
W - Wrecker

Symbols: P - Passenger Car
T - Truck
W - Wrecker

RULES OF THE DEPARTMENT

1. A motor vehicle operator may be assigned to drive only those types of vehicles on which he has been cleared. No one but a motor vehicle operator may be assigned to drive a Department vehicle.

2. Private cars may not be used for Department business.

3. The motor vehicle dispatcher shall keep a daily record of overtime credits of all operators under his supervision to be sure that no operator acquires more than 150 hours of overtime credit. An assignment which involves overtime should be given, wherever possible, to the operator with the least overtime credit.

4. A vehicle due for preventive maintenance must be sent to the repair shop on the date it is due for preventive maintenance, except when a vehicle has been in the repair shop during the previous month.

5. All available vehicles are to be assigned to jobs as requested, with none held in reserve.

11. An official who is requesting a truck and operator for the three days beginning May 26th   11.___
    indicates to you that some overtime may be necessary for the operator, but he cannot
    predict how many hours of overtime will be needed. Under these circumstances, the
    MOST logical man for you to choose for this assignment would be operator

    A. Allen   B. Boyd   C. Diggs   D. First

12. The vehicle which does NOT have to be sent to the shop for preventive maintenance on   12.___
    the date it is due is vehicle number

    A. 23   B. 25   C. 27   D. 29

13. As dispatcher, you receive a request on May 25th for a truck and motor vehicle operator   13.___
    for a job that will take three days, from May 26th through May 28th.
    The vehicle that it would be BEST for you to choose on May 25th for this assignment is
    vehicle number

    A. 28   B. 27   C. 22   D. 20

14. On May 25th, right after all the vehicles have left the garage on daily assignment, you   14.___
    receive a call from your Commissioner's secretary. She tells you that an emergency has
    come up and asks you for a car to be ready in fifteen minutes to take a messenger with
    important papers to be delivered to the Commissioner who is waiting for the papers at a
    court in another borough.
    Of the following, the BEST thing for you to do, after explaining to the secretary that you
    have no cars available, is to

    A. advise her she should give you advance notice the next time so that you can
       reserve a car for the messenger
    B. offer to drive the messenger yourself in your private car
    C. promise to get a car from another department
    D. suggest that the messenger use public transportation

15. To give you more leeway in assigning your operators to the available equipment, it would   15.___
    be MOST practical for you to

    A. ask your supervisor to assign two additional motor vehicle operators to the garage
    B. have additional operators cleared on the wrecker
    C. suggest to your supervisor that rule 3 be abolished
    D. suggest to your supervisor that rule 1 be abolished

16. Other things being equal, the operator who should probably be of MOST value to you, as   16.___
    the dispatcher, is

    A. Cohen   B. Diggs   C. First   D. Hanson

17. The factor which indicates MOST strongly that there may not be enough operators   17.___
    assigned to this garage is the

    A. amount of overtime accumulated
    B. excess of number of vehicles over number of operators
    C. incomplete vacation schedule
    D. number of operators cleared on trucks

18. When dispatching men and equipment in the morning, it would be BEST for you to first dispatch men who

    A. are cleared on 1 vehicle
    B. are cleared on 2 vehicles
    C. are cleared on 3 vehicles
    D. have already had their vacations

18.____

19. The second week in June, you receive a call for an operator and wrecker.
    It is better to dispatch Boyd rather than First because

    A. he has already had his vacation
    B. he has less overtime
    C. he is not cleared on trucks
    D. unless there are special reasons, you might as well assign the men in alphabetical order for easier record keeping

19.____

20. You have requests for 6 passenger cars and 2 trucks for jobs on May 25th. All of these jobs will probably take the full day but none will require any overtime.
    How many of these requests for May 25th would you have to refuse?

    A. None
    B. One
    C. Two
    D. More than two

20.____

KEY (CORRECT ANSWERS)

1.	B	11.	D
2.	A	12.	A
3.	D	13.	B
4.	B	14.	D
5.	C	15.	B
6.	D	16.	C
7.	C	17.	A
8.	A	18.	A
9.	C	19.	C
10.	B	20.	B

TEST 4

DIRECTIONS: Each question or incomplete statement is followed by several suggested answers or completions. Select the one that BEST answers the question or completes the statement. *PRINT THE LETTER OF THE CORRECT ANSWER IN THE SPACE AT THE RIGHT.*

1. In a program of switching tires on a vehicle at regular intervals to give longer tire life, the BEST system to follow is   1.___

   A.   B.   C.   D.

2. If an engine misfires when it is operated at low speed, the order in which the items below should be inspected, tested, and adjusted is   2.___

   A. breaker contact points, distributor cap and rotor, high voltage wires, spark plugs
   B. distributor cap and rotor, breaker contact points, spark plugs, high voltage wires
   C. high voltage wires, spark plugs, breaker contact points, distributor can and rotor
   D. spark plugs, high voltage wires, distributor cap and rotor, breaker contact points

3. An operator complains that the headlights on his vehicle flare up and then dim as the speed of the vehicle changes.
   The MOST probable cause is   3.___

   A. a burned out fuse or defective circuit breaker
   B. a defective dimmer switch
   C. a loose connection in the headlight wiring
   D. weak bulbs

4. A can of motor oil is marked *S.A.E. 20-20W.*
   This indicates that   4.___

   A. a mistake was made, and the oil should not be used
   B. chemicals have been added to winterize the oil
   C. the oil may be used both in medium temperatures and in winter weather
   D. the oil should be used when the temperature is between 20 degrees below and 20 degrees above zero

5. A specific gravity reading of 1280 at 80° F means that a battery is   5.___

   A. fully discharged   B. nearing a discharged condition
   C. about half charged   D. fully charged

6. If a generator constantly charges at a high rate, it is MOST probably due to a(n)   6.___

   A. defective regulator   B. dirty commutator
   C. too tight fan belt adjustment   D. overcharged battery

7. In the servicing of spark plugs, it is IMPORTANT to

   A. bend the center electrode rather than the side electrode when adjusting the spark plug gap
   B. clean the spark plug recess in the cylinder head with a brush or compressed air after a spark plug has been removed
   C. make sure that each spark plug has only one gasket
   D. use an adjustable wrench to tighten a spark plug in its hole

7.____

8. If air gets into the lines of a hydraulic brake system, the MOST likely result will be

   A. a spongy pedal   B. grabbing brakes
   C. locked brakes   D. a hard pedal

8.____

9. In hooking test ammeters and voltmeters into a circuit, the ammeter

   A. should be connected in parallel and the voltmeter in series
   B. should be connected in series and the voltmeter in parallel
   C. and voltmeter should be connected in parallel
   D. and voltmeter should be connected in series

9.____

10. When brakes are correctly adjusted but one wheel takes hold before the others, it is MOST likely that the

    A. cup on the wheel cylinder has swelled
    B. relief port on the master cylinder isn't working
    C. push rod adjustment is faulty
    D. brake fluid has leaked into the lining

10.____

11. Racing an automobile engine on cold mornings to warm it up is

    A. *bad* practice, because there is poor lubrication of moving parts
    B. *good* practice, because the oil will reach moving parts faster
    C. *bad* practice, because it will form sludge in the engine
    D. *good* practice, because it will allow liquid gasoline to reach the crankcase

11.____

12. Using anti-freeze solution for more than a single season is

    A. *bad* practice, because it will cause excessive rust
    B. *good* practice, because it will be economical
    C. *bad* practice, because it will raise the boiling point
    D. *good* practice, because it will not clog the cooling system

12.____

13. The one of the following which is NOT usually a purpose of a preventive maintenance program for a fleet of automotive vehicles is

    A. a greater margin of safety in the operation of the vehicles
    B. easier and more comfortable driving
    C. improved mechanical ability of vehicle operators
    D. increased economy in vehicle operations

13.____

14. The one of the following which will NOT help improve gasoline mileage is 14.___

    A. driving at high speeds
    B. even acceleration
    C. keeping tires at recommended pressure
    D. using light oil in winter

15. An abnormally cool brake drum on one wheel after the vehicle has been in operation would MOST probably indicate a(n) 15.___

    A. dragging shoe
    B. improperly adjusted brake drum
    C. non-functioning brake
    D. underlubricated bearing

16. The pitman arm is part of the 16.___

    A. brake shoe assembly   B. driving axle
    C. fan belt assembly   D. steering mechanism

17. When he returns to the garage at the end of his shift, a motor vehicle operator complains to you that the engine *skips* on the car he is driving.
    When you prepare your requisition for a check-up of this vehicle, it is LEAST important for you to ask for a check of the 17.___

    A. battery   B. carburetor
    C. condenser   D. fuel line

18. In a garage where a vehicle preventive maintenance program is in operation, the one of the following which it is MOST important to do right away without waiting for next checkup is 18.___

    A. adjusting brakes that pull unevenly
    B. changing oil and lubrication to summer or winter grades
    C. checking spark plugs
    D. replacing an oil-soaked water hose

19. To test whether every cylinder has good compression, the instrument that should be used is a 19.___

    A. vacuum gauge   B. gas analyzer
    C. creeper   D. vent ball

20. It is generally recommended that the radiator of a passenger vehicle be flushed out 20.___

    A. every 1,000 miles   B. every fall and spring
    C. every 2,000 miles   D. once a year

KEY (CORRECT ANSWERS)

1. A
2. D
3. C
4. C
5. D

6. A
7. C
8. A
9. B
10. D

11. A
12. A
13. C
14. A
15. C

16. D
17. A
18. A
19. A
20. B

———

EXAMINATION SECTION
TEST 1

DIRECTIONS: Each question or incomplete statement is followed by several suggested answers or completions. Select the one that BEST answers the question or completes the statement. *PRINT THE LETTER OF THE CORRECT ANSWER IN THE SPACE AT THE RIGHT.*

1. Suppose that a new motor vehicle operator has been assigned to you, the dispatcher. It is your responsibility to see that he understands how to fill out the forms he is required to use.
Of the following, the BEST way to do this would be to

   A. ask an experienced driver to tell him about the forms
   B. explain the purpose of each form to the new operator, and show him how to fill them out
   C. give the new man a copy of each form, so that he can study them
   D. tell the new man that filling out forms is simple, and that he should just follow the instructions on each form

   1.____

2. As a dispatcher, you may from time to time be faced with an important job problem.
The usual way of solving a job problem includes the following four steps:
   I. Seeing what the facts mean in relation to the problem
   II. Choosing the best solution
   III. Getting all the important facts relating to the problem
   IV. Finding possible solutions

   If the above four numbered steps were arranged in the order in which they should be taken, the CORRECT order would be

   A. IV, III, I, II   B. IV, I, III, II
   C. III, I, IV, II   D. I, IV, III, II

   2.____

3. Of the following, it is LEAST desirable that a dispatcher

   A. correct a driver for a minor rule violation, even if it is the first time that the driver broke the rule and no harm was done
   B. discuss with any new drivers he supervises some situations that may come up in their work and how to handle them
   C. encourage the drivers he supervises to ask him questions about any of his instructions that they do not understand
   D. observe for a few days the mistakes one of his drivers makes and then discuss these mistakes with him

   3.____

4. Suppose you receive a telephone call from an employee who complains that, while being driven on official business, he was treated rudely by the driver.
As the dispatcher who supervises this driver, which of the following actions should you take FIRST?

   A. Tell the caller that you will have the driver write him a letter of apology
   B. Tell the caller that you will have the driver telephone him to apologize
   C. Ask the other drivers you supervise if this driver is generally discourteous
   D. Try to get the details of the incident from the caller and from the driver

   4.____

5. When a certain dispatcher has to criticize one of his drivers, he makes a practice of doing it in private.
This practice is GENERALLY

   A. *good;* private criticism can help save the driver unnecessary embarrassment
   B. *bad;* open criticism helps develop among the drivers a feeling of being treated fairly
   C. *good;* private criticism leaves no hard feelings between the driver and the dispatcher
   D. *bad;* open criticism keeps the drivers on their toes

6. A certain dispatcher often issues orders in the form of a request rather than in the form of a command.
This is

   A. *good;* it lets the driver decide the best way to carry out such an order
   B. *poor;* it shows that the dispatcher lacks sufficient self-confidence
   C. *good;* it helps to create good will with the drivers
   D. *poor;* it puts the responsibility on the drivers to decide which job to do first

7. For a dispatcher to judge the performance of a driver exclusively on how well he drives, his safety record, and his neatness of appearance would be

   A. *undesirable;* there are other important factors to consider also
   B. *desirable;* these factors are objective and eliminate personal bias
   C. *undesirable;* these factors should have been judged before the driver was appointed
   D. *desirable;* this method stresses on-the-job performance

8. Suppose you discover that you have unfairly criticized one of the drivers you supervise.
Of the following, the BEST thing for you to do would be to

   A. think of some indirect way to let the driver know you realize that he was not at fault
   B. admit your mistake to the driver, and apologize
   C. overlook some offense that the driver commits in the future
   D. make up for it by giving this driver better assignments for a short time

9. A driver, who otherwise does a rather good job, is starting to arrive late for work too often. You, as the dispatcher, have called him in to talk to him about it.
Which of the following would be BEST for you to do?

   A. Let him know right away that there are no excuses for being late this much
   B. Discuss these latenesses with him but also mention good points in his work
   C. Give him a strong warning of punishment in order to stop the habit right away
   D. Tell him that he ought to improve to keep the other drivers from complaining

10. A year ago you corrected one of the men you supervise for driving carelessly while in the garage. Since then he has been careful not to repeat such actions.
To remind this driver once in a while about that careless act would be

    A. *good;* it will help to keep him from doing it again
    B. *bad;* it suggests to this subordinate that you have a bad memory
    C. *good;* he will know that you have not forgotten an important infraction
    D. *bad;* the incident is over and he has not done anything like it since

11. Lately one of the drivers that you supervise has not been doing as good a job as he used to do. He asks whether he may discuss with you a problem that has been bothering him. He says he thinks that the problem has been affecting his work. But after he tells you the problem, you feel that this is really a minor problem and that he has somehow failed to consider certain alternatives open to him.
Of the following, the FIRST thing you should do is to

   A. examine with him possibilities for solving the problem
   B. tell him it is a minor problem
   C. tell him the solution to the problem
   D. explain to him that he must not let such problems disturb him in his work

11.____

12. Suppose that you, the dispatcher, instruct a motor vehicle operator to make a delivery and to use a certain route which you believe is the fastest and shortest. The driver then says that he knows a shorter, faster route.
Of the following, it would be BEST for you to

   A. tell the driver to follow your route and not question the orders of his supervisor
   B. assign this delivery to a driver who agrees that your route is best
   C. ask your supervisor to decide which is the best route so the driver will know that you are open-minded
   D. have the driver describe the other route and let him use it if it seems at least as good as yours

12.____

13. Your department has just made a major policy change affecting work procedures for the 30 men under your supervision, and they do not yet know about it. You wish to reduce or eliminate lasting negative reactions and to gain as much acceptance of this policy change as possible.
Which of the following is the BEST method to use to accomplish this purpose?

   A. Circulate a memo to them describing the policy change in detail
   B. Call a meeting with them to inform them thoroughly of the policy change, and to answer questions
   C. Make clear to the men that the policy change was not your idea, but that it must be followed
   D. Announce the policy change at a meeting and end the meeting before objections can be raised

13.____

14. A driver asks you, the dispatcher, about a suggestion he plans to send in to the employees' suggestion program. You doubt whether his suggestion can be used because you think it will be unacceptable to most employees; that they will resist its use.
Of the following, the BEST thing for you to do would be to tell him

   A. why you do not think he should send in the suggestion
   B. your doubts about the suggestion, but encourage him to send it in anyway
   C. that you think it is a good suggestion and that he should send it in
   D. not to send in the suggestion unless he can think of some way to get employees to accept it

14.____

15. A dispatcher should periodically check the procedures and practices in his garage to see whether any changes should be made.
Which of the following is the MAIN reason for checking in this manner?

15.____

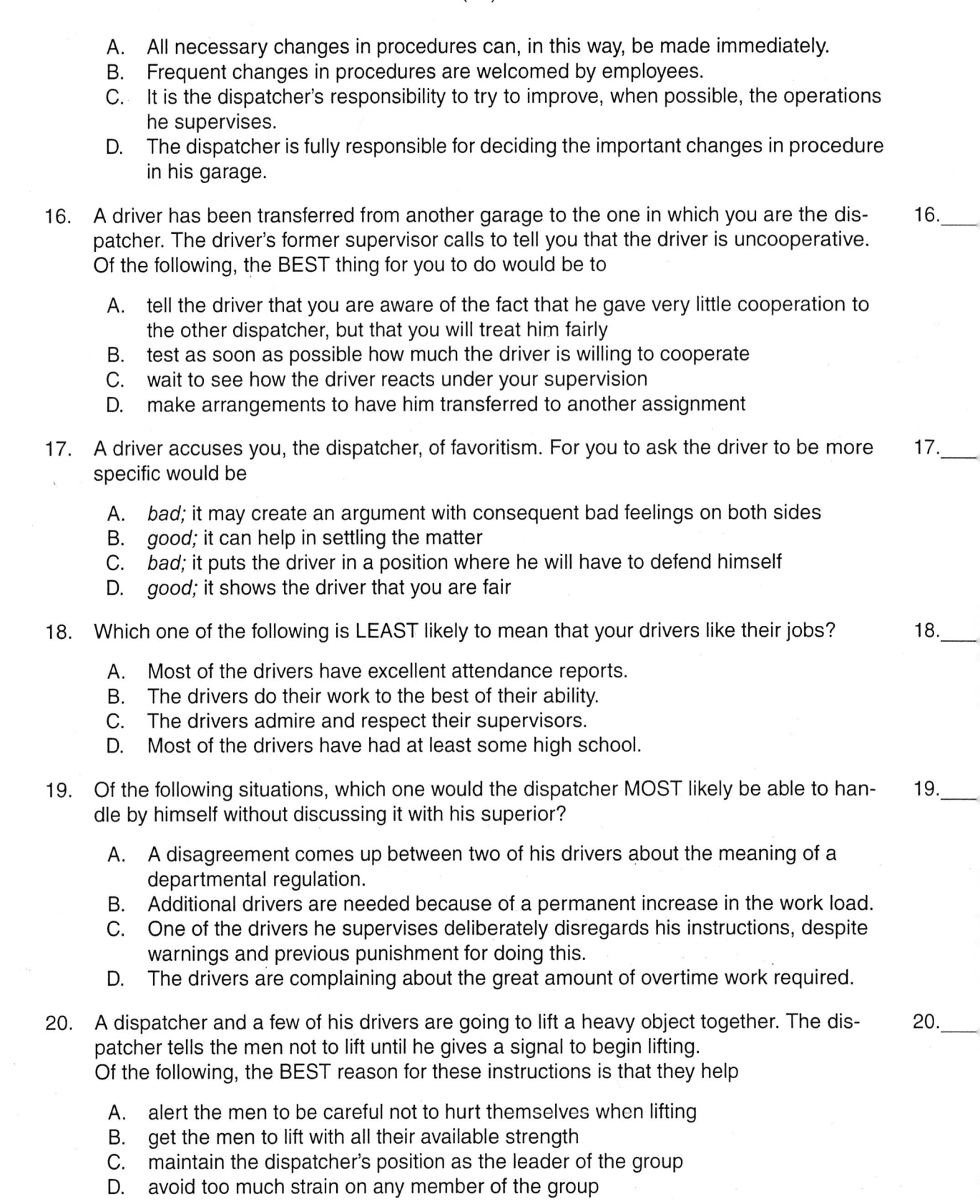

A. All necessary changes in procedures can, in this way, be made immediately.
B. Frequent changes in procedures are welcomed by employees.
C. It is the dispatcher's responsibility to try to improve, when possible, the operations he supervises.
D. The dispatcher is fully responsible for deciding the important changes in procedure in his garage.

16. A driver has been transferred from another garage to the one in which you are the dispatcher. The driver's former supervisor calls to tell you that the driver is uncooperative.
Of the following, the BEST thing for you to do would be to

    A. tell the driver that you are aware of the fact that he gave very little cooperation to the other dispatcher, but that you will treat him fairly
    B. test as soon as possible how much the driver is willing to cooperate
    C. wait to see how the driver reacts under your supervision
    D. make arrangements to have him transferred to another assignment

17. A driver accuses you, the dispatcher, of favoritism. For you to ask the driver to be more specific would be

    A. *bad;* it may create an argument with consequent bad feelings on both sides
    B. *good;* it can help in settling the matter
    C. *bad;* it puts the driver in a position where he will have to defend himself
    D. *good;* it shows the driver that you are fair

18. Which one of the following is LEAST likely to mean that your drivers like their jobs?

    A. Most of the drivers have excellent attendance reports.
    B. The drivers do their work to the best of their ability.
    C. The drivers admire and respect their supervisors.
    D. Most of the drivers have had at least some high school.

19. Of the following situations, which one would the dispatcher MOST likely be able to handle by himself without discussing it with his superior?

    A. A disagreement comes up between two of his drivers about the meaning of a departmental regulation.
    B. Additional drivers are needed because of a permanent increase in the work load.
    C. One of the drivers he supervises deliberately disregards his instructions, despite warnings and previous punishment for doing this.
    D. The drivers are complaining about the great amount of overtime work required.

20. A dispatcher and a few of his drivers are going to lift a heavy object together. The dispatcher tells the men not to lift until he gives a signal to begin lifting.
Of the following, the BEST reason for these instructions is that they help

    A. alert the men to be careful not to hurt themselves when lifting
    B. get the men to lift with all their available strength
    C. maintain the dispatcher's position as the leader of the group
    D. avoid too much strain on any member of the group

KEY (CORRECT ANSWERS)

1.	B	11.	A
2.	C	12.	D
3.	D	13.	B
4.	D	14.	B
5.	A	15.	C
6.	C	16.	C
7.	A	17.	B
8.	B	18.	D
9.	B	19.	A
10.	D	20.	D

TEST 2

DIRECTIONS: Each question or incomplete statement is followed by several suggested answers or completions. Select the one that BEST answers the question or completes the statement. *PRINT THE LETTER OF THE CORRECT ANSWER IN THE SPACE AT THE RIGHT.*

1. The EASIEST and QUICKEST way of finding which spark plug is bad and causing an engine to miss is to

    A. remove each plug and examine it
    B. replace each plug, one at a time, with a new one
    C. check each plug with a timing light
    D. short circuit each plug, one at a time

    1.____

2. A pressure cap is used in an automotive cooling system to

    A. measure the water pressure
    B. prevent cold water from reaching the engine
    C. raise the boiling point of the water
    D. aid circulation of water in the cooling system

    2.____

3. The necessity to frequently add large amounts of water to a car storage battery is MOST likely an indication that the

    A. charging rate is too high
    B. charging rate is too low
    C. battery connection is loose
    D. ground connection is loose

    3.____

4. Inspection of an automobile tire shows that the center treads have had more wear than the side treads.
   The MOST common cause for this condition is

    A. too much camber   B. cornering
    C. overinflation   D. underinflation

    4.____

5. Graphite is a recommended lubricant for automotive

    A. springs   B. car door locks
    C. differentials   D. steering shafts

    5.____

6. The ignition coil on a gasoline engine

    A. transforms low voltage to high voltage
    B. prevents sparking at the breaker points
    C. limits charging voltage on the battery
    D. prevents excessive flow of current to the spark plugs

    6.____

7. The MAIN function of a thermostat in the radiator of an automobile is to

    A. prevent cold water from circulating between the engine and the radiator
    B. permit full flow of cooling water to the engine when starting the engine up
    C. prevent cooling water from overheating
    D. alert the driver that the engine is overheating

    7.____

8. The one of the following automotive components or systems that is NOT considered a part of the *power train* is the

8.____

   A. propeller shaft
   B. ignition system
   C. transmission
   D. clutch

9. Suppose in your garage records are kept of the vehicular accidents your men have while driving at work. In addition to the number of accidents each man has, which of the following facts in the records would be the MOST important for comparing drivers on their success in avoiding driving accidents while working?
The

9.____

   A. number of years of driving experience of each man
   B. number of miles driven by each driver on the job
   C. gasoline consumption of each vehicle
   D. age of the drivers assigned to the garage

10. A department has asked dispatchers to study the standard forms and reports they fill out each day, and to make recommendations for revision.
Which of the following is the BEST reason for a dispatcher to suggest that certain information no longer be asked on such forms?

10.____

   A. The information is no longer applicable to this department.
   B. Although the information is accurate, it becomes outdated after a while.
   C. The information is difficult to evaluate on the level of the dispatcher.
   D. The information requested can only be estimated at ninety-eight percent accuracy.

Questions 11-18.

DIRECTIONS: Questions 11 through 18 are to be answered according to the information given in the notes and map that appear on Page 3 following.

NOTES

A circle with a number inside (3) indicates a street work crew.
A cross (X) indicates an entrance and exit.
Arrows on streets indicate (→) one-way and (↔) two-way streets.
No U-turns are permitted.
Disregard the width of the streets, avenues, and boulevards in arriving at your answers.
Assume that for each standard block shown on the map, the length (from street to street) is twice as big as the width (from avenue to avenue).

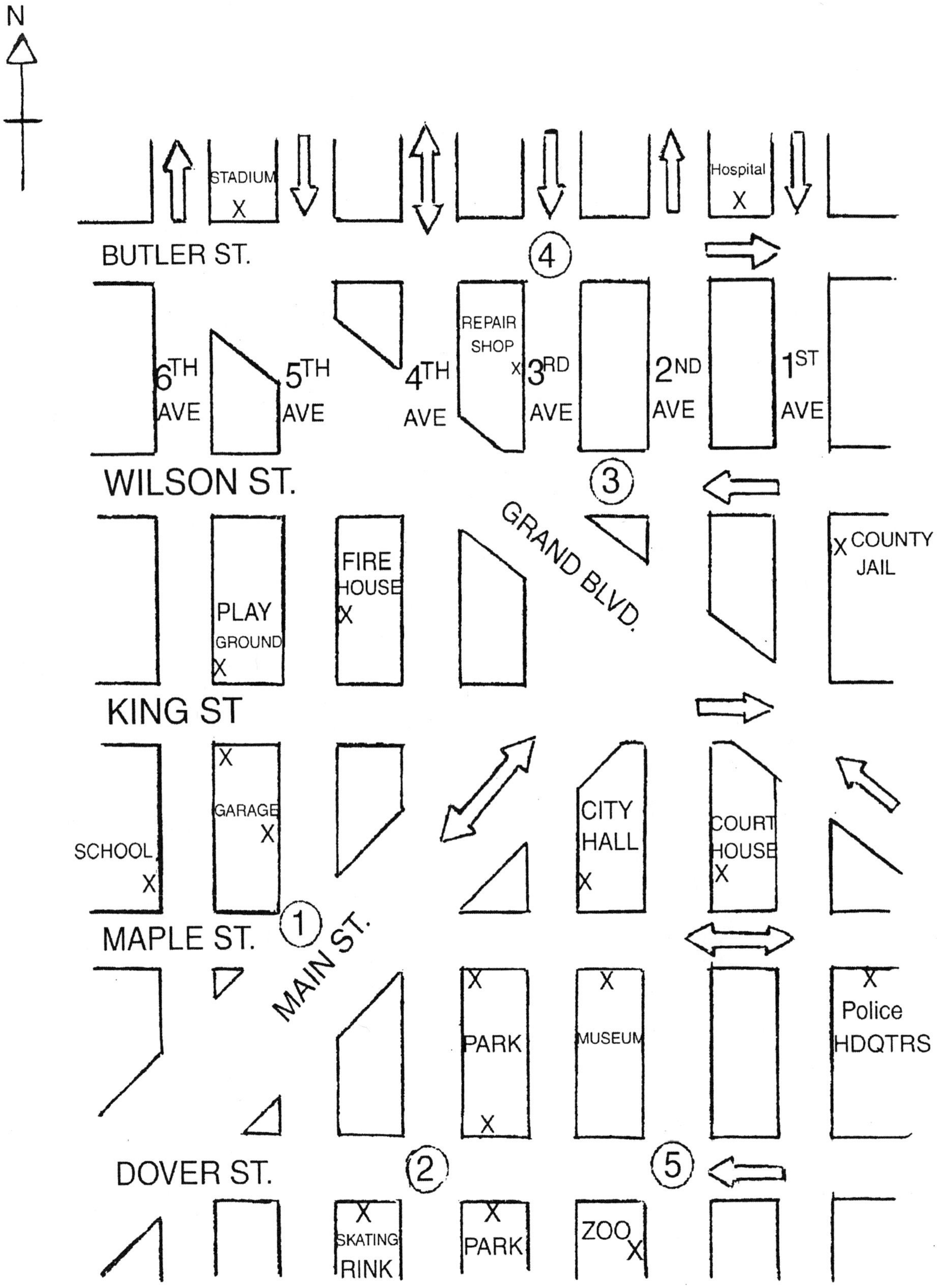
N
STADIUM
Hospital
BUTLER ST.
4
REPAIR
SHOP
6TH AVE
5TH AVE
4TH AVE
3RD AVE
2ND AVE
1ST AVE
WILSON ST.
3
GRAND BLVD.
COUNTY
JAIL
FIRE
HOUSE
PLAY
GROUND
KING ST
GARAGE
SCHOOL
CITY
HALL
COURT
HOUSE
1
MAPLE ST.
MAIN ST.
PARK
MUSEUM
Police
HDQTRS
2
DOVER ST.
5
SKATING
RINK
PARK
ZOO

11. A driver should turn left when exiting from the   11.____

    A. court house   B. playground
    C. stadium   D. repair shop

12. An operator, facing west on Wilson St. and 2nd Ave., wants to drive to Dover St. and 6th   12.____
    Ave.
    The SHORTEST allowable route for him to take is

    A. Wilson St., 3rd Ave., and Main St.
    B. Wilson St., 5th Ave., and Dover St.
    C. Wilson St., 3rd Ave., Maple St., 5th Ave., and Dover St.
    D. 2nd Ave., Grand Blvd., and Main St.

13. The SHORTEST allowable route for driving from the repair shop exit to the garage   13.____
    entrance is to use Third Ave.,

    A. Maple St., and 6th Ave.
    B. and King St.
    C. Main St., and 5th Ave.
    D. Wilson St., and 5th Ave.

14. An emergency repair has to be made in front of the entrance to the fire house and a work   14.____
    crew is needed there immediately. The dispatcher is told to send the crew that can reach
    the fire house entrance first, using the shortest allowable driving distance.
    Which crew should he send?
    Crew

    A. 1   B. 2   C. 3   D. 4

15. Which describes BEST the location of the museum in relation to the school?   15.____
    The museum is located _____ of the school.

    A. southwest   B. southeast   C. northwest   D. northeast

16. Work Crew 5 will be finished with its job at 1 P.M. and has to join Work Crew 3 for the rest   16.____
    of the day. Work Crew 4 will also be finished at 1 P.M. and must join Work Crew 2 for the
    rest of the day. The driver of the truck is to start from inside the garage, take Work Crews
    5 and 4 to their new locations, and return into the garage. Of the following choices, the
    driver will cover the SHORTEST allowable route if he picks up crew

    A. 5, drops off crew 5 at crew 3, picks up crew 4, drops off crew 4 at crew 2
    B. 4, picks up crew 5, drops off crew 5 at crew 3, drops off crew 4 at crew 2
    C. 4, drops off crew 4 at crew 2, picks up crew 5, drops off crew 5 at crew 3
    D. 5, picks up crew 4, drops off crew 5 at crew 3, drops off crew 4 at crew 2

17. One operator is assigned to pick up a city official at the hospital and drive him to the   17.____
    entrance to City Hall. The SHORTEST allowable route to take from the hospital is Butler
    St., First Ave.,

    A. Maple St., and Third Ave.
    B. Wilson St. 2nd Ave., Grand Blvd., Main St., and Third Ave.
    C. Maple St., Main St., and Third Ave.
    D. Wilson St., and Third Ave.

18. Of the following, which entrance is the SHORTEST allowable driving distance from the school exit?
    The entrance to

    A. the hospital
    B. police headquarters
    C. the County Jail
    D. the museum

Questions 19-20.

DIRECTIONS: A city vehicle has been involved in an accident and a diagram of the accident has been prepared. Answer Questions 19 and 20 according to the information given in the diagram and notes below.

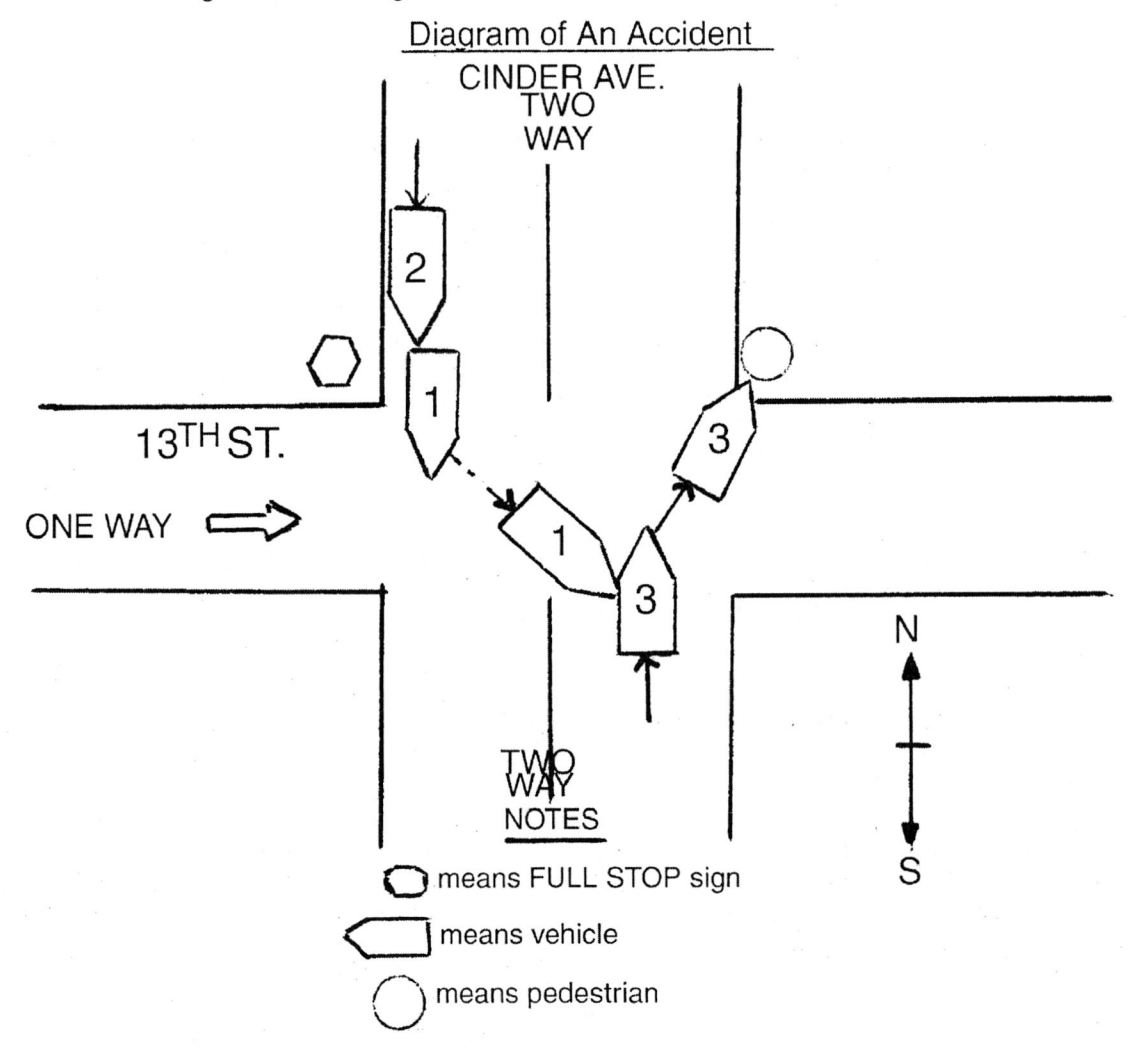

Diagram of An Accident

(Diagram shows CINDER AVE. running north-south (TWO WAY) intersecting with 13TH ST. running east-west (ONE WAY, eastbound). Vehicle #1 travels south on Cinder Ave., Vehicle #2 travels south on Cinder Ave. behind #1, Vehicle #3 travels north. After accident, Vehicle #1 deflects southeast. A FULL STOP sign (hexagon) is on the northwest corner, and a pedestrian (circle) is on the northeast corner.)

NOTES

⬡ means FULL STOP sign

⬟ means vehicle

◯ means pedestrian

Solid arrow (←) means direction of travel before accident.

Broken arrow (←--) means direction of travel after accident. Vehicle #1 is the city vehicle.

19. The FULL STOP sign is located on the _____ corner of the intersection.

    A. northeast   B. northwest   C. southeast   D. southwest

20. If the driver of the city vehicle was following driving regulations, it is MOST likely that at the time he was hit he was   20.____

    A. making a right turn
    B. making a left turn
    C. standing still
    D. driving down Cinder Avenue

KEY (CORRECT ANSWERS)

1.	D	11.	C
2.	C	12.	A
3.	A	13.	D
4.	C	14.	C
5.	B	15.	B
6.	A	16.	A
7.	A	17.	D
8.	B	18.	D
9.	B	19.	B
10.	A	20.	D

TEST 3

DIRECTIONS: Each question or incomplete statement is followed by several suggested answers or completions. Select the one that BEST answers the question or completes the statement. *PRINT THE LETTER OF THE CORRECT ANSWER IN THE SPACE AT THE RIGHT.*

Questions 1-19.

DIRECTIONS: In each of Questions 1 through 19, choose the lettered word which means MOST NEARLY the same as the word in capital letters.

1. APPRAISE 1.____
   A. inform   B. evaluate   C. increase   D. decrease

2. IMPARTIAL 2.____
   A. strange   B. funny   C. fair   D. bad

3. INCENTIVE 3.____
   A. cash   B. fire   C. messenger   D. motive

4. INSUBORDINATE 4.____
   A. confusing   B. disobedient
   C. important   D. smart

5. NEGLIGENT 5.____
   A. careless   B. painful   C. cruel   D. untidy

6. REVISION 6.____
   A. change   B. decision   C. dream   D. retreat

7. SEMIANNUALLY 7.____
   A. four times in a year   B. three times in a year
   C. twice in a year   D. every other year

8. UTILIZE 8.____
   A. break   B. cook   C. reduce   D. use

9. VAGUE 9.____
   A. new   B. sure   C. old   D. uncertain

10. CENTRIFUGAL 10.____
    A. moving away from a center
    B. moving toward a center
    C. having a center
    D. without a center

11. INDUCE   11.____
    A. cause   B. stop   C. name   D. signal

12. PERTINENT   12.____
    A. wise   B. stormy
    C. relevant   D. understood

13. ENUMERATE   13.____
    A. free   B. count   C. postpone   D. obey

14. DEPLETE   14.____
    A. hide   B. order   C. purchase   D. empty

15. DIVERSE   15.____
    A. average   B. varied   C. faulty   D. hollow

16. MESH   16.____
    A. engage   B. skip   C. spin   D. use

17. DISMANTLE   17.____
    A. lock up   B. forget about
    C. look over   D. take apart

18. INCIDENTAL   18.____
    A. casual   B. necessary
    C. infrequent   D. needless

19. ELASTIC   19.____
    A. resilient   B. reserved
    C. tranquil   D. sterile

20. Truck A has been driven 38,742.3 miles, Truck B has been driven 24,169.7 miles, Truck C has been driven 41,286.4 miles, Truck D has been driven 15,053.5 miles, and Truck E has been driven 8,407.0 miles.   20.____
    The total mileage of these five trucks combined is MOST NEARLY _____ miles.

    A. 127,650   B. 127,660   C. 128,650   D. 128,660

21. Suppose that the trucks in a certain garage used a total of 86,314 gallons of gas in 1991 and 8,732 gallons less in 1992.   21.____
    If they used a total of 72,483 gallons of gas in 1993, how much LESS gas was used in 1993 than in 1992?
    _____ gallons.

    A. 5,099   B. 5,109   C. 5,199   D. 5,209

22. A driver averaged 17 miles for each gallon of gas used one week and 26 miles the next week.   22.____
    If he used 38.9 gallons during the first week and 27.6 during the second, the TOTAL number of miles he drove in these two weeks was _____ miles.

A. 1,266.3   B. 1,322.6   C. 1,378.9   D. 1,435.2

23. In Garage A, 87 drivers worked a total of 427 hours overtime. In Garage B, 53 drivers worked a total of 245 hours overtime.
Compared to the average overtime worked per man in Garage B, the average overtime worked per man in Garage A was MOST NEARLY _____ of an hour _____ .

    A. 2/10; more   B. 2/10; less
    C. 3/10; more   D. 3/10; less

24. The scale on a map indicates that every 1 5/8 inches on the map represents 5 miles. If two locations are 13 inches apart on the map, what is the distance between them, in miles?

    A. 30   B. 35   C. 40   D. 45

25. If a car is traveling on a highway at a steady speed of 35 miles an hour, how many miles will it go in a period of 24 minutes?
_____ miles.

    A. 13   B. 14   C. 15   D. 16

26. An employee's annual salary is $7,625.
If he receives a 5.4% salary increase, his new annual salary will be

    A. $7,992.50   B. $8,036.75
    C. $8,147.25   D. $8,169.00

27. Of the 60 drivers assigned to a garage, 1/6 of them live in County A, 1/4 of them live in County B, 1/5 of them live in County C, and the rest live in County D.
How many of the drivers live in County D?

    A. 22   B. 23   C. 24   D. 25

28. Driver Green travels 33 miles along express highways at an average speed of 44 miles an hour to get to his destination. Driver Smith travels 28 miles through traffic at an average speed of 21 miles an hour to get to the same destination.
If Mr. Smith starts his trip a half hour before Mr. Green, he will reach the destination _____ Mr. Green.

    A. 5 minutes before   B. at the same time as
    C. 5 minutes after   D. 10 minutes after

29. A 210 foot by 120 foot parking lot is reduced in size by construction of a 36 foot by 54 foot building at one of its corners.
The area left for parking is MOST NEARLY _____ square yards.

    A. 1,800   B. 2,600   C. 22,800   D. 23,300

30. A dispatcher works a total of 44 hours, spending 17 on Special Project A, 13 on Special Project B, and the rest on his usual duties.
The percentage of time he spends on the two special projects is MOST NEARLY

    A. 68%   B. 69%   C. 70%   D. 71%

31. A driver, dispatched from the garage at 8:15 A.M., arrived at his first destination 35 minutes later. He waited 50 minutes at this location before he could go on to his next destination. It took him one hour and 40 minutes traveling time to get to this second location. He then took an hour lunch period before driving back to the garage, a trip that took 45 minutes.
What time did the driver return to the garage?
_____ P.M.

    A. 12:25   B. 12:45   C. 1:05   D. 1:25

Questions 32-35.

DIRECTIONS: Questions 32 through 35 are to be answered according to the information given in the following passage.

ACCIDENT PRONENESS

Accident proneness is a subject deserving much more attention than it has received. Studies have shown a high incidence of accidents to be associated with particular employees who are called accident prone. Such employees, according to these studies, behave on their jobs in ways which make them likely to have more accidents than would normally be expected.

It is important to point out the difference between the employee who is a "repeater" and the one who is truly accident prone. It is obvious that any person assigned to work about which he knows little will be liable to injury until he does learn the "how" of the job. Few workers left completely on their own will develop adequate safe practices. Therefore, they must be trained. Only those who fail to respond to proper training should be regarded as accident prone.

The dangers of an occupation should also be considered when judging an accident record. For a crane operator, a record of five accidents in a given period of time may not indicate accident proneness, while, in the case of a clerk, two accidents over the same period of time may be excessive. There are the repeaters whose accident records can be explained by correctible physical defects, by correctible unsafe plant or machine conditions, or by assignment to work for which they are not suited because they cannot meet all the job's physical requirements. Such repeaters cannot be fairly called "accident prone." A diagnosis of accident proneness should not be lightly made, but should be based on all of these considerations.

32. According to the above passage, studies have shown that accident prone employees

    A. work under unsafe physical conditions
    B. act in unsafe ways on the job
    C. are not usually physically suited for their jobs
    D. work in the more dangerous occupations

33. According to the above passage, a person who is accident prone

    A. has received proper training which has not reduced his tendency toward accidents
    B. repeats the same accident several times over a short period of time
    C. experiences excessive anxiety about dangers in his occupation
    D. ignores unsafe but correctible machine conditions

34. According to the above passage, MOST persons who are given work they know little about

    A. will eventually learn on their own sufficient safety practices to follow
    B. work safely if they are not accident prone
    C. must be trained before they develop adequate safety methods
    D. should be regarded as accident prone until they become familiar with the job

35. According to the above passage, to effectively judge the accident record of an employee, one should consider

    A. the employee's age and physical condition
    B. that five accidents are excessive
    C. the type of dangers that are natural to his job
    D. the difficulty level of previous occupations held by the employee

Questions 36-39.

DIRECTIONS: Questions 36 through 39 are to be answered according to the information given in the following paragraph.

FIRES

The four types of fives are called Class A, Class B, Class C, and Class D. Examples of Class A fires are paper, cloth, or wood fires. The types of extinguishers used on Class A fires are foam, soda acid, or water. Class B fires are those in burning liquids. They require a smothering action for extinguishment. Carbon dioxide, dry chemical, vaporizing liquid, or foam are the types of extinguishers that are used on burning liquids. Electrical fires, such as in motors and switches, are Class C fires. A non-conducting extinguishing agent must be used for this kind of fire. Therefore, carbon dioxide, dry chemical, or vaporizing liquid extinguishers are used. Fires in motor vehicles are Class D fires, and carbon dioxide, dry chemical, or vaporizing liquid extinguishers should be used on them.

36. According to the information in the above paragraph, a fire in a can full of gasoline would be a Class _____ fire.

    A. D   B. C   C. B   D. A

37. In the above paragraph, the extinguishers recommended are entirely the same for Class _____ and Class _____ fires.

    A. B; D   B. C; D   C. B; C   D. A; B

38. According to the information in the above paragraph, a water extinguisher would MOST likely be suitable for use on which one of the following fires? A(n)

    A. fire in a truck engine
    B. fire in an electrical switch
    C. oil fire
    D. lumber fire

39. According to the information in the above paragraph, dry chemical   39._____

    A. should not be used on a burning liquid fire
    B. is a conducting extinguishing agent
    C. should not be used on a fire in a car
    D. smothers fires to put them out

Questions 40-45.

DIRECTIONS: The table below shows the initial requests made by staff for vacation. It is to be used with the Rules and Guidelines to make the decisions and judgments called for in each of Questions 40 through 45.

VACATION REQUESTS FOR THE ONE YEAR PERIOD
FROM
MAY 1, YEAR X, THROUGH APRIL 30, YEAR Y

NAME	WORK ASSIGNMENT	DATE APPOINTED	ACCUMULATED ANNUAL LEAVE DAYS	VACATION PERIODS REQUESTED
DeMarco	MVO	Mar. 2003	25	May 3-21; Oct. 25-Nov. 5
Moore	Dispatcher	Dec. 1997	32	May 24-June 4; July 12-16
Kingston	MVO	Apr. 2007	28	May 24-June 11; Feb. 7-25
Green	MVO	June 2006	26	June 7-18; Sept. 6-24
Robinson	MVO	July 1998	30	June 28-July 9; Nov. 15-26
Reilly	MVO	Oct. 2009	23	July 5-9; Jan. 31-Mar. 3
Stevens	MVO	Sept. 1996	31	July 5-23; Oct. 4-29
Costello	MVO	Sept. 1998	31	July 5-30; Oct. 4-22
Maloney	Dispatcher	Aug. 1992	35	July 5-Aug. 6; Nov. 1-5
Hughes	Director	Feb. 1990	38	July 26-Sept. 3
Lord	MVO	Jan. 2010	20	Aug. 9-27; Feb. 7-25
Diaz	MVO	Dec. 2009	28	Aug. 9-Sept. 10
Krimsky	MVO	May 2006	22	Oct. 18-22; Nov. 22-Dec. 10

RULES AND GUIDELINES

1. The two dispatchers cannot be on vacation at the same time, nor can a dispatcher be on vacation at the same time as the director.

2. For the period June 1 through September 30, not more than three MVO's can be on vacation at the same time.

3. For the period October 1 through May 31, not more than two MVO's at a time can be on vacation.

4. In cases where the same vacation time is requested by too many employees for all of them to be given the time under the rules, the requests of those who have worked the longest will be granted.

5. No employee may take more leave days than the number of annual leave days accumulated and shown in the table.

6. All vacation periods shown in the table and described in the questions below begin on a Monday and end on a Friday.

7. Employees work a five day week (Monday through Friday). They are off weekends and holidays with no charges to leave balances. When a holiday falls on a Saturday or Sunday, employees are given the following Monday off without charge to annual leave.

8. Holidays: May 31   October 25   January 1
              July 4   November 2   February 12
              September 6   November 25   February 21
              October 11   December 25

9. An employee shall be given any part of his initial requests that is permissible under the above rules and shall have first right to it despite any further adjustment of schedule.

40. Until adjustments in the vacation schedule can be made, the vacation dates that can be approved for Krimsky are

    A. Oct. 18-22; Nov. 22-Dec. 10
    B. Oct. 18-22; Nov. 29-Dec. 10
    C. Oct. 18-22 only
    D. Nov. 22-Dec. 10 only

41. Until adjustments in the vacation schedule can be made, the vacation dates that can be approved for Maloney are

    A. July 5-Aug. 6; Nov. 1-5
    B. July 5-23; Nov. 1-5
    C. July 5-9; Nov. 1-5
    D. Nov. 1-5 only

42. According to the table, Lord wants a vacation in August and another in February. Until adjustments in the vacation schedule can be made, he can be allowed to take _____ of the August vacation _____ of the February vacation.

    A. all; but none
    B. all; and almost half
    C. almost all; and almost half
    D. almost half; and all

43. Costello cannot be given all the vacation he has requested because

    A. the MVO's who have more seniority than he has have requested time he wishes
    B. he does not have enough accumulated annual leave
    C. a dispatcher is applying for vacation at the same time as Costello
    D. there are five people who want vacation in July

44. According to the table, how many leave days will DeMarco be charged for his vacation from October 25 through November 5?

    A. 10   B. 9   C. 8   D. 7

45. How many leave days will Moore use if he uses the requested vacation allowable to him under the rules?

    A. 9   B. 10   C. 14   D. 15

KEY (CORRECT ANSWERS)

1. B	11. A	21. A	31. C	41. B
2. C	12. C	22. C	32. B	42. A
3. D	13. B	23. C	33. A	43. B
4. B	14. D	24. C	34. C	44. C
5. A	15. B	25. B	35. C	45. A
6. A	16. A	26. B	36. C	
7. C	17. D	27. B	37. B	
8. D	18. A	28. C	38. D	
9. D	19. A	29. B	39. D	
10. A	20. B	30. A	40. D	

EXAMINATION SECTION
TEST 1

DIRECTIONS: Each question or incomplete statement is followed by several suggested answers or completions. Select the one that BEST answers the question or completes the statement. *PRINT THE LETTER OF THE CORRECT ANSWER IN THE SPACE AT THE RIGHT.*

1. The problem with driving the car in neutral is that 1.____

   A. you lose needed motor control
   B. the car will not go fast enough
   C. the car would not ride as smooth
   D. you would not be able to go up a hill

2. At 40 MPH, you should allow _____ car lengths between your car and the one ahead. 2.____

   A. four   B. eight   C. twelve   D. sixteen

3. Your taillight must be visible at night for _____ feet. 3.____

   A. 200   B. 350   C. 500   D. 400

4. The driver's left hand and arm are extended upward. This hand signal means that the driver plans to 4.____

   A. turn left
   B. turn right
   C. come to a stop
   D. go straight ahead

5. Which of the following are used on some highways to direct drivers into the proper lanes for turns? 5.____

   A. Flashing red lights
   B. White lines on the side of the road
   C. White arrows in the middle of the lanes
   D. Flashing yellow lights

6. When you want to overtake and pass another vehicle, you should 6.____

   A. change lanes quickly so the other driver will see you
   B. signal and pass when safe to do so
   C. wait for a signal from the other driver
   D. stay close behind so you need less time to pass

7. If you drive past your exit on an expressway, you should 7.____

   A. drive to the next exit and leave the expressway
   B. make a U-turn at the nearest emergency turn area
   C. make a U-turn at the next service area
   D. pull onto the shoulder, then back up to the exit

8. A flashing yellow light means 8.____

   A. come to a full stop
   B. proceed with caution
   C. merging traffic
   D. pedestrian crossing

9. You are waiting in the intersection to complete a left turn. You should

    A. drive around the rear of a car if it blocks you
    B. signal and keep your wheels straight
    C. flash your headlights so the driver will let you get through
    D. signal and keep your wheels turned to the left

10. Alcohol affects

    A. recovery from headlight glare
    B. judgment of distances
    C. reaction time
    D. all of the above

11. A red and white triangular sign at an intersection means

    A. always come to a full stop at the intersection
    B. look both ways as you cross the intersection
    C. slow down and be prepared to stop if necessary
    D. slow down if an emergency vehicle is approaching

12. When driving at 60 MPH, a driver will be able to stop his car in _____ feet.

    A. 67 B. 120 C. 190 D. 400

13. After you have passed a car, you should return to the right lane when you

    A. see the front bumper of the other car in your mirror
    B. see the other car's headlights come on
    C. have put your turn signal on
    D. have turned your headlights on

14. You may pass another vehicle on the right if it is waiting to

    A. park at the curb
    B. turn into a driveway on the right
    C. turn right
    D. turn left

15. Expressways have *expressway entrance lanes* (acceleration lanes) so that drivers can

    A. reach the proper speed before blending with traffic
    B. test their brakes before driving at expressway speeds
    C. test the pickup of their cars
    D. stop at the end to wait for a traffic opening

16. Night driving is dangerous because

    A. some traffic signs are less visible at night
    B. more vehicles are on the road at night
    C. street lights tend to blur our vision
    D. the distance we can see ahead is reduced

17. Assuming that the street is level, after you have finished parallel parking in a space between two other cars, you should

    A. leave your front wheels turned toward the curb
    B. straighten your front wheels and leave room between cars
    C. move as far forward in the space as possible
    D. make sure your car almost touches the car behind you

18. You drive along a street and hear a siren. You cannot immediately see the emergency vehicle.
    You should

    A. pull to the curb until you are sure it is not on your street
    B. speed up and turn at the next intersection
    C. keep driving until you see the vehicle
    D. slow down but don't stop until you see it

19. If you leave ignition keys in an unattended vehicle,

    A. you must leave the meter running
    B. you commit a traffic infraction
    C. it is alright as long as you have your parking brake set
    D. you should leave them in the event the car has to be moved

20. The ones who *always* have the right of way are

    A. motorists   B. pedestrians
    C. cyclists   D. animals

21. On a road where there are no sidewalks, a pedestrian should walk

    A. on the shoulder of the road, facing traffic
    B. on the shoulder of the road, going with the traffic
    C. in the gutter alongside of the road
    D. in the nearest clear space next to the road

22. To signal for help on the New York State Thruway,

    A. flash your headlights on and off
    B. flash your brake lights on and off
    C. tie a white cloth to the left hand door handle of the car
    D. stand on the road and flag down the first oncoming car

23. The MAIN use to which a driver's horn should be put is

    A. to let the other driver know the light is green
    B. in passing other cars or as a warning
    C. if the driver is in a hurry
    D. so that pedestrians will give you the right of way

24. If a car is traveling at 40 MPH, it needs _____ feet to stop.

    A. 30   B. 67   C. 120   D. 190

25. When a tire blows out, 25.___
    A. take your foot from the gas and hold the steering wheel as steadily as possible
    B. brake firmly until you bring the car to a stop
    C. disengage your clutch and use your brakes to reduce speed
    D. give more gas and hold the steering wheel as steadily as possible

---

KEY (CORRECT ANSWERS)

1.	A	11.	C
2.	A	12.	D
3.	C	13.	A
4.	B	14.	D
5.	C	15.	A
6.	B	16.	D
7.	A	17.	B
8.	B	18.	A
9.	B	19.	B
10.	D	20.	B

21. A
22. C
23. B
24. C
25. A

TEST 2

DIRECTIONS: Each question or incomplete statement is followed by several suggested answers or completions. Select the one that BEST answers the question or completes the statement. *PRINT THE LETTER OF THE CORRECT ANSWER IN THE SPACE AT THE RIGHT.*

1. When a driver sees or hears a vehicle with a flashing red light on, siren blowing, or bell ringing, he should

    A. give it the right of way
    B. speed up and drive on
    C. stop in his lane
    D. stop and direct traffic, if there is no police officer

    1.____

2. When approaching a stopped school bus with red lights flashing, a driver should

    A. pass the bus with due caution
    B. pass the bus only on the left
    C. stop at least 8 feet behind and wait until the bus proceeds
    D. stop and then go if all is clear

    2.____

3. Before making a turn, a driver should signal for _____ ft.

    A. 50 B. 100 C. 150 D. 75

    3.____

4. The general rule with regard to right of way at intersections is that the car _____ has the right of way.

    A. going straight ahead   B. on the main road
    C. on the right   D. making a turn

    4.____

5. You should be _____ ft. from a vehicle you are overtaking before switching your headlights to low beam.

    A. 100 B. 200 C. 250 D. 350

    5.____

6. Unless a sign indicates otherwise, a driver must park _____ ft. from a fire hydrant.

    A. 5 B. 10 C. 15 D. 9

    6.____

7. When parking parallel to the curb, the wheels must be no more than _____ inches away from the curb.

    A. 6 B. 12 C. 18 D. 24

    7.____

8. If a police officer at an intersection gives a signal for you to proceed although the traffic signal is against you, the driver should obey

    A. the traffic signal
    B. whichever he wants
    C. the police officer
    D. the pedestrian who may be crossing

    8.____

9. An octagonal (8-sided) sign means to

    A. reduce speed
    B. proceed with caution
    C. yield the right of way
    D. stop and proceed with caution

10. When approaching a flashing red traffic signal, a driver should

    A. proceed with caution
    B. stop and then proceed with caution
    C. pull over to the side of the road
    D. reduce speed

11. When nearing an intersection marked with a *Yield Right of Way* sign, the driver must

    A. yield the right of way to pedestrians
    B. yield the right of way to all commercial traffic
    C. yield the right of way to all horse-drawn vehicles
    D. slow down and allow all cross traffic to proceed before him

12. If a signal light changes from green to yellow as a driver nears an intersection, he should

    A. try to get through the intersection before the red light comes on
    B. prepare to stop
    C. keep his speed the same
    D. speed up and rush through the intersection

13. A flashing yellow or amber light differs in meaning from a flashing red light in that yellow means _____ while red means _____.

    A. proceed with caution; stop and then proceed
    B. try to stop; stop and then proceed
    C. proceed with caution; stop
    D. stop; proceed at will

14. Diamond-shaped signs indicate

    A. cattle crossing ahead
    B. stop and then proceed with caution
    C. reduce speed for curves, hills or narrow bridges
    D. railroad crossing ahead

15. The rectangular (square) signs mean

    A. proceed with caution   B. railroad crossing ahead
    C. yield right of way   D. danger, slow down

16. A broken line painted on the highway means that a driver

    A. must not cross it at any time
    B. may cross it to pass provided traffic permits
    C. may cross it to pass, even on hills
    D. must not cross it on weekends

17. A double solid line on the highway means that a driver

    A. may cross it any time
    B. may cross it only if he is on the main road
    C. must never cross it
    D. must never cross it unless traffic permits

18. The highway sign shaped like an inverted pyramid means

    A. stop
    B. slow down, and proceed with caution
    C. danger
    D. yield right of way

19. The shape of the highway sign which means that a driver is approaching a railroad crossing is

    A. square   B. round
    C. diamond   D. rectangular

20. A driver may follow a fire engine on its way to a fire _____ ft. in a city, _____ ft. in a rural area.

    A. 200; 500   B. 100; 500   C. 20; 400   D. 100; 50

21. Parking lights should be used when a driver

    A. is driving in well-lighted areas
    B. leaves the car parked in a driveway
    C. parks the car on a road facing traffic
    D. parks the car on a road going with the traffic

22. When passing a playground, park or other area where children are playing or walking,

    A. stop and then proceed with caution
    B. slow down and proceed with caution
    C. blow horn and make sure they see you
    D. blow horn, stop, and then proceed with caution

23. If a driver is parked parallel to the curb on a busy street, he may open the doors on the traffic side

    A. when the traffic light turns red
    B. between the hours of sunrise and sunset
    C. if he looks very carefully
    D. when no traffic is approaching

24. When following another car on a superhighway,

    A. do not tailgate
    B. try to follow at the same speed
    C. watch out for littering
    D. make sure you do not lose sight of it

25. When driving in heavy fog at night, a driver should use his

    A. upper headlight beams
    B. lower headlight beams
    C. uppers, in addition to fog lights
    D. lowers, in addition to fog lights

26. A driver may drive at the MAXIMUM speed limit whenever

    A. his car is in good condition
    B. there is an emergency
    C. he is on a New York State road unless otherwise marked
    D. he is escorted by a state policeman

27. At night when you meet an oncoming vehicle with blinding, bright lights, the SAFEST action to take is to

    A. turn your head away so that you don't have to look at the lights
    B. cast your gaze at the right side of the road, stay near it and slow down
    C. put on your brightest lights so as to counteract his
    D. put on your dark glasses

28. To get a car out of a skid,

    A. press the gas gently as you turn the wheels in the direction of the skid
    B. press the brakes and try to stop the vehicle
    C. press the gas hard so as to pull out of the skid
    D. turn the wheels as fast as you can in the direction you want

29. A driver should stay at least _____ car length(s) behind the car ahead of him for every _____ MPH.

    A. 2; 20   B. 2; 10   C. 1; 20   D. 1; 10

30. A driver can avoid being poisoned by the monoxide gas from his exhaust by

    A. always making sure he keeps the car windows closed
    B. keeping a window of the car open to allow fresh air in
    C. making sure he always uses the best grade gasoline
    D. boring an extra hole in the exhaust pipe

KEY (CORRECT ANSWERS)

1.	A	16.	B
2.	C	17.	C
3.	B	18.	D
4.	C	19.	B
5.	B	20.	A
6.	C	21.	C
7.	B	22.	B
8.	C	23.	D
9.	D	24.	A
10.	B	25.	B
11.	D	26.	C
12.	B	27.	B
13.	A	28.	A
14.	C	29.	D
15.	A	30.	B

MAP READING
EXAMINATION SECTION
TEST 1

DIRECTIONS: Each question or incomplete statement is followed by several suggested answers or completions. Select the one that BEST answers the question or completes the Statement. *PRINT THE LETTER OF THE CORRECT ANSWER IN THE SPACE AT THE RIGHT.*

Questions 1-5.

DIRECTIONS: Questions 1 through 5 are to be answered SOLELY on the basis of the following information and map.

An employee may be required to assist civilians who seek travel directions or referral to city agencies and facilities.

The following is a map of part of a city, where several public offices and other institutions are located. Each of the squares represents one city block. Street names are as shown. If there is an arrow next to the street name, it means the street is one-way only in the direction of the arrow. If there is no arrow next to the street name, two-way traffic is allowed.

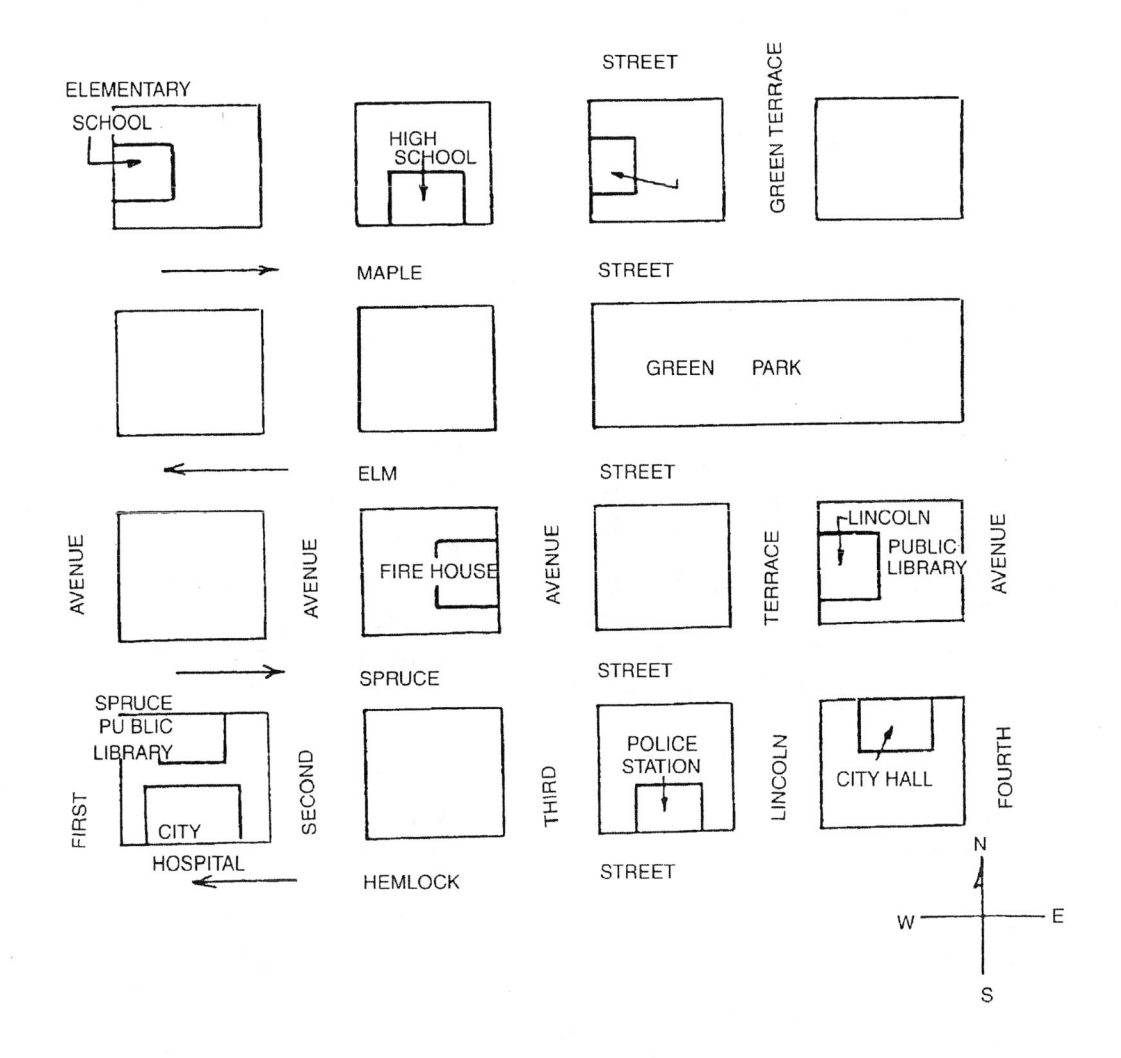

1. A woman whose handbag was stolen from her in Green Park asks a firefighter at the firehouse where to go to report the crime.
   The firefighter should tell the woman to go to the

   A. police station on Spruce Street
   B. police station on Hemlock Street
   C. city hall on Spruce Street
   D. city hall on Hemlock Street

2. A disabled senior citizen who lives on Green Terrace telephones the firehouse to ask which library is closest to her home.
   The firefighter should tell the senior citizen it is the

   A. Spruce Public Library on Lincoln Terrace
   B. Lincoln Public Library on Spruce Street
   C. Spruce Public Library on Spruce Street
   D. Lincoln Public Library on Lincoln Terrace

3. A woman calls the firehouse to ask for the exact location of City Hall.
   She should be told that it is on

   A. Hemlock Street, between Lincoln Terrace and Fourth Avenue
   B. Spruce Street, between Lincoln Terrace and Fourth Avenue
   C. Lincoln Terrace, between Spruce Street and Elm Street
   D. Green Terrace, between Maple Street and Pine Street

4. A delivery truck driver is having trouble finding the high school to make a delivery. The driver parks the truck across from the firehouse on Third Avenue facing north and goes into the firehouse to ask directions.
   In giving directions, the firefighter should tell the driver to go _____ to the school.

   A. north on Third Avenue to Pine Street and then make a right
   B. south on Third Avenue, make a left on Hemlock Street, and then make a right on Second Avenue
   C. north on Third Avenue, turn left on Elm Street, make a right on Second Avenue and go to Maple Street, then make another right
   D. north on Third Avenue to Maple Street, and then make a left

5. A man comes to the firehouse accompanied by his son and daughter. He wants to register his son in the high school and his daughter in the elementary school. He asks a firefighter which school is closest for him to walk to from the firehouse.
   The firefighter should tell the man that the

   A. high school is closer than the elementary school
   B. elementary school is closer than the high school
   C. elementary school and high school are the same distance away
   D. elementary school and high school are in opposite directions

Questions 6-8.

DIRECTIONS: Questions 6 through 8 are to be answered SOLELY on the basis of the following map and information. The flow of traffic is indicated by the arrows. If there is only one arrow shown, then traffic flows in the direction indicated by the arrow. If there are two arrows, then traffic flows in both directions. You must follow the flow of traffic

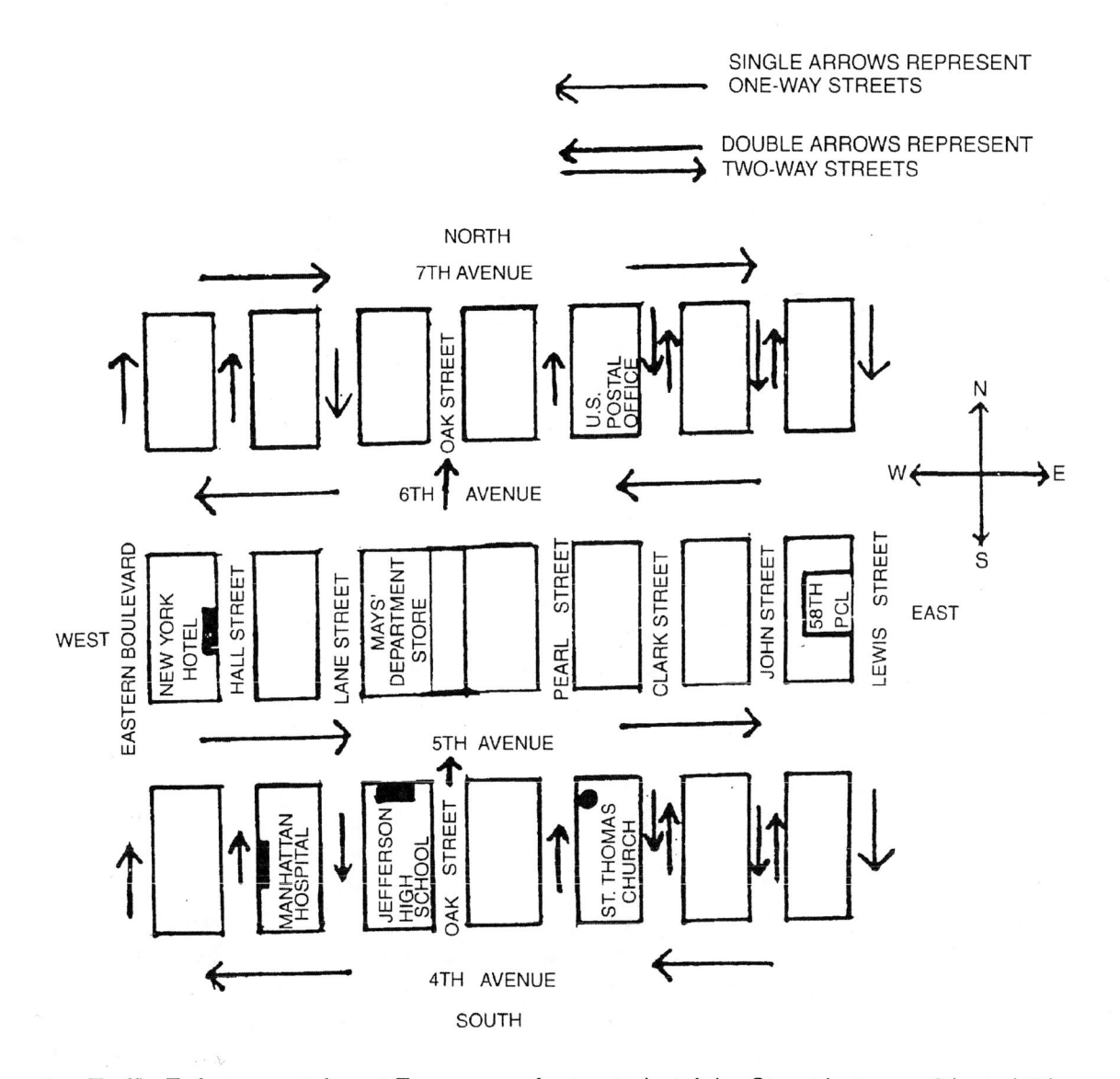

SINGLE ARROWS REPRESENT ONE-WAY STREETS

DOUBLE ARROWS REPRESENT TWO-WAY STREETS

6. Traffic Enforcement Agent Fox was on foot patrol at John Street between 6th and 7th Avenues when a motorist driving southbound asked her for directions to the New York Hotel, which is located on Hall Street between 5th and 6th Avenues. Which one of the following is the SHORTEST route for Agent Fox to direct the motorist to take, making sure to obey all traffic regulations?
Travel _____ to the New York Hotel.

   A. north on John Street, then east on 7th Avenue, then north on Lewis Street, then west on 4th Avenue, then north on Eastern Boulevard, then east on 5th Avenue, then north on Hall Street
   B. south on John Street, then west on 6th Avenue, then south on Eastern Boulevard, then east on 5th Avenue, then north on Hall Street

6._____

C. south on John Street, then west on 6th Avenue, then south on Clark Street, then east on 4th Avenue, then north on Eastern Boulevard, then east on 5th Avenue, then north on Hall Street
D. south on John Street, then west on 4th Avenue, then north on Hall Street

7. Traffic Enforcement Agent Murphy is on motorized patrol on 7th Avenue between Oak Street and Pearl Street when Lt. Robertson radios him to go to Jefferson High School, located on 5th Avenue between Lane Street and Oak Street. Which one of the following is the SHORTEST route for Agent Murphy to take, making sure to obey all the traffic regulations?
Travel east on 7th Avenue, then south on _____, then east on 5th Avenue to Jefferson High School.

A. Clark Street, then west on 4th Avenue, then north on Hall Street
B. Pearl Street, then west on 4th Avenue, then north on Lane Street
C. Lewis Street, then west on 6th Avenue, then south on Hall Street
D. Lewis Street, then west on 4th Avenue, then north on Oak Street

8. Traffic Enforcement Agent Vasquez was on 4th Avenue and Eastern Boulevard when a motorist asked him for directions to the 58th Police Precinct, which is located on Lewis Street between 5th and 6th Avenues.
Which one of the following is the SHORTEST route for Agent Vasquez to direct the motorist to take, making sure to obey all traffic regulations.
Travel north on Eastern Boulevard, then east on _____ on Lewis Street to the 58th Police Precinct.

A. 5th Avenue, then north
B. 7th Avenue, then south
C. 6th Avenue, then north on Pearl Street, then east on 7th Avenue, then south
D. 5th Avenue, then north on Clark Street, then east on 6th Avenue, then south

Questions 9-13.

DIRECTIONS: Questions 9 through 13 are to be answered SOLELY on the basis of the following map and the following information.

Toll collectors answer motorists' questions concerning directions by reading a map of the metropolitan area. Although many alternate routes leading to destinations exist on the following map, you are to choose the MOST direct route of those given.

9. A motorist driving from the Bronx over the Triborough Bridge wants to go to LaGuardia Airport in Queens.
   The officer should direct him to

   A. Grand Central Parkway
   B. F.D.R. Drive
   C. Shore Parkway
   D. Flatbush Avenue

10. A motorist driving from Manhattan through the Queens Midtown Tunnel would travel DIRECTLY onto

    A. Shore Parkway
    B. F.D.R. Drive
    C. Long Island Expressway
    D. Atlantic Avenue

11. A motorist traveling north over the Marine Parkway Bridge should take which route to reach Coney Island?

    A. Shore Parkway East
    B. Belt Parkway West
    C. Linden Boulevard
    D. Ocean Parkway

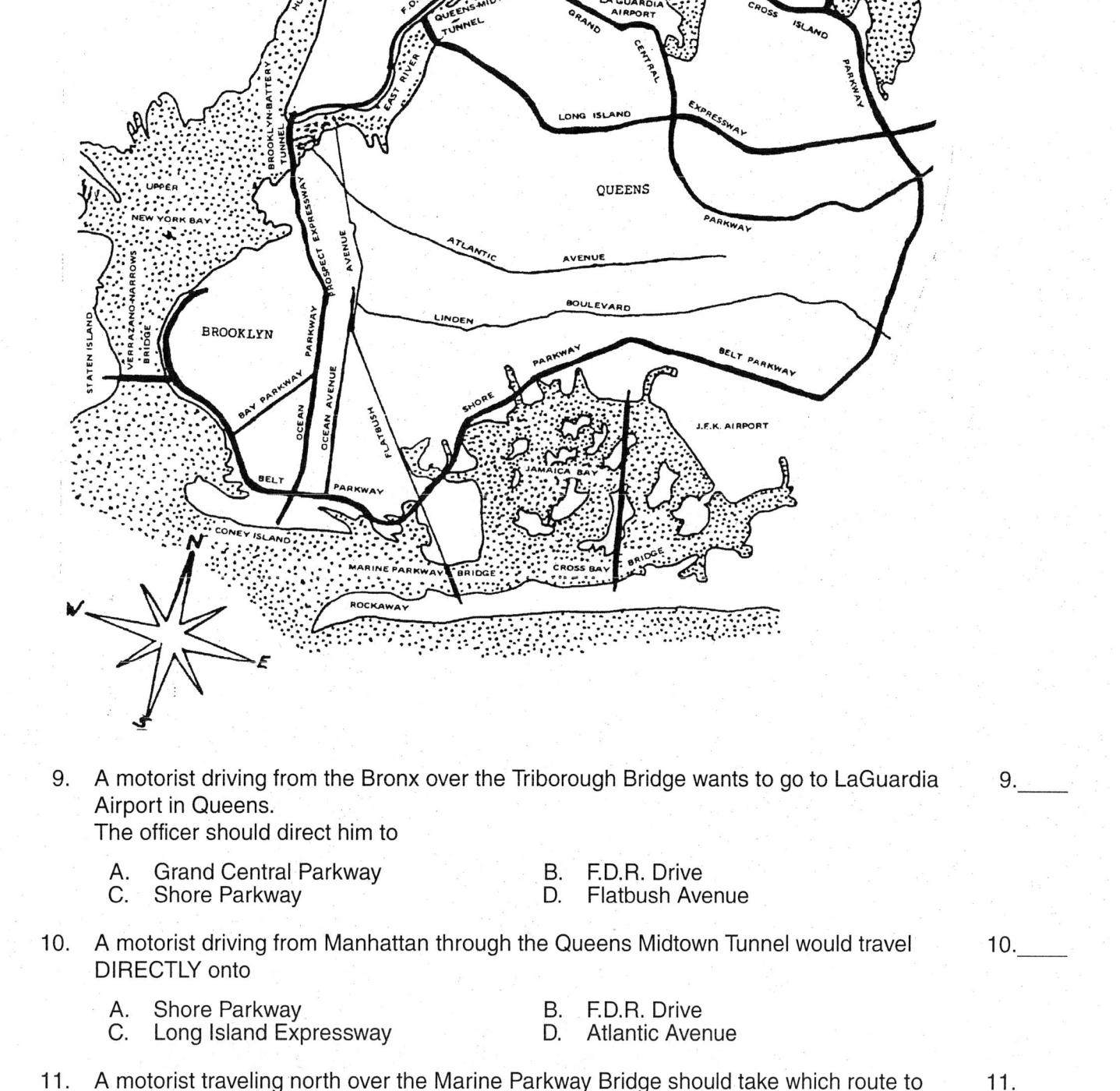

12. Which facility does NOT connect the Bronx and Queens?   12.____

    A. Triborough Bridge   B. Bronx-Whitestone Bridge
    C. Verrazano-Narrows Bridge   D. Throgs-Neck Bridge

13. A motorist driving from Manhattan arrives at the toll booth of the Brooklyn-Battery Tunnel   13.____
    and asks directions to Ocean Parkway.
    To which one of the following routes should the motorist FIRST be directed?

    A. Atlantic Avenue   B. Bay Parkway
    C. Prospect Expressway   D. Ocean Avenue

Questions 14-16.

DIRECTIONS: Questions 14 through 16 are to be answered SOLELY on the basis of the following map. The flow of traffic is indicated by the arrows. If there is only one arrow shown, then traffic flows only in the direction indicated by the arrow. If there are two arrows, then traffic flows in both directions. You must follow the flow of traffic.

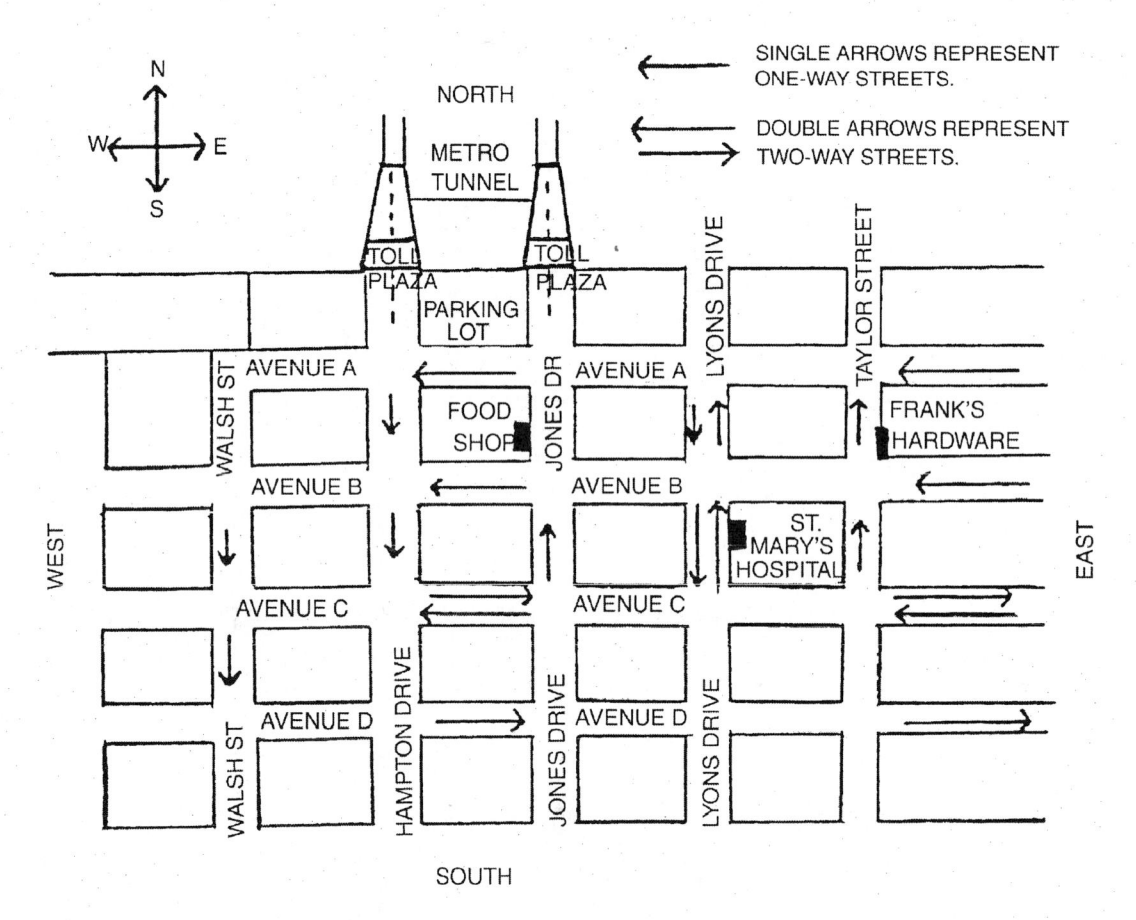

14. A motorist is exiting the Metro Tunnel and approaches the bridge and tunnel officer at the   14.____
    toll plaza. He asks the officer how to get to the food shop on Jones Drive. Which one of the following is the SHORTEST route for the motorist to take, making sure to obey all traffic regulations?
    Travel south on Hampton Drive, then left on _____ on Jones Drive to the food shop.

A.	Avenue A, then right	B.	Avenue B, then right
C.	Avenue D, then left	D.	Avenue C, then left

15. A motorist heading south pulls up to a toll booth at the exit of the Metro Tunnel and asks Bridge and Tunnel Officer Evans how to get to Frank's Hardware Store on Taylor Street. Which one of the following is the SHORTEST route for the motorist to take, making sure to obey all traffic regulations?
    Travel south on Hampton Drive, then east on

    A. Avenue B to Taylor Street
    B. Avenue D, then north on Taylor Street to Avenue B
    C. Avenue C, then north on Taylor Street to Avenue B
    D. Avenue C, then north on Lyons Drive, then east on Avenue B to Taylor Street

15.____

16. A motorist is exiting the Metro Tunnel and approaches the toll plaza. She asks Bridge and Tunnel Officer Owens for directions to St. Mary's Hospital.
    Which one of the following is the SHORTEST route for the motorist to take, making sure to obey all traffic regulations?
    Travel south on Hampton Drive, then _____ on Lyons Drive to St. Mary's Hospital.

    A. left on Avenue D, then left
    B. right on Avenue A, then left on Walsh Street, then left on Avenue D, then left
    C. left on Avenue C, then left
    D. left on Avenue B, then right

16.____

Questions 17-18.

DIRECTIONS: Questions 17 and 18 are to be answered SOLELY on the basis of the map which appears on the following page. The flow of traffic is indicated by the arrows. If there is only one arrow shown, then traffic flows only in the direction indicated by the arrow. If there are two arrows shown, then traffic flows in both directions. You must follow the flow of traffic.

SINGLE ARROWS REPRESENT ONE-WAY STREETS.

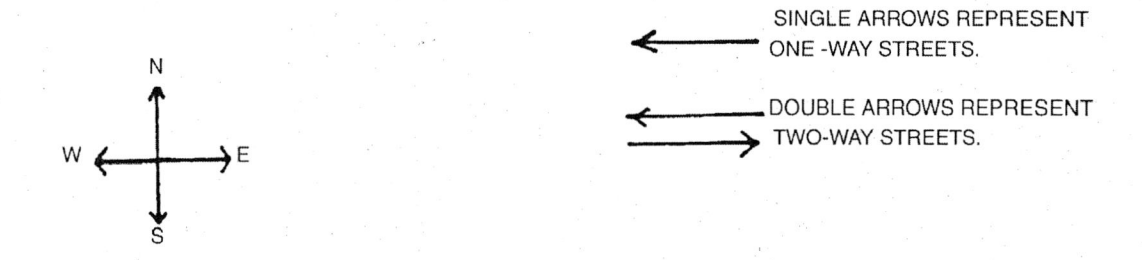

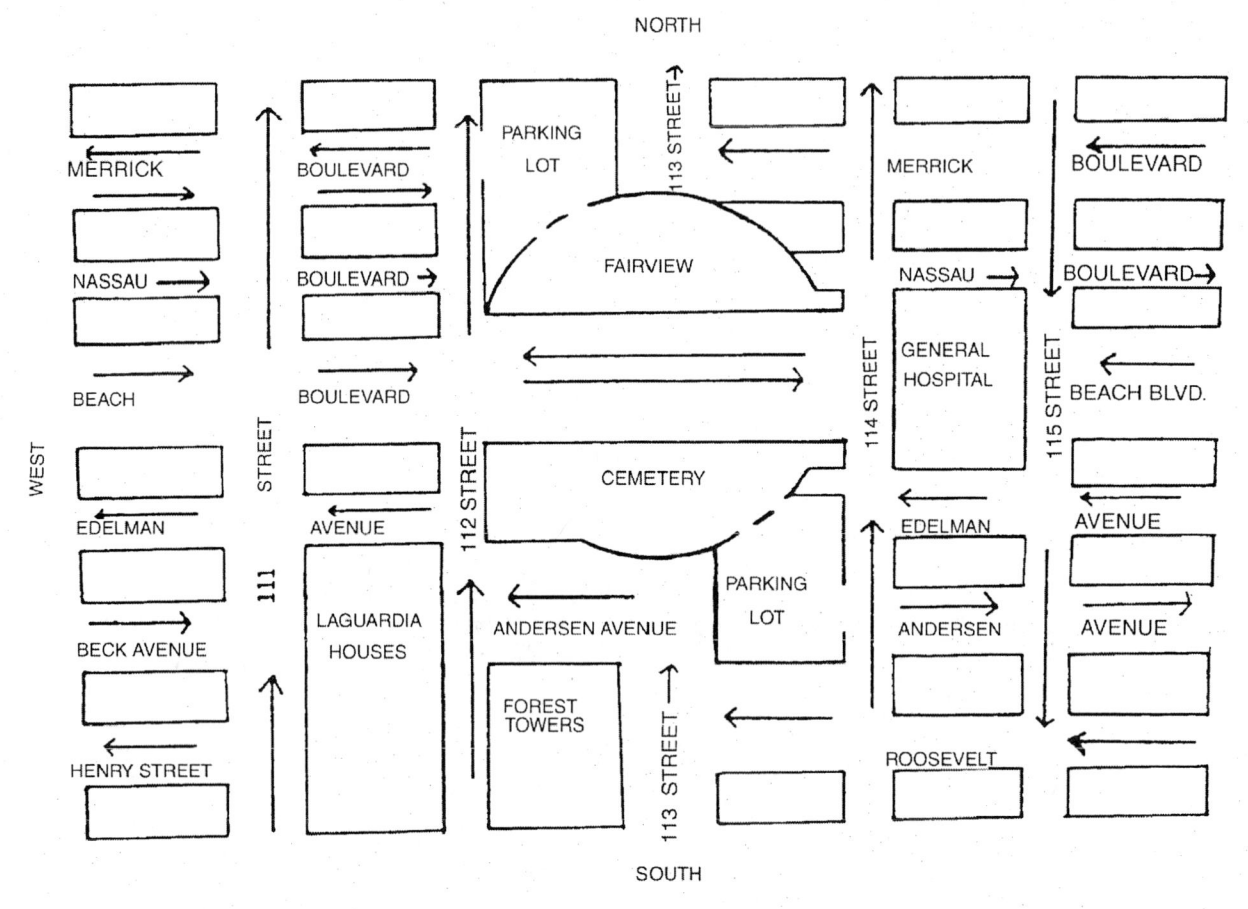

DOUBLE ARROWS REPRESENT TWO-WAY STREETS.

17. Police Officers Glenn and Albertson are on 111th Street at Henry Street when they are dispatched to a past robbery at Beach Boulevard and 115th Street.
Which one of the following is the SHORTEST route for the officers to follow in their patrol car, making sure to obey all traffic regulations?
Travel north on 111th Street, then east on _____ south on 115th Street.

    A. Edelman Avenue, then north on 112th Street, then east on Beach Boulevard, then north on 114th Street, then east on Nassau Boulevard, then one block
    B. Beach Boulevard, then north on 114th Street, then east on Nassau Boulevard, then one block
    C. Merrick Boulevard, then two blocks
    D. Nassau Boulevard, then south on 112th Street, then east on Beach Boulevard, then north on 114th Street, then east on Nassau Boulevard, then one block

17._____

18. Later in their tour, Officers Glenn and Albertson are driving on 114th Street. If they make a left turn to enter the parking lot at Andersen Avenue, and then make a u-turn, in what direction would they now be headed?

    A. North   B. South   C. East   D. West

18.____

Questions 19-20.

DIRECTIONS: Questions 19 and 20 are to be answered SOLELY on the basis of the following map. The flow of traffic is indicated by the arrows. If there is only one arrow shown, then traffic flows only in the direction indicated by the arrow. If there are two arrows shown, then traffic flows in both directions. You must follow the flow of traffic.

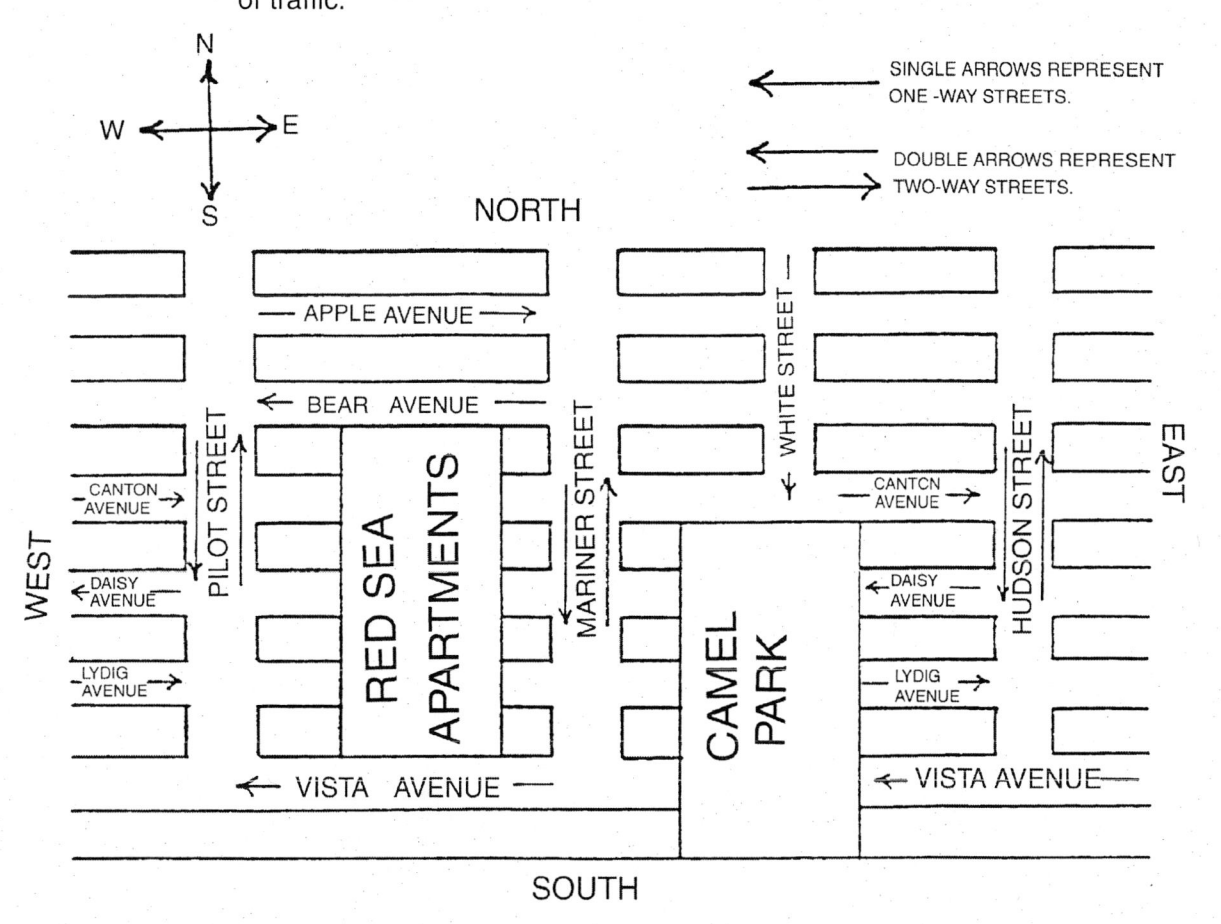

19. You are located at Apple Avenue and White Street. You receive a call to respond to the corner of Lydig Avenue and Pilot Street.
Which one of the following is the MOST direct route for you to take in your patrol car, making sure to obey all traffic regulations?
Travel _____ on Pilot Street.

19.____

    A. two blocks south on White Street, then one block east on Canton Avenue, then one block north on Hudson Street, then three blocks west on Bear Avenue, then three blocks south
    B. one block south on White Street, then two blocks west on Bear Avenue, then three blocks south

C. two blocks west on Apple Avenue, then four blocks south
D. two blocks south on White Street, then one block west on Canton Avenue, then three blocks south on Mariner Street, then one block west on Vista Avenue, then one block north

20. You are located at Canton Avenue and Pilot Street. You receive a call of a crime in progress at the intersection of Canton Avenue and Hudson Street.
Which one of the following is the MOST direct route for you to take in your patrol car, making sure to obey all traffic regulations?
Travel

   A. two blocks north on Pilot Street, then two blocks east on Apple Avenue, then one block south on White Street, then one block east on Bear Avenue, then one block south on Hudson Street
   B. three blocks south on Pilot Street, then travel one block east on Vista Avenue, then travel three blocks north on Mariner Street, then travel two blocks east on Canton Avenue
   C. one block north on Pilot Street, then travel three blocks east on Bear Avenue, then travel one block south on Hudson Street
   D. two blocks north on Pilot Street, then travel three blocks east on Apple Avenue, then travel two blocks south on Hudson Street

KEY (CORRECT ANSWERS)

1.	B	11.	B/D
2.	D	12.	C
3.	B	13.	C
4.	C	14.	D
5.	A	15.	C
6.	D	16.	C
7.	A	17.	B
8.	B	18.	C
9.	A	19.	B
10.	C	20.	D

EXAMINATION SECTION
TEST 1

DIRECTIONS: Each question or incomplete statement is followed by several suggested answers or completions. Select the one that BEST answers the question or completes the statement. *PRINT THE LETTER OF THE CORRECT ANSWER IN THE SPACE AT THE RIGHT.*

1. A *basic* method of operation that a *good* supervisor should follow is to   1.____

    A. check the work of subordinates constantly to make sure they are not making exceptions to the rules
    B. train subordinates so they can handle problems that come up regularly themselves and come to him only with special cases
    C. delegate to subordinates only those duties which he cannot do himself
    D. issue directions to subordinates only on special matters

2. To do a *good* job of performance evaluation, it is BEST for a supervisor to   2.____

    A. compare the employee's performance to that of another employee doing similar work
    B. give greatest weight to instances of unusually good or unusually poor performance
    C. leave out any consideration of the employee's personal traits
    D. measure the employee's performance against standard performance requirements

3. Of the following, the MOST important reason for a supervisor to have private face to face discussions with subordinates about their performance is to   3.____

    A. help employees improve their work
    B. give special praise to employees who perform well
    C. encourage the employees to compete for higher performance ratings
    D. discipline employees who perform poorly

4. Of the following, the CHIEF purpose of a probationary period for a new employee is to allow time for   4.____

    A. finding out whether the selection processes are satisfactory
    B. the employee to make adjustments in his home circumstances made necessary by the job
    C. the employee to decide whether he wants a permanent appointment
    D. determining the fitness of the employee to continue in the job

5. When a subordinate resigns his job, it is MOST important to conduct an exit interview in order to   5.____

    A. try to get the employee to remain on the job
    B. learn the true reasons for the employee's resignation
    C. see that the employee leaves with a good opinion of the agency
    D. ask the employee if he would consider a transfer

6. Chronic lateness of employees is generally LEAST likely to be due to   6.____

    A. distance of job location from home   B. poor personnel administration
    C. unexpressed employee grievances   D. low morale

7. Of the following, the LEAST effective stimulus for motivating employees toward inproved performance over a long-range period is

   A. their sense of achievement
   B. their feeling of recognition
   C. opportunity for their self-development
   D. an increase in salary

8. Suppose that NOT ONE of a group of employees has turned in an idea to the employees suggestion system during the past year.
   The *most probable* reason for this situation is that the

   A. money awards given for suggestions used are not high enough to make employees interested
   B. employees in this group are not able to develop any good ideas
   C. supervisor of these employees is not doing enough to encourage them to take part in the program
   D. methods and procedures of operation do not need improvement

9. A subordinate tells you that he is having trouble concentrating on his work due to a personal problem at home.
   Of the following, it would be BEST for you to

   A. refer him to a community service agency
   B. listen quietly to the story because he may just need a sympathetic ear
   C. tell him that you cannot help him because the problem is not job related
   D. ask him questions about the nature of the problem and tell him how you would handle it

10. For you as a supervisor to give each of your subordinates *exactly* the same type of supervision is

    A. *advisable,* because doing this insures fair and impartial treatment of each individual
    B. *not advisable,* because individuals like to think that they are receiving better treatment than others
    C. *advisable,* because once a supervisor learns how to deal with a subordinate who brings a problem to him, he can handle another subordinate with this problem in the same way
    D. *not advisable,* because each person is different and there is no one supervisory procedure for dealing with individuals that applies in every case

11. A senior employee under your supervision tells you that he is reluctant to speak to one of his subordinates about his poor work habits, because this worker is "strong-willed" and he does not want to antagonize him.
    For you to offer to speak to the subordinate about this matter yourself would be

    A. *advisable,* since you are in a position of greater authority
    B. *inadvisable,* since handling this problem is a basic supervisory responsibility of the senior employee
    C. *advisable,* since the senior employee must work more closely with the worker than you do
    D. *inadvisable,* since you should not risk antagonizing the employee yourself

12. Some of your subordinates have been coming to you with complaints you feel are unimportant. For you to hear their stories out is

    A. *poor practice,* you should spend your time on more important matters
    B. *good practice,* this will increase your popularity with your subordinates
    C. *poor practice,* subordinates should learn to come to you only with major grievances
    D. *good practice,* it may prevent minor complaints from developing into major grievances

13. Assume that an agency has an established procedure for handling employee grievances. An employee in this agency, comes to his immediate supervisor with a grievance. The supervisor investigates the matter and makes a decision.
    However, the employee is not satisfied with the decision made by the supervisor. The BEST action for the supervisor to take is to

    A. tell the employee he will review the matter further
    B. remind the employee that he is the supervisor and the employee must act in accordance with his decision
    C. explain to the employee how he can carry his complaint forward to the next step in the grievance procedure
    D. tell the employee he will consult with his own superiors on the matter

14. Subordinate employees and senior employees often must make quick decisions while in the field. The supervisor can BEST help subordinates meet such situations by

    A. training them in the appropriate action to take for every problem that may come up
    B. limiting the areas in which they are permitted to make decisions
    C. making certain they understand clearly the basic policies of the bureau and the department
    D. delegating authority to make such decisions to only a few subordinates on each level

15. Studies have shown that the CHIEF cause of failure to achieve success as a supervisor is

    A. an unwillingness to delegate authority to subordinates
    B. the establishment of high performance standards for subordinates
    C. the use of discipline that is too strict
    D. showing too much leniency to poor workers

16. When a supervisor delegates to a subordinate certain work that he normally does himself, it is MOST important that he give the subordinate

    A. responsibility for also setting the standards for the work to be done
    B. sufficient authority to be able to carry out the assignment
    C. written, step-by-step instructions for doing the work
    D. an explanation of one part of the task at a time

17. It is particularly important that disciplinary actions be equitable as between individuals. This statement *implies* that

    A. punishment applied in disciplinary actions should be lenient
    B. proposed disciplinary actions should be reviewed by higher authority
    C. subordinates should have an opportunity to present their stories before penalties are applied
    D. penalties for violations of the rules should be standardized and consistently applied

17.____

18. You discover that from time to time a number of false rumors circulate among your subordinates.
    Of the following, the BEST way for you to handle this situation is to

    A. ignore the rumors since rumors circulate in every office and can never be eliminated
    B. attempt to find those responsible for the rumors and reprimand them
    C. make sure that your employees are informed as soon as possible about all matters that affect them
    D. inform your superior about the rumors and let him deal with the matter

18.____

19. Supervisors who allow the "halo effect" to influence their evaluations of subordinates are *most likely* to

    A. give more lenient ratings to older employees who have longer service
    B. let one highly favorable or unfavorable trait unduly affect their judgment of an employee
    C. evaluate all employees on one trait before considering a second
    D. give high evaluations in order to avoid antagonizing their subordinates

19.____

20. For a supervisor to keep records of reprimands to subordinates about infractions of the rules is

    A. *good practice,* because these records are valuable to support disciplinary actions recommended or taken
    B. *poor practice,* because such records are evidence of the supervisor's inability to maintain discipline
    C. *good practice,* because such records indicate that the supervisor is doing a good job
    D. *poor practice,* because the best way to correct subordinates is to give them more training

20.____

21. When a new departmental policy has been established, it would be MOST advisable for you, as a supervisor, to

    A. distribute a memo which states the new policy and instruct your subordinates to read it
    B. explain specifically to your subordinates how the policy is going to affect them
    C. make sure your subordinates understand that you are not responsible for setting the policy
    D. tell your subordinates whether you agree or disagree with the policy

21.____

22. As a supervisor, you receive several complaints about the rude conduct of a subordinate. The FIRST action you should take is to

    A. request his transfer to another office
    B. prepare a charge sheet for disciplinary action
    C. assign a senior employee to work with him for a week
    D. interview the employee to determine possible reason, and warn that correction is necessary

23. A supervisor is *most likely* to get subordinates to work cooperatively toward accomplishing bureau goals if he

    A. creates an atmosphere that contributes to their feeling of security
    B. backs up subordinates even when they occasionally disobey regulations
    C. shows interest in subordinates by helping them solve their personal problems
    D. uses an authoritarian or "bossy" approach to supervision

24. A supervisor is holding a staff meeting with his senior employees to try to find an acceptable solution to a problem that has come up.
    Of the following, the CHIEF role of the supervisor at this meeting should be to

    A. see that every member of the group contributes at least one suggestions
    B. act as chairman of the meeting, but take no other active part to avoid influencing the senior employees
    C. keep the participants from wandering off into discussions of irrelevant matters
    D. make certain the participants hear his views on the matter at the beginning of the meeting

25. An employee shows you a certificate that he has just received for completing two years of study in conversational Spanish. As his supervisor, it would be BEST for you to

    A. put a note about this accomplishment in his personnel folder
    B. assign him to areas in which people of Spanish origin live
    C. congratulate him on this accomplishment, but tell him frankly that you doubt this is likely to have any direct bearing on his work
    D. encourage him to continue his studies and become thoroughly fluent in speaking the language

KEY (CORRECT ANSWERS)

1.	B	11.	B
2.	D	12.	D
3.	A	13.	C
4.	D	14.	C
5.	B	15.	A
6.	A	16.	B
7.	D	17.	D
8.	C	18.	C
9.	B	19.	B
10.	D	20.	A

21. B
22. D
23. A
24. C
25. A

———

TEST 2

DIRECTIONS: Each question or incomplete statement is followed by several suggested answers or completions. Select the one that BEST answers the question or completes the statement. *PRINT THE LETTER OF THE CORRECT ANSWER IN THE SPACE AT THE RIGHT.*

1. Of the following, the factor affecting employee morale which the immediate supervisor is LEAST able to control is   1.____

    A. handling of grievances
    B. fair and impartial treatment of subordinates
    C. general presonnel rules and regulations
    D. accident prevention

2. When one of your workers does outstanding work, you should   2.____

    A. explain to your other employees that you expect the same kind of work of them
    B. praise him for his work so that he will know it is appreciated
    C. say nothing, because other employees may think you are showing favoritism
    D. show him how his work can be improved still more so that he will not sit back

3. For you as a supervisor to consider a suggestion from a probationary worker for improving a procedure would be   3.____

    A. *poor practice,* because this employee is too new on the job to know much about it
    B. *good practice,* because you may be able to share credit for the suggestion
    C. *poor practice,* because it may hurt the morale of the older employees
    D. *good practice,* because the suggestion may be worthwhile

4. If you find you must criticize the work of one of your workers, it would be BEST for you to   4.____

    A. mention the good points in his work as well as the faults
    B. caution him that he will receive an unsatisfactory performance report unless his work improves
    C. compare his work to that of the other agents you supervise
    D. apologize for making the criticism

5. As a senior employee which one of the following matters would it be BEST for you to talk over with your supervisor before you take final action?   5.____

    A. One of the workers you supervise continues to disregard your instructions repeatedly in spite of repeated warnings
    B. One of your workers tells you he wants to discuss a personal problem
    C. A probationary employee tells you he does not understand a procedure
    D. One of your workers tells you he disagrees with the way you rate his work

6. If one of your subordinates asks you a question about a department rule and you do not know the answer, you should tell him that   6.____

    A. he should try to get the information himself
    B. you do not have the answer, but you will get it for him as soon as you can
    C. he should ask you the question again a week from now
    D. he should put the question in writing

7. If, as a supervisor, you realize that you have been unfair in criticizing one of your subordinates, the BEST action for you to take is to

   A. say nothing, but overlook some error made by this employee in the future
   B. be frank and tell the employee that you are sorry for the mistake you made
   C. let the employee know in some indirect way without admitting your mistake, that you realize he was not at fault
   D. say nothing, but be more careful about criticizing subordinates in the future

8. Of the following, the MOST important reason for a supervisor to write an accident report as soon as possible after an accident has happened is to

   A. make sure that important facts about the accident are not forgotten
   B. avoid delay in getting compensation for the injured person
   C. get adequate medical treatment for the injured person
   D. keep department accident statistics up to date

9. In any matter which may require disciplinary action, the FIRST responsibility of the supervisor is to

   A. decide what penalty should be applied for the offense
   B. refer the matter to a higher authority for complete investigation
   C. place the interests of the department above those of the employee
   D. investigate the matter fully to get all the facts

10. Suppose you find it necessary to criticize one of the subordinates you supervise. You should

    A. send an official letter to his home
    B. speak to him about the matter privately
    C. speak to him at a staff meeting
    D. ask another worker who is friendly with him to talk to him about the matter

11. Some of your subordinates have been coming to you with complaints you feel are unimportant. For you to hear their stories out is

    A. *poor practice,* you should spend your time on more important matters
    B. *good practice,* this will increase your popularity with your subordinates
    C. *poor practice,* subordinates should learn to come to you only with major grievances
    D. *good practice,* it may prevent minor complaints from developing into major grievances

12. Suppose that NOT ONE of a group of employees has turned in an idea to the employees' suggestion system during the past year. The *most probable* reason for this situation is that the

    A. supervisor of these employees is not doing enough to encourage them to take part in this program
    B. employees in this group are not able to develop any good ideas
    C. money awards given for suggestions used are not high enough to make employees interested
    D. methods and procedures of operation do not need improvement

13. For you as a supervisor to give each of your subordinates *exactly* the same type of supervision is

    A. *advisable,* because doing this insures fair and impartial treatment of each individual
    B. *not advisable,* because each person is different and there is no one supervisory procedure for dealing with individuals that applies in every case
    C. *advisable,* because once a supervisor learns how to deal with a subordinate who brings a problem to him, he can handle another subordinate with this problem in the same way
    D. *not advisable,* because individuals like to think that they are receiving better treatment than others

14. In evaluating personnel, a supervisor should keep in mind that the MOST important objective of performance evaluations is to

    A. encourage employees to compete for higher performance ratings
    B. give recognition to employees who perform well
    C. help employees improve their work
    D. discipline employees who perform poorly

15. A subordinate tells you that he is having trouble concentrating on his work due to a personal problem at home. Of the following, it would be BEST for you to

    A. refer him to a community service agency
    B. listen quietly to the story because he may just need a sympathetic ear
    C. tell him that you cannot help him because the problem is not job-related
    D. ask him some questions about the nature of the problem and tell him how you would handle it

16. To do a good job of performance evaluation, it is BEST for a supervisor to

    A. measure the employee's performance against standard performance requirements
    B. compare the employee's performance to that of another employee doing similar work
    C. leave out any consideration of the employee's personal traits
    D. give greatest weight to instances of unusually good or unusually poor performance

17. It is particularly important that disciplinary actions be equitable as between individuals. This statement *implies* that

    A. punishment applied in disciplinary actions should be lenient
    B. proposed disciplinary actions should be reviewed by higher authority
    C. subordinates should have an opportunity to present their stories before penalties are applied
    D. penalties for violations of the rules should be standardized and consistently applied

18. Assume that an agency has an established procedure for handling employee grievances. An employee in this agency comes to his immediate supervisor with a grievance. The supervisor investigates the matter and makes a decision. However, the employee is not satisfied with the decision made by the supervisor.
    The BEST action for the supervisor to take is to

A. tell the employee he will review the matter further
B. remind the employee that he is the supervisor and the employee must act in accordance with his decision
C. explain to the employee how he can carry his complaint forward to the next step in the grievance procedure
D. tell the employee he will consult with his own superiors on the matter

19. Of the following, the CHIEF purpose of a probationary period for a new employee is to allow time for

    A. finding out whether the selection processes are satisfactory
    B. determining the fitness of the employee to continue in the job
    C. the employee to decide whether he wants a permanent appointment
    D. the employee to make adjustments in his home circumstances made necessary by the job

20. Of the following, the subject that would be MOST important to include in a "break-in" program for new employees is

    A. explanation of rules, regulations and policies of the agency
    B. Instruction in the agency's history and programs
    C. explanation of the importance of the new employees' own particular job
    D. explanation of the duties and responsibilities of the employee

21. Suppose a new employee under your supervision seems slow to learn and is making mistakes in performing his duties. Your FIRST action should be to

    A. pass this information on to the bureau director
    B. reprimand the worker so he will not repeat these mistakes
    C. find out whether this worker understands your instructions
    D. note these facts for future reference when writing up the monthly performance evaluation

22. In training new employees to do a certain job it would be LEAST desirable for you to

    A. demonstrate how the job is done, step by step
    B. encourage the workers to ask questions if they aren't clear about any point
    C. tell them about the various mistakes other agents have made in doing this job
    D. have the workers do the job, explaining to you what they are doing and why

23. One of the workers under your supervision is resentful when you ask her to remove her jangling bracelets before she starts her tour of duty.
    Of the following, the BEST explanation you can give her for the rule against wearing such jewelry while on duty is that

    A. the jewelry may create a safety hazard
    B. employees must give up certain personal liberties if they want to keep their jobs
    C. workers cannot perform their duties as efficiently if they wear distracting jewelry
    D. citizens may receive an unfavorable impression of the department

24. Of the following, the LEAST important reason for having a department handbook and a bureau standard operating procedure is to

    A. help in training new employees
    B. provide a source of reference for department and bureau rules and procedures
    C. prevent errors in work by providing clear guidelines
    D. make the supervisor's job easy

25. On inspecting your squad prior to their tour of duty, you note an employee improperly and unacceptably dressed.
    The FIRST action you should take is to

    A. call the employee aside and insist on immediate correction if possible
    B. notify the district commander right away
    C. have the employee submit a memorandum explaining the reason for the improper uniform
    D. permit the employee to proceed on duty but warn him not to let this happen again

KEY (CORRECT ANSWERS)

1.	C	11.	D
2.	B	12.	A
3.	D	13.	B
4.	A	14.	C
5.	A	15.	B
6.	B	16.	A
7.	B	17.	D
8.	A	18.	C
9.	D	19.	B
10.	B	20.	D

21. C
22. C
23. D
24. D
25. A

SUPERVISION STUDY GUIDE

Social science has developed information about groups and leadership in general and supervisor-employee relationships in particular. Since organizational effectiveness is closely linked to the ability of supervisors to direct the activities of employees, these findings are important to executives everywhere.

IS A SUPERVISOR A LEADER?

First-line supervisors are found in all large business and government organizations. They are the men at the base of an organizational hierarchy. Decisions made by the head of the organization reach them through a network of intermediate positions. They are frequently referred to as part of the management team, but their duties seldom seem to support this description.

A supervisor of clerks, tax collectors, meat inspectors, or securities analysts is not charged with budget preparation. He cannot hire or fire the employees in his own unit on his say-so. He does not administer programs which require great planning, coordinating, or decision making.

Then what is he? He is the man who is directly in charge of a group of employees doing productive work for a business or government agency. If the work requires the use of machines, the men he supervises operate them. If the work requires the writing of reports, the men he supervises write them. He is expected to maintain a productive flow of work without creating problems which higher levels of management must solve. But is he a leader?

To carry out a specific part of an agency's mission, management creates a unit, staffs it with a group of employees and designates a supervisor to take charge of them. Management directs what this unit shall do, from time to time changes directions, and often indicates what the group should not do. Management presumably creates status for the supervisor by giving him more pay, a title, and special priviledges.

Management asks a supervisor to get his workers to attain organizational goals, including the desired quantity and quality of production. Supposedly, he has authority to enable him to achieve this objective. Management at least assumes that by establishing the status of the supervisor's position it has created sufficient authority to enable him to achieve these goals -- not his goals, nor necessarily the group's, but management's goals.

In addition, supervision includes writing reports, keeping records of membership in a higher-level administrative group, industrial engineering, safety engineering, editorial duties, housekeeping duties, etc. The supervisor as a member of an organizational network, must be responsible to the changing demands of the management above him. At the same time, he must be responsive to the demands of the work group of which he is a member. He is placed in the difficult position of communicating and implementing new decisions, changed programs and revised production quotas for his work group, although he may have had little part in developing them.

It follows, then, that supervision has a special characteristic: achievement of goals, previously set by management, through the efforts of others. It is in this feature of the supervisor's job that we find the role of a leader in the sense of the following definition: *A leader is that person who most effectively influences group activities toward goal setting and goal achievements.*

This definition is broad. It covers both leaders in groups that come together voluntarily and in those brought together through a work assignment in a factory, store, or government agency. In the natural group, the authority necessary to attain goals is determined by the group membership and is granted by them. In the working group, it is apparent that the establishment of a supervisory position creates a predisposition on the part of employees to accept the authority of the occupant of that position. We cannot, however, assume that mere occupancy confers authority sufficient to assure the accomplishment of an organization's goals.

Supervision is different, then, from leadership. The supervisor is expected to fulfill the role of leader but without obtaining a grant of authority from the group he supervises. The supervisor is expected to influence the group in the achieving of goals but is often handicapped by having little influence on the organizational process by which goals are set. The supervisor, because he works in an organizational setting, has the burdens of additional organizational duties and restrictions and requirements arising out of the fact that his position is subordinate to a hierarchy of higher-level supervisors. These differences between leadership and supervision are reflected in our definition: *Supervision is basically a leadership role, in a formal organization, which has as its objective the effective influencing of other employees.*

Even though these differences between supervision and leadership exist, a significant finding of experimenters in this field is that supervisors must be leaders to be successful.

The problem is: How can a supervisor exercise leadership in an organizational setting? We might say that the supervisor is expected to be a natural leader in a situation which does not come about naturally. His situation becomes really difficult in an organization which is more eager to make its supervisors into followers rather than leaders.

LEADERSHIP: NATURAL AND ORGANIZATIONAL

Leadership, in its usual sense of *natural* leadership, and supervision are not the same. In some cases, leadership embraces broader powers and functions than supervision; in other cases, supervision embraces more than leadership. This is true both because of the organization and technical aspects of the supervisor's job and because of the relatively freer setting and inherent authority of the natural leader.

The natural leader usually has much more authority and influence than the supervisor. Group members not only follow his command but prefer it that way. The employee, however, can appeal the supervisor's commands to his union or to the supervisor's superior or to the personnel office. These intercessors represent restrictions on the supervisor's power to lead.

The natural leader can gain greater membership involvement in the group's objectives, and he can change the objectives of the group. The supervisor can attempt to gain employee support only for management's objectives; he cannot set other objectives. In these instances leadership is broader than supervision.

The natural leader must depend upon whatever skills are available when seeking to attain objectives. The supervisor is trained in the administrative skills necessary to achieve management's goals. If he does not possess the requisite skills, however, he can call upon management's technicians.

A natural leader can maintain his leadership, in certain groups, merely by satisfying members' need for group affilation. The supervisor must maintain his leadership by directing and organizing his group to achieve specific organizational goals set for him and his group by management. He must have a technical competence and a kind of coordinating ability which is not needed by many natural leaders.

A natural leader is responsible only to his group which grants him authority. The supervisor is responsible to management, which employs him, and, also, to the work group of which he is a member. The supervisor has the exceedingly difficult job of reconciling the demands of two groups frequently in conflict. He is often placed in the untenable position of trying to play two antagonisic roles. In the above instances, supervision is broader than leadership.

ORGANIZATIONAL INFLUENCES ON LEADERSHIP

The supervisor is both a product and a prisoner of the organization wherein we find him. The organization which creates the supervisor's position also obstructs, restricts, and channelizes the exercise of his duties. These influences extend beyond prescribed functional relationships to specific supervisory behavior. For example, even in a face-to-face situation involving one of his subordinates, the supervisor's actions are controlled to a great extent by his organization. His behavior must conform to the organization policy on human relations, rules which dictate personnel procedures, specific prohibitions governing conduct, the attitudes of his own superior, etc. He is not a free agent operating within the limits of his work group. His freedom of action is much more circumscribed than is generally admitted. The organizational influences which limit his leadership actions can be classified as structure, prescriptions, and proscriptions.

The organizational structure places each supervisor's position in context with other designated positions. It determines the relationships between his position and specific positions which impinge on his. The structure of the organization designates a certain position to which he looks for orders and information about his work. It gives a particular status to his position within a pattern of statuses from which he perceives that (1) certain positions are on a par, organizationally, with his, (2) other positions are subordinate, and (3) still others are superior. The organizational structure determines those positions to which he should look for advice and assistance, and those positions to which he should give advice and assistance.

For instance, the organizational structure has predetermined that the supervisor of a clerical processing unit shall report to a supervisory position in a higher echelon. He shall have certain relationships with the supervisors of the work units which transmit work to and receive work from his unit. He shall discuss changes and clarification of procedures with certain staff units, such as organization and methods, cost accounting, and personnel. He shall consult supervisors of units which provide or receive special work assignments.

The organizational structure, however, establishes patterns other than those of the relationships of positions. These are the patterns of responsibility, authority, and expectations.

The supervisor is responsible for certain activities or results; he is presumably invested with the authority to achieve these. His set of authority and responsibility is interwoven with other sets to the end that all goals and functions of the organization are parceled out in small, manageable lots. This, of course, establishes a series of expectations: a single supervisor can perform his particular set of duties only upon the assumption that preceding or contiguous sets of duties have been, or are being, carried out. At the same time, he is aware of the expectations of others that he will fulfill his functional role.

The structure of an organization establishes relationships between specified positions and specific expectations for these positions. The fact that these relationships and expectations are established is one thing; whether or not they are met is another.

PRESCRIPTIONS AND PROSCRIPTIONS

But let us return to the organizational influences which act to restrict the supervisor's exercise of leadership. These are the prescriptions and proscriptions generally in effect in all organizations, and those peculiar to a single organization. In brief these are the *thous shalt's* and the *thou shalt not's*.

Organizations not only prescribe certain duties for individual supervisory positions, they also prescribe specific methods and means of carrying out these duties and maintaining management-employee relations. These include rules, regulations, policy, and tradition. It does no good for the supervisor to say, *This seems to be the best way to handle such-and such,* if the organization has established a routine for dealing with problems. For good or bad, there are rules that state that firings shall be executed in such a manner, accompanied by a certain notification; that training shall be conducted, and in this manner. Proscriptions are merely negative prescriptions: you may not discriminate against any employee because of politics or race; you shall not suspend any employee without following certain procedures and obtaining certain approvals.

Most of these prohibitions and rules apply to the area of interpersonal relations, precisely the area which is now arousing most interest on the part of administrators and managers. We have become concerned about the contrast between formally prescribed relationships and interpersonal relationships, and this brings us to the often discussed informal organization.

FORMAL AND INFORMAL ORGANIZATIONS

As we well know, the functions and activities of any organization are broken down into individual units of work called positions. Administrators must establish a pattern which will link these positions to each other and relate them to a system of authority and responsibility. Man-to-man are spelled out as plainly as possible for all to understand. Managers, then, build an official structure which we call the formal organization.

In these same organizations employees react individually and in groups to institutionally determined roles. John, a worker, rides in the same car pool as Joe, a foreman. An unplanned communication develops. Harry, a machinist, knows more about highspeed machining than his foreman or anyone else in his shop. An unofficial tool boss comes into being. Mary, who fought with Jane is promoted over her. Jane now ignores Mary's directions. A planned relationship fails to develop. The employees have built a structure which we call the informal organization.

Formal organization is a system of management-prescribed relations between positions in an organization.

Informal organization is a network of unofficial relations between people in an organization.

These definitions might lead us to the absurd conclusion that positions carry out formal activities and that employees spend their time in unofficial activities. We must recognize that organizational activities are in all cases carried out by people. The formal structure provides a needed framework within which interpersonal relations occur. What we call informal organization is the complex of normal, natural relations among employees. These personal relationships may be negative or positive. That is, they may impede or aid the achievement of organizational, goals. For example, friendship between two supervisors greatly increases the probability of good cooperation and coordination between their sections. On the other hand, *buck passing* nullifies the formal structure by failure to meet a prescribed and expected responsibility.

It is improbable that an ideal organization exists where all activities are acarried out in strict conformity to a formally prescribed pattern of functional roles. Informal organization arises because of the incompleteness and ambiguities in the network of formally prescribed relationships, or in response to the needs or inadequacies of supervisors or managers who hold prescribed functional roles in an organization. Many of these relationships are not prescribed by the organizational pattern; many cannot be prescribed; many should not be prescribed.

Management faces the problem of keeping the informal organization in harmony with the mission of the agency. One way to do this is to make sure that all employees have a clear understanding of and are sympathetic with that mission. The issuance of organizational charts, procedural manuals, and functional descriptions of the work to be done by divisions and sections helps communicate management's plans and goals. Issuances alone, of course, cannot do the whole job. They should be accompanied by oral discussion and explanation. Management must ensure that there is mutual understanding and acceptance of charts and procedures. More important is that management acquaint itself with the attitudes, activities, and peculiar brands of logic which govern the informal organization. Only through this type of knowledge can they and supervisors keep informal goals consistent with the agency mission.

SUPERVISION, STATUS, AND FUNCTIONAL ROLE

A well-established supervisor is respected by the employees who work with him. They defer to his wishes. It is clear that a superior-subordinate relationship has been established. That is, status of the supervisor has been established in relation to other employees of the same work group. This same supervisor gains the respect of employees when he behaves in a certain manner. He will be expected generally, to follow the customs of the group in such matters as dress, recreation, and manner of speaking. The group has a set of expectations as to his behavior. His position is a functional role which carries with it a collection of rights and obligations.

The position of supervisor usually has a status distinct from the individual who occupies it: it is much like a position description which exists whether or not there is an incumbent. The status of a supervisory position is valued higher than that of an employee position both because of the functional role of leadership which is assigned to it and because of the status symbols of titles, rights, and privileges which go with it.

Social ranking, or status, is not simple because it involves both the position and the man. An individual may be ranked higher than others because of his education, social background, perceived leadership ability, or conformity to group customs and ideals. If such a man is ranked higher by the members of a work group than their supervisor, the supervisor's effectiveness may be seriously undermined.

If the organization does not build and reinforce a supervisor's status, his position can be undermined in a different way. This will happen when managers go around rather than through the supervisor or designate him as a straw boss, acting boss, or otherwise not a real boss.

Let us clarify this last point. A role, and corresponding status, establishes a set of expectations. Employees expect their supervisor to do certain things and to act in certain ways. They are prepared to respond to that expected behavior. When the supervisor's behavior does not conform to their expectations, they are surprised, confused, and ill-at-ease. It becomes necessary for them to resolve their confusion, if they can. They might do this by turning to one of their own members for leadership. If the confusion continues, or their attempted solutions are not satisfactory, they will probably become a poorly motivated, non-cohesive group which cannot function very well.

COMMUNICATION AND THE SUPERVISOR

In a recent survey railroad workers reported that they rarely look to their supervisors for information about the company. This is startling, at least to us, because we ordinarily think of the supervisor as the link between management and worker. We expect the supervisor to be the prime source of information about the company. Actually, the railroad workers listed the supervisor next to last in the order of their sources of information. Most suprising of all, the supervisors, themselves, stated that rumor and unofficial contacts were their principal sources of information. Here we see one of the reasons why supervisors may not be as effective as management desires.

The supervisor is not only being bypassed by his work group, he is being ignored, and his position weakened, by the very organization which is holding him responsible for the activities of his workers. If he is management's representative to the employee, then management has an obligation to keep him informed of its activities. This is necessary if he is to carry out his functions efficiently and maintain his leadership in the work group. The supervisor is expected to be a source of information; when he is not, his status is not clear, and employees are dissatisfied because he has not lived up to expectations.

By providing information to the supervisor to pass along to employees, we can strengthen his position as leader of the group, and increase satisfaction and cohesion within the group. Because he has more information than the other members, receives information sooner, and passes it along at the proper times, members turn to him as a source and also provide him with information in the hope of receiving some in return. From this we can see an increase in group cohesiveness because:

- Employees are bound closer to their supervisor because he is *in the know*

- there is less need to go outside the group for answers

- employees will more quickly turn to the supervisor for enlightenment.

The fact that he has the answers will also enhance the supervisor's standing in the eyes of his men. This increased sta,tus will serve to bolster his authority and control of the group and will probably result in improved morale and productivity.

The foregoing, of course, does not mean that all management information should be given out. There are obviously certain policy determinations and discussions which need not or cannot be transmitted to all supervisors. However, the supervisor must be kept as fully informed as possible so that he can answer questions when asked and can allay needless fears and anxieties. Further, the supervisor has the responsibility of encouraging employee questions and submissions of information. He must be able to present information to employees so that it is clearly understood and accepted. His attitude and manner should make it clear that he believes in what he is saying, that the information is necessary or desirable to the group, and that he is prepared to act on the basis of the information.

SUPERVISION AND JOB PERFORMANCE

The productivity of work groups is a product; employees' efforts are multiplied by the supervision they receive. Many investigators have analyzed this relationship and have discovered elements of supervision which differentiate high and low production groups. These researchers have identified certain types of supervisory practices which they classify as *employee-centered* and other types which they classify as *production centered*.

The difference between these two kinds of supervision lies not in specific practices but in the approach or orientation to supervision. The employee-centered supervisor directs most of his efforts toward increasing employee motivation. He is concerned more with realizing the potential energy of persons than with administrative and technological methods of increasing efficiency and productivity. He is the man who finds ways of causing employees to want to work harder with the same tools. These supervisors emphasize the personal relations between their employees and themselves.

Now, obviously, these pictures are overdrawn. No one supervisor has all the virtues of the ideal type of employee-centered supervisor. And, fortunately, no one supervisor has all the bad traits found in many production-centered supervisors. We should remember that the various practices that researchers have found which distinguish these two kinds of supervision represent the many practices and methods of supervisors of all gradations between these extremes. We should be careful, too, of the implications of the labels attached to the two types. For instance, being production-centered is not necessarily bad, since the principal responsibility of any supervisor is maintaining the production level that is expected of his work group. Being employee-centered may not necessarily be good, if the only result is a happy, chuckling crew of loafers. To return to the researchers's findings, employee-centered supervisors:

- Recommend promotions, transfers, pay increases
- Inform men about what is happening in the company
- Keep men posted on how well they are doing
- Hear complaints and grievances sympathetically
- Speak up for subordinates

Production-centered supervisors, on the other hand, don't do those things. They check on employees more frequently, give more detailed and frequent instructions, don't give reasons for changes, and are more punitive when mistakes are made. Employee-centered supervisors were reported to contribute to high morale and high production, whereas production-centered supervision was associated with lower morale and less production.

More recent findings, however, show that the relationship between supervision and productivity is not this simple. Investigators now report that high production is more frequently associated with supervisory practices which combine employee-centered behavior with concern for production. (This concern is not the same, however, as anxiety about production, which is the hallmark of our production-centered supervisor.) Let us examine these apparently contradictory findings and the premises from which they are derived.

SUPERVISION AND MORALE

Why do supervisory activities cause high or low production? As the name implies, the activities of the employee-centered supervisor tend to relate him more closely and satisfactorily to his workers. The production-centered supervisor's practices tend to separate him from his group and to foster antagonism. An analysis of this difference may answer our question.

Earlier, we pointed out that the supervisor is a type of leader and that leadership is intimately related to the group in which it occurs. We discover, now, that an employee-centered supervisor's primary activities are concerned with both his leadership and his group membership. Such a supervisor is a member of a group and occupies a leadership role in that group.

These facts are sometimes obscured when we speak of the supervisor as management's representative, or as the organizational link between management and the employee, or as the end of the chain of command. If we really want to understand what it is we expect of the supervisor, we must remember that he is the designated leader of a group of employees to whom he is bound by interaction and interdependence.

Most of his actions are aimed, consciously or unconsciously, at strengthening membership ties in the group. This includes both making members more conscious that he is a member of their grout) and causing members to identify themselves more closely with the group. These ends are accomplished by:

> making the group more attractive to the worker: they
>> find satisfaction of their needs for recognition,
>> friendship, enjoyable work, etc.;
>
> maintaining open communication: employees can express
>> their views and obtain information about the organization.
>
> giving assistance: members can seek advice on
>> personal problems as well as their work; and
>
> acting as a buffer between the group and management:
>> he speaks up for his men and explains the reasons
>> for management's decisions.

Such actions both strengthen group cohesiveness and solidarity and affirm the supervisor's leadership position in the group.

DEFINING MORALE

This brings us back to a point mentioned earlier. We had said that employee-centered supervisors contribute to high morale as well as to high production. But how can we explain units which have low morale and high productivity, or vice versa? Usually production and morale are considered separately, partly because they are measured against different criteria and partly because, in some instances, they seem to be independent of each other.

Some of this difficulty may stem from confusion over definitions of morale. Morale has been defined as, or measured by, absences from work, satisfaction with job or company, dissension among members of work groups, productivity, apathy or lack of interest, readiness to help others, and a general aura of happiness as rated by observers. Some of these criteria of morale are not subject to the influence of the supervisor, and some of them are not clearly related to productivity. Definitions like these invite findings of low morale coupled with high production.

Both productivity and morale can be influenced by environmental factors not under the control of group members or supervisors. Such things as plant layout, organizational structure and goals, lighting, ventilation, communications, and management planning may have an adverse or desirable effect.

We might resolve the dilemma by defining morale on the basis of our understanding of the supervisor as leader of a group; morale is the degree of satisfaction of group members with their leadership. In this light, the supervisor's employee-centered activities bear a clear relation to morale. His efforts to increase employee identification with the group and to strengthen his leadership lead to greater satisfaction with that leadership. By increasing group cohesiveness and by demonstrating that his influence and power can aid the group, he is able to enhance his leadership status and afford satisfaction to the group.

SUPERVISION, PRODUCTION, AND MORALE

> There are factors within the organization itself which determine whether increased production is possible:

Are production goals expressed in terms understandable to employees and are they realistic?

Do supervisors responsible for production respect the agency mission and production goals?

If employees do not know how to do the job well, does management provide a trainer--often the supervisor--who can teach efficient work methods?

There are other factors within the work group which determine whether increased production will be attained:

Is leadership present which can bring about the desired level of production?

Are production goals accepted by employees as reasonable and attainable?

If group effort is involved, are members able to coordinate their efforts?

Research findings confirm the view that an employee-centered supervisor can achieve higher morale than a production-centered supervisor. Managers may well ask what is the relationship between this and production?

Supervision is production-oriented to the extent that it focuses attention on achieving organizational goals, and plans and devises methods for attaining them; it is employee-centered to the extent that it focuses attention on employee attitudes toward those goals, and plans and works toward maintenance of employee satisfaction.

High productivity and low morale result when a supervisor plans and organizes work efficiently but cannot achieve high membership satisfaction. Low production and high morale result when a supervisor, though keeping members satisfied with his leadership, either has not gained acceptance of organizational goals or does not have the technical competence to achieve them.

The relationship between supervision, morale, and productivity is an interdependent one, with the supervisor playing an integrating role due to his ability to influence productivity and morale independently of each other.

A supervisor who can plan his work well has good technical knowledge, and who can install better production methods can raise production without necessarily increasing group satisfaction. On the other hand, a supervisor who can motivate his employees and keep them satisfied with his leadership can gain high production in spite of technical difficulties and environmental obstacles.

CLIMATE AND SUPERVISION

Climate, the intangible environment of an organization made up of attitudes, beliefs, and traditions, plays a large part in morale, productivity, and supervision. Usually when we speak of climate and its relationship to morale and productivity, we talk about the merits of *democratic* versus *authoritarian* climate. Employees seem to produce more and have higher morale in a democratic climate, whereas in an authoritarian climate, the reverse seems to be true or so the researchers tell us. We would do well to determine what these terms mean to supervision.

Perhaps most of our difficulty in understanding and applying these concepts comes from our emotional reactions to the words themselves. For example, authoritarian climate is usually painted as the very blackest kind of dictatorship. This not surprising, because we are usually expected to believe that it is invariably bad. Conversely, democratic climate is drawn to make the driven snow look impure by comparison.

Now these descriptions are most probably true when we talk about our political processes, or town meetings, or freedom of speech. However the same labels have been used by social scientists in other contexts and have also been applied to government and business organizations, without, it seems, any recognition that the meanings and their social values may have changed somewhat .

For example, these labels were used in experiments conducted in an informal class room setting using 11 year old boys as subjects. The descriptive labels applied to the climate of the setting as well as the type of leadership practiced. When these labels were transferred to a management setting it seems that many presumed that they principally meant the king of leadership rather than climate. We can see that there is a great difference between the experimental and management settings and that leadership practices for one might be inappropriate for the other.

It is doubtful that formal work organizations can be anything but authoritarian, in that goals are set by management and a hierarchy exists through which decisions and orders from the top are transmitted downward. Organizations are authoritarian by structure and need: direction and control are placed in the hands of a few in order to gain fast and efficient decision making. Now this does not mean to describe a dictatorship. It is merely the recognition of the fact that direction of organizational affairs comes from above. It should be noted that leadership in some natural groups is, in this sense, authoritarian.

Granting that formal organizations have this kind of authoritarian leadership, can there be a democratic climate? Certainly there can be, but we would want to define and delimit this term. A more realistic meaning of democratic climate in organizations is, the use of permissive and participatory methods in management-employee relations. That is, a mutual exchange of information and explanation with the granting of individual freedom within certain restricted and defined limits. However, it is not our purpose to debate the merits of authoritarianism versus democracy. We recognize that within the small work group there is a need for freedom from constraint and an increase in participation in order to achieve organizational goals within the framework of the organizational environment.

Another aspect of climate is best expressed by this familiar, and true saying: actions speak louder than words. Of particular concern to us is this effect of management climate on the behavior of supervisors, particularly in employee-centered activities.

There have been reports of disappointment with efforts to make supervisors more employee-centered. Managers state that, since research has shown ways of improving human relations, supervisors should begin to practice these methods. Usually a training course in human relations is established, and supervisors are given this training. Managers then sit back and wait for the expected improvements, only to find that there are none.

If we wish to produce changes in the supervisor's behavior, the climate must be made appropriate and rewarding to the changed behavior. This means that top-level attitudes and behavior cannot deny or contradict the change we are attempting to effect. Basic changes in organizational behavior cannot be made with any permanence, unless we provide an environment that is receptive to the changes and rewards those persons who do change.

IMPROVING SUPERVISION

Anyone who has read this far might expect to find *A Dozen Rules for Dealing With Employees* or *29 Steps to Supervisory Success*. We will not provide such a list.

Simple rules suffer from their simplicity. They ignore the complexities of human behavior. Reliance upon rules may cause supervisors to concentrate on superficial aspects of their relations with employees. It may preclude genuine understanding.

The supervisor who relies on a list of rules tends to think of people in mechanistic terms. In a certain situation, he uses *Rule No. 3*. Employees are not treated as thinking and feeling persons, but rather as figures in a formula: Rule 3 applied to employee X = Production.

Employees usually recognize mechanical manipulation and become dissatisfied and resentful. They lose faith in, and respect for, their supervisor, and this may be reflected in lower morale and productivity.

We do not mean that supervisors must become social science experts if they wish to improve. Reports of current research indicate that there are two major parts of their job which can be strengthened through self-improvement: (1) Work planning, including technical skills. (2) Motivation of employees.

The most effective supervisors combine excellence in the administrative and technical aspects of their work with friendly and considerate personal relations with their employees.

CRITICAL PERSONAL RELATIONS

Later in this chaper we shall talk about administrative aspects of supervision, but first let us comment on *friendly and considerate personal relations*. We have discussed this subject throughout the preceding chapters, but we want to review some of the critical supervisory influences on personal relations.

Closeness of Supervision

The closeness of supervision has an important effect on productivity and morale. Mann and Dent found that supervisors of low-producing units supervise very closely, while high-producing supervisors exercise only general supervision. It was found that the low-producing supervisors:

- o check on employees more frequently
- o give more detailed and frequent instructions
- o limit employee's freedom to do job in own way.

Workers who felt less closely supervised reported that they were better satisfied with their jobs and the company. We should note that the manner or attitude of the supervisor has an important bearing on whether employees perceive supervision as being close or general.

These findings are another way of saying that supervision does not mean standing over the employee and telling him what to do and when and how to do it. The more effective supervisor tells his employees what is required, giving general instructions.

COMMUNICATION

Supervisors of high-production units consider communication as one of the most important aspects of their job. Effective communication is used by these supervisors to achieve better interpersonal relations and improved employee motivation. Low-production supervisors do not rate communication as highly important.

High-producing supervisors find that an important aid to more effective communication is listening. They are ready to listen to both personal problems or interests and questions about the work. This does not mean that they are *nosey* or meddle in their employees' personal lives, but rather that they show a willingness to listen, and do listen, if their employees wish to discuss problems.

These supervisors inform employees about forthcoming changes in work; they discuss agency policy with employees; and they make sure that each employee knows how well he is doing. What these supervisors do is use two-way communication effectively. Unless the supervisor freely imparts information, he will not receive information in return.

Attitudes and perception are frequently affected by communication or the lack of it. Research surveys reveal that many supervisors are not aware of their employees' attitudes, nor do they know what personal reactions their supervision arouses. Through frank discussions with employees, they have been surprised to discover employee beliefs about which they were ignorant. Discussion sometimes reveals that the supervisor and his employees have totally different impressions about the same event. The supervisor should be constantly on the alert for misconceptions about his words and deeds. He must remember that, although his actions are perfectly clear to himself, they may be, and frequently are, viewed differently by employees.

Failure to communicate information results in misconceptions and false assumptions. What you say and how you say it will strongly affect your employees' attitudes and perceptions. By giving them available information you can prevent misconceptions; by discussion, you may be able to change attitudes; by questioning; you can discover what the perceptions and assumptions really are. And it need hardly be added that actions should conform very closely to words.

If we were to attempt to reduce the above discussion on communication to rules, we would have a long list which would be based on one cardinal principle: Don't make assumptions!

- o Don't assume that your employees know; tell them.
- o Don't assume that you know how they feel; find out.
- o Don't assume that they understand; clarify.

20 SUPERVISORY HINTS

1. Avoid inconsistency.
2. Always give employees a chance to explain their actions before taking disciplinary action. Don't allow too much time for a "cooling off" period before disciplining an employee.
3. Be specific in your criticisms.
4. Delegate responsibility wisely.
5. Do not argue or lose your temper, and avoid being impatient.
6. Promote mutual respect and be fair, impartial and open-minded.
7. Keep in mind that asking for employees' advice and input can be helpful in decision making.
8. If you make promises, keep them.
9. Always keep the feelings, abilities, dignity and motives of your staff in mind.
10. Remain loyal to your employees' interests.
11. Never criticize employees in front of others, or treat employees like children.
12. Admit mistakes. Don't place blame on your employees, or make excuses.
13. Be reasonable in your expectations, give complete instructions, and establish well-planned goals.
14. Be knowledgeable about office details and procedures, but avoid becoming bogged down in details.
15. Avoid supervising too closely or too loosely. Employees should also view you as an approachable supervisor.
16. Remember that employees' personal problems may affect job performance, but become involved only when appropriate.
17. Work to develop workers, and to instill a feeling of cooperation while working toward mutual goals.
18. Do not overpraise or underpraise, be properly appreciative.
19. Never ask an employee to discipline someone for you.
20. A complaint, even if unjustified, should be taken seriously.

SCHOOL BUS FLEET OPERATIONS

Contents

Chapter — Page

1 Planning for Safety — 1
Choosing pickup and delivery points. Planning special activity trips. Supervisor responsibilities.

2 Establishing the Safety Program — 4
Developing safety guidelines.

3 Providing Local Direction — 6
The role of the local school board. The role of the school superintendent.

4 Supervising the School Bus Fleet — 9
Qualifications of a supervisor. Supervising drivers. Purchasing and maintaining vehicles. The supervisor's role in public relations. Keeping up-to-date.

5 Selecting the School Bus Driver — 15
Who should screen applicants? What type of person makes a safe school bus driver?

6 Training the School Bus Driver — 20
What to include and where to find it. Types of training: initial, refresher, and remedial. Psycho-physical testing.

7 Motivating the School Bus Driver — 26
Set a good example. Show real interest. Use competition effectively. Recognize good work.

SCHOOL BUS FLEET OPERATIONS

CHAPTER 1

Planning for Safety

More than a quarter million school buses operate over three billion miles annually. They carry more than 21 million elementary and secondary pupils each day. School transportation, therefore, is a giant in the U.S. transportation industry.

This giant is made up of many divisions. Most school transportation is operated by the school district or by a contractor-operated school bus service.

Getting and keeping uniform, adequate, standards of vehicle and driver operation pose a tremendous challenge to the public and private sectors of the industry. The needs of school systems vary because the needs of the population centers they serve vary.

Although responsibility for guidance and results lies at the state level, supervision of school bus service involves the county, city, and local school districts. As a result, problems can arise from incomplete communication or lack of direction.

In addition to the normal problems of transportation, there are parental and political influences to consider. Whether school transportation is a function of the school system or is provided through contract service, basic standards must be met to protect pupil passengers.

Conflicting traffic laws and differences in local operating policies and practices confuse the motoring public. They can impede the normal traffic flow and imperil the lives they were designed to protect. Uniform national standards are necessary to guide local regulation of school bus operating conditions and schedules in the traffic stream.

Choosing Pickup and Delivery Points

In rural districts, pickup locations are scattered and frequently far apart. Routes and pickup points should be planned for the least interference with the normal traffic flow. Traffic delays caused by frequent bus stops, or by the need to allow pupils to cross the highway, should be kept to a minimum. When the school transportation system repeatedly interrupts traffic, other drivers grow impatient and may be tempted to violate local conditions of control.

Political pressure for special privileges or unusual, frequent, personalized bus stops should not be permitted by school authorities or local traffic officials.

In suburban districts, the school system should follow the pattern of transit operations, creating minimum interference with traffic on arterial or collector streets. Corner pickups at traffic-controlled locations should be encouraged. When possible, the young passengers should cross streets at locations where crossing protection is a community responsibility instead of the bus driver's. To reduce interference with the normal traffic flow, lightly traveled streets should be used for pupil pickup points in suburban operations.

Uniform operating policies also must be established to regulate transportation by special activity buses. Area discharge points away from the heavy traffic of arterial and collector streets should be designated. Parents should understand that they must pick up their children at these points or permit them to make their own arrangements to get home.

Planning Special Activity Trips

When school buses are scheduled for special events and activities outside the community, "protection routes" should be mapped out and drivers should be required to follow them. Supervisors should plan routes with these factors in mind: traffic volume on the available alternate routes; dangerous intersections; railroad crossings; sharp curves; steep hills; one-lane bridges; and narrow pavements.

Pupils on special activity trips should be supervised and controlled by a person *other* than the bus driver. Principals should assign one or more staff members to each bus who have demonstrated their supervision and control of pupils under special circumstances. The bus driver should be free to concentrate on driving duties.

Supervisor Responsibilities

Supervisor responsibilities are varied. Among them is having a written set of specifications for new vehicle purchases. The person responsible for the specifications should consider the number of pupils to be transported, the general climatic conditions in the area, and the type of terrain in which the vehicle will be used.

Special training is needed to be an effective supervisor. Also, continuous in-service training is necessary to update knowledge and maintain competence.

Knowing the operating policies and procedures is essential. Each employee is entitled to a detailed description of his or her duties, and should know who can provide special instruction and assistance when the unexpected or unusual occurs.

Vehicle accidents do not "just happen." They are usually the cumulative result of poor environmental conditions and faulty driving habits or attitudes. Although most adverse environmental factors cannot be controlled, they can be compensated for by teaching drivers the principles of defensive driving. It also would help to recognize bad driving habits as they develop, and correct them before they contribute to accidents.

The experience of bus, truck, and passenger fleet operators demonstrates that drivers need help and encouragement to be safe. Management must formulate and enforce specific policies to regulate vehicle operation and maintenance. (See Chapter 3, "Providing Local Direction.") Drivers need constant in-service training in safe driving techniques and attitudes. Drivers are motivated to perform safely when they feel that their safety records are important and that good safety performance is recognized and appreciated.

CHAPTER 2

Establishing the Safety Program

Safety programs must begin at the top. If top management is not genuinely interested in the safety program or is unwilling to provide supervisory time and funds for implementation, the program will fail. In many cases, it will not even get started.

Increasing attention has been focused on highway safety by the creation of the National Highway Traffic Safety Administration within the federal government, and by establishment of guidelines covering the vehicle, the driver, and the highway.

To assure their constituents that these guidelines are met, state governments must establish standards and regulations and provide leadership and direction in training.

The role of most state Departments of Education is to help schools provide education for safe and efficient living in our society. An extension of this role lies in the area of pupil transportation. State Departments of Education must take the lead in establishing criteria for driver selection and training, and promulgate rules and regulations governing the transportation of pupils. States must provide guidelines for obtaining funds for both transportation and instruction.

Developing Safety Guidelines

Leadership must provide comprehensive safety programs for school transportation. Minimum standards must be established for safety and efficiency.

1. Standards must be established for buses and equipment. In many instances they should exceed the established national minimums.
2. Maintenance standards must be set and enforced by rigid, periodic vehicle inspections, made by competent personnel, to guarantee that vehicles are maintained in safe operating condition, consistent with standards for new vehicles. Superficial annual inspection by un-

trained personnel cannot meet this need.
3. Driver qualifications must be established, and mental and physical standards and strict licensing procedures must be set and adhered to, for the protection of the pupils who ride the buses.
4. Mandatory driver training schools or workshops should be established.
5. Basic rules and regulations governing transportation of pupils should be established. They should state the extent of transportation services provided, who has authority at various levels of responsibility, and expected safe pupil behavior.

These minimum requirements should apply to all public and private school transportation in the state. Personnel and funds must be available to implement these programs and provide for supervision and inspection.

Leadership at the state level should maintain liaison with the departments of public instruction, public safety, motor vehicles, and state highways. It also should provide for adequate training facilities, seminars, and specialized courses to be conducted for individuals at all levels of responsibility.

CHAPTER 3

Providing Local Direction

The top officials of the school administration must want a safe transportation system in order to achieve it. They must be thoroughly familiar with the mechanics of good fleet safety programs and must apply proven principles of driver selection, training, and supervision.

Driver interest is a direct reflection of the degree of interest the administration shows. For this reason, members of the school board, the school superintendent, and other school officials must demonstrate their sincere interest in the safety program. They must convince newly hired drivers that they demand safe, efficient operation at all times. They should personally present safe driving awards to deserving drivers to let them know that everyone in the school district appreciates their professional achievement.

The Role of the Local School Board

Local school board officials must decide that they want safe, dependable pupil transportation, and channel that determination through the school administration and the driver safety supervisor to the school bus drivers. They must show their interest by participating in such safety program activities as driver award dinners and meetings.

Because local conditions and situations vary, school boards need to establish local policies that are within the framework of policies established at the state level. Definite policies will elevate the system's safety and efficiency and enlist the understanding and cooperation of other school personnel and the public. Policy statements should define areas and the extent of responsibility. They should specify the following:

1. The supervisor's qualifications, responsibilities, and authority, which includes attendance at safety seminars, training courses, and national, regional, and state safety meetings that are important for the fleet safety supervisor's development and efficiency;
2. The extent of the supervisor's responsibility for liaison with other administrators, the public, the schools, the Department of Public

Safety, and the news media;
3. Minimum requirements for driver selection and training;
4. The extent of the driver's responsibility and authority for the safety and conduct of pupils using school bus transportation (e.g., research and experience indicate that school board policy should prohibit pupils from standing in any part of the bus while it is moving);
5. The extent of service, including who is entitled to transportation, and conditions under which it will be provided;
6. Provisions for extracurricular transportation and its relation to the regular transportation program policy. (These should provide for minimum interference with the normal traffic flow on arterial or collector highways and streets and for preplanning of routes by the supervisor, so that hazardous routes and areas are avoided.)
7. Equipment replacement schedule (or basis), defining standards and stating who is responsible for writing specifications for the purchase of new buses;
8. Standards for bus maintenance and the facilities needed to accomplish a maintenance program;
9. Budget allocated to cover the services that are demanded.

The Role of the School Superintendent

The school superintendent should:
1. Recommend transportation needs to the school board and provide a factual basis for establishing transportation policies.
2. Show interest in a good accident control program, and expect continuing interest from all employees; the superintendent should attend some of the driver safety meetings and participate in safe driver award presentations.
3. Outline authority and responsibilities of all participants in the transportation system and require strict conformance with policies.
4. Provide specific guidelines for driver recruitment, training, and supervision, and for maintenance control.
5. Involve schools and parents in the transportation safety program by requiring schools to teach pupils how to ride safely and by including transportation discussion in P.T.A. meetings. (Parents can play a vital role in the safety program. They can learn about the program and demonstrate their interest by requiring their children to obey safety rules and to cooperate fully with the school transportation system.)

NOTE: In parochial school transportation systems, the school superintendent, or the person in charge of the diocese or parish, should provide this stimulus and guidance.

Top administrative interest and continuity are equally essential for public school-, parochial school-, and contract-operated fleet safety program. Administration must demand constant emphasis on accident prevention from all transportation system employees.

CHAPTER 4

Supervising the School Bus Fleet

The superintendent should appoint a school transportation safety supervisor in each school district. Supervision might be a part-time job in small fleets, but in many fleets, supervision requires much time and ability. In some large fleets, more than one person may be needed to provide adequate supervision.

The vehicle, its maintenance, and the driver are the factors that determine the safety and efficiency of the school transportation program. It is impossible to avoid accidents when any of these ingredients are neglected. The supervisor is the catalyst that makes these factors produce results. The right individual, with proper training and adequate support, will produce the safety and efficiency necessary for pupil passenger protection.

The checklists that follow treat the qualifications, responsibilities, authority, and performance of the school transportation supervisor.

Qualifications of a Supervisor

Here is a checklist to help evaluate the experience and training needed for a school transportation supervisor. Individual supervisors may find areas in which they need to increase their efforts.

1. Has the supervisor had formal training in fleet supervision? Did he or she attend a school or have in-service training?
2. Does he or she have previous experience in fleet safety supervision? Supervising a commercial fleet, a bus fleet, a delivery service fleet, or another type of fleet?
3. Does he or she have an aptitude for and an interest in the work? What can the supervisor offer to the job?
4. Does he or she have the ability to get along well with other people?
5. Does he or she have public speaking experience?

Supervising Drivers

How does a supervisor's job responsibilities and authority to carry them out compare with other supervisors in similar positions? Consider his or her authority and responsibility in the supervision of your drivers.

Is your supervisor:
1. Authorized to take charge of the drivers?
2. Allowed ample time for proper supervision?
3. Responsible for selection of new drivers?
4. Responsible for planning and implementing the driver training program?
5. Responsible for transportation records?
6. Responsible for accident investigation including the following?
    a. Establishing preventability
    b. Establishing an accident review committee

Here is a brief self-test for the driver supervisor:
How do you rate your own performance in the supervision of your drivers?
1. Do you use the accident report to counsel the driver involved in an accident?
2. Are you able to use accident reports in remedial training of drivers?
3. Can you recognize substandard performance and symptoms of accidents-in-the-making? Such as the following:
    a. Errors in the performance of work
    b. Changes in everyday behavior and manners
    c. Changes in simple habits of a routine nature
    d. Near-accidents
4. Are you alert in your personal observations of driver performance?
5. Do you carefully check reports received from drivers, pupils, school authorities, parents, police, and others involved, to determine the validity of the report and the need for counseling?
6. Can you check reasons for substandard performance?
7. Do you spend your time helping your drivers to drive safely, instead of merely determining preventability after an accident?
8. Are you capable of establishing a program of counseling and retraining?
9. Do you know all the laws and regulations that are applicable to school bus fleet operation?
10. Do you keep posted on innovations, research, and new techniques in school transportation?

11. Have you built "flexibility" into your operation so it can handle unexpected emergencies?

How to spot driver errors

Drivers are capable of committing any number of errors that can have serious consequences. The supervisor should know what these errors are, how they can be spotted, and how to prevent them. Supervision is more than the art of getting things done through people—it is the art of getting them done well.

There are a number of specific driving errors that frequently lead to accidents. A list of these errors was compiled from a survey of more than 150 of the nation's top fleet safety professionals. To help the supervisor recognize these errors and head off accidents *before* they occur, review the errors that are listed in the section, "Driving Errors."

Because each fleet of school buses transports pupils and uses the public streets and highways, its drivers have a special obligation to operate within the law. Violations of traffic laws cannot be condoned. Violations may not only expose the pupil passengers to serious hazards, but may also reflect badly on the school system. Repeated violations by individual drivers should be cause for their dismissal.

Purchasing and Maintaining Vehicles

The supervisor's authority and responsibility for vehicles usually includes both purchasing and maintenance.

Purchasing

School buses must be properly selected and equipped to assure the safe and efficient operation of the school transportation program. The supervisor's knowledge of bus routes, pupils to be transported, special environmental or operational conditions, and maintenance factors qualifies him or her to prepare specifications for bus purchases or to assist another person who is knowledgeable about school buses and components to prepare specifications.

The school board should provide guidelines to help make the best selection. The following questions will help to evaluate purchasing procedures:

1. Are local minimum standards in effect?
2. Are needs in excess of minimum standards considered?
3. Are local vehicle specifications written?
4. Are specifications carefully explained to each prospective bidder?
5. Does policy require rejection of any bid that does not meet specifications, even when it is the lowest bid?
6. Do specifications reflect consideration of the required bus capacity and the environmental factors affecting the operation—such as hills, average temperature, and type of roadway?
7. Do specifications reflect careful evaluation of safety factors such as horsepower, tires, service brake effort, special emergency and parking brakes, defrosters and windshield washers?
8. Are the advantages of power steering and automatic transmissions (with built-in retarders) considered?
9. Do specifications rule out, on the basis of size or performance, components that have previously caused problems or concern in vehicle operation and maintenance?
10. Does the transportation supervisor prepare vehicle specifications, or assist in their preparation?

Maintaining

Preventive maintenance plays a vital part in the safety and efficiency of the school transportation program. It is as much a part of the safety supervisor's responsibility as other facets of the program. School buses must be kept in top mechanical condition.

Proper vehicle maintenance ensures dependability, maximum life, peak performance, and safety. Both sound operating policies and adequate maintenance will help control fleet accidents and costs. Efficient supervision makes the safe method a part of everyday operations.

The following questions will help you to determine whether you have what is necessary for good maintenance:
1. Are you in charge of maintenance facilities, vehicles, and mechanics?
2. If your school district operates the school bus fleet, are the facilities adequate to maintain today's school buses? If a contractor operates the fleet, is maintenance quality high?
3. Do you have the financial support necessary to keep shop equipment up-to-date and to retain well-trained, experienced mechanics?

If you are responsible for maintenance, answer the following ques-

tions to determine the quality of your maintenance operation:
1. Are buses scheduled for regular mileage or time-interval preventive maintenance inspections?
2. Are drivers required to make pretrip inspections?
3. Are drivers required to report all defects in writing?
4. Is immediate attention given to all reported defects?
5. Are mechanics required to sign each repair order and be responsible for maintenance quality?
6. Are drivers required to road test completed repairs before loading pupils?
7. Are individual drivers held personally responsible for vehicle abuse?

8. Are mechanics fully qualified?
9. Do they receive periodic instruction and in-service training?
10. Do they keep abreast of the latest equipment maintenance procedures and the techniques? (Much of this information is available from manufacturers and suppliers at little or no cost to the mechanics or the fleet.)
11. Are the buses and equipment, including warning devices, maintained so they operate as originally intended?
12. Does inadequate maintenance ever prevent a bus from operating or contribute to irregular schedules?
13. Has lack of adequate maintenance ever contributed to an accident —or near accident—in your fleet?

The Supervisor's Role in Public Relations

The school transportation supervisor also is responsible for the fleet's public image. The supervisor should make the drivers feel they share the responsibility for good public relations. Courtesy and safety are inseparable in the operation of motor vehicles. They are an important part of the school bus operator's job.

The following checklist will serve as a guide for combining the efforts of the fleet service, school, pupils, and parents for a safe and efficient school transportation program.
1. Are bus routes planned to eliminate as many traffic hazards as possible, including traffic interference, sharp curves, and railroad crossings?

2. Are routes planned to provide minimum time on the bus?
3. Are the smallest children given the most consideration in keeping to a minimum the distances they have to walk?
4. Are school authorities asked to cooperate with staggered school hours for greater fleet utilization and less pupil time away from home?
5. Are pupils taught the safe way to approach, ride, and leave a bus? Are emergency drills conducted?
6. Does the supervisor actively seek parental cooperation by participating in P.T.A. and civic club meetings?
7. Does the supervisor and other school authorities explain transportation policies and problems to parents and teachers?
8. Are influential parents and civic-minded persons given the opportunity to observe the driver training program and bus maintenance facilities?
9. Does the supervisor take advantage of opportunities for favorable publicity through news media?
10. Do drivers extend driving courtesies to other motorists?
11. Are buses kept clean and painted?

Keeping Up-to-Date

Although a supervisor's initial qualifications and experience may be excellent, his or her safety education must be continuous to do a good job. Every school transportation supervisor must keep professionally up-to-date.

The following checklist focuses on some important factors of a supervisor's in-service training. Does the supervisor:
1. Keep current on school bus safety research?
2. Have adequate funds to obtain publications and papers giving research results and conclusions?
3. Apply these findings to upgrading the safety and efficiency of the fleet?
4. Maintain contact with bus and bus equipment manufacturers?
5. Use fleet operation safety innovations as they are proven and become available?
6. Keep abreast of the latest techniques and programs for the selection, training, and supervision of drivers and maintenance of vehicles?
7. Attend state, regional, and national safety meetings?
8. Attend fleet and safety supervision seminars?
9. Periodically attend courses in safety supervision?

CHAPTER 5

Selecting the School Bus Driver

The goal in driver selection should be to provide the highest possible transportation service quality and safety by selecting school bus drivers who will improve the fleet's record and performance.

Few occupations involve a greater need for good safety attitude. The school bus driver has both the responsibility of a professional driver and responsibility for the well-being of every pupil who rides the school bus.

Driver selection, training, and motivation must be designed to prevent accidents. Before discussing the qualities to look for when seeking applicants, we must examine the qualifications of the person responsible for hiring.

Who Should Screen Applicants?

Personnel selection is a demanding task requiring skill, tact, and training. It must be performed by a qualified person who can exercise good judgment and take the time and trouble to screen applicants thoroughly. If no staff member is trained in personnel selection, it is advisable to send a staff member for training to fill this role.

Even individuals with "natural ability" in this area should be encouraged to enroll in refresher courses, seminars, and workshops to hone their skills and to acquire current personnel recruitment techniques. Recruitment sources, methods and channels of communication must be thoroughly explored and understood. Such training would be valuable not only for selecting drivers, but also for other jobs that need filling over a period of time.

If possible, the transportation supervisor should be the person responsible for driver selection.

What Kind of Person Makes a Safe School Bus Driver?

A school bus operator does not need the stature and endurance of a professional athlete, but certain physical and mental characteristics are required for good job performance.

Physical characteristics

Because of the configuration of the driver's compartment in school buses, the size of the driver should be considered. The driver needs sufficient height to reach the hand- and foot-operated controls, and to see easily both inside and outside the vehicle.

Requirements should be determined by the school bus fleet supervisor, the contractor, the school district, and the state director of public transportation.

The following Bureau of Motor Carrier Safety requirements are a minimum for commercial truck drivers. Minimums for school bus drivers should be no less stringent.

1. No loss of foot, leg, hand, or arm.
2. No mental, nervous, organic, or functional disease that is likely to interfere with safe driving.
3. No impairment in the use of foot, leg, fingers, hand, or arm, or other physical defect or limitation likely to interfere with safe driving.
4. Visual acuity not less than 20/40 (Snellen), in both eyes with or without glasses; a field of vision, not less than 140 degrees in a horizontal plane; and the ability to distinguish the colors red, green, and yellow.
5. Hearing should be such that, measured by an audiometric device, there is an average hearing loss in the better ear no greater than 40 dB at 500 Hz, 1000 Hz, and 2000 Hz with or without a hearing aid.
6. Not addicted to narcotics or habit-forming drugs, or to excessive use of alcoholic beverages.

DISQUALIFYING CONDITIONS

Emotional instability	Hernia
Convulsion disorder	Back injuries
Diabetes	Cardiovascular disease

Some states have physical requirements that equal or exceed the Bureau of Motor Carrier Safety Regulations. If your state is one of these, see that your drivers meet those requirements. If physical requirements in your state are less stringent, have your local school board establish adequate physical qualifications to provide the reasonable safeguards you need.

Mental characteristics

The American Medical Association's Committee on Medical Aspects of Automobile Injuries and Deaths reports that persons with an intelligence quotient (IQ) below 70 are more susceptible to accidents than are individuals with an average IQ of 100 or higher. This is especially true when they are faced with emergency situations requiring accurate judgment or decisive action. Low-IQ drivers might also be difficult to supervise and could make poor witnesses in case of an accident.

It is also known that highly intelligent drivers are likely to have accidents—not because they do not drive well, but because their minds are so active they find it difficult to concentrate while driving a vehicle. To these drivers, personal mental distraction can be more dangerous than external physical distraction.

Obeying traffic regulations and extending courtesies to pedestrians and other motorists is essential for both safe driving and good public relations. Conversely, there is a close correlation between repeated traffic violations and repeated accidents.

The driver must be able to find satisfaction in the job and get along well with others. A new employee brings to the job skill, aptitude, and, sometimes, negative personality traits. The new driver who gets along well with others contributes to the morale of the entire group, helps keep pupil discipline problems at a minimum, and is valuable in maintaining the fleet's good public image.

Other considerations

Drivers differ in the degree that they maintain or abuse their vehicles. Because many school transportation systems operate on limited budgets, evidence of this trait in an applicant should be carefully evaluated. Conservation of the vehicle reduces the expense of maintaining it in a safe and operable condition, extends its useful life and service, and contributes to a more accurate schedule. The vehicle that is abused breaks down more often on the route and is frequently in the shop for repairs. As a consequence, schedules are delayed. Frequent schedule irregularities disrupt school teaching programs, antagonize parents and students and lower the fleet's service image. No school district can afford an unreliable and irregular bus schedule.

The emotionally mature employee makes the best and safest driver. Permitting an immature person to operate school buses is dangerous. Maturity does not always correspond directly with the age of a driver. Safe drivers of any age recognize and accept their full responsibility for the operation of the bus and the safety of their pupil passengers.

Another important point to consider is the employee's emotional health. Family and other personal problems and responsibilities often can affect on-the-job performance. Personal troubles can distract one's attention from driving. Anger, carried to the job, can cause a driver to disregard common sense, courtesy, and caution.

The applicant's maturity is reflected in his attitude. An immature person blames others for past accidents and always is ready to blame the other party for disagreements or misunderstandings. The mature person shows an interest in people's opportunities, needs and interests. Interest in the problems and welfare of others contributes to a driver's ability to get along with pupils. The immature person is easily irritated, and cannot be expected to act for the safety and best interest of the pupil passengers and others at all times. Patience and understanding indicate a person can be responsible for the transportation of pupils.

Therefore, check an applicant's past record carefully. If there are discrepancies between the applicant's statements and previous employment records, try to reconcile the differences. Try to learn about the person's attitude, health, dependability, and loyalty during this check.

Traffic convictions and reportable accidents are usually on file in the state where they occur. It is worth the time and effort to check with the motor vehicle department in any state where the applicant has lived or has been licensed to operate a motor vehicle. Request that the department check the applicant's record at the National Driver Register Service. Checking the register will enable you to find any instances of license suspension or revocation, regardless of where they have occurred. A driver's real attitude toward safety and authority often is reflected in the records of the person's violations and accidents.

In summary, careful driver selection consists of seeking the following qualities in each applicant:
1. Physical fitness.
2. Good adjustment and emotional stability.
3. Size and stature to fit the job.
4. Impeccable references.

5. Neat appearance.
6. Congenial personality.
7. Acceptable driving skill, or capability of being trained.
8. No record of repeated traffic violations or preventable vehicular accidents.
9. Honesty, punctuality, and dependability.

CHAPTER 6

Training the School Bus Driver

The most important ingredient in an efficient school transportation service is safe driving. The skill, attitude, and knowledge necessary for safe driving and control of pupils must be developed through a driver training program. The training program must cover everything the driver needs to know to do the job well.

Driver instruction begins with the first contact with the supervisor, whose attitude toward the total safety program will be reflected in the driver's performance. Effective training establishes a standard of performance in all areas, including safe driving.

Three types of driver training are essential: initial training, refresher training, and remedial training. However, before discussing them, let us discuss the subject areas that should be included in training and the sources for training materials.

What To Include and Where To Find It

There are many approaches to training. In developing a fleet training program, be sure to include management policies, all the functions of the fleet, local laws and ordinances, state laws and regulations, and pertinent *Bureau of Motor Carrier Safety Regulations*.

Material is available from many sources. Be sure the material chosen covers the subject thoroughly and in an interesting manner. Because it will be presented to new drivers, it must be revised to keep it up-to-date. Some of the factors determining the extent and frequency of any revision are audience reaction, the subsequent performance of trainees, changing needs of the fleet, changes in administrative policies, changes in the extent and type of service rendered by the fleet, and changes in local and state laws and regulations.

Resources

. Films and selected video tapes are available either by purchase or rental to help the supervisor or other instructor teach proper driving techniques, including defensive driving.

Defensive Driving Course

The Defensive Driving Course emphasizes the six positions of the two-car crash. Each year, one of 12 drivers is involved in a two-car accident. This represents over 80 percent of the total number of accidents annually.

A two-car crash may involve you with another vehicle (*a*) ahead of you, (*b*) behind you, (*c*) meeting you head on, (*d*) meeting you at an intersection, (*e*) passing you, or (*f*) being passed by you. The Defensive Driving Course teaches a simple defense to prevent accident involvement in any of these six situations. Application of these principles can help each school bus driver avoid accidents.

The films that teach the six positions of the two-car crash can be purchased for your training materials library and used to teach defensive driving to your fleet for years to come.

Accidents may have many contributing factors, but in almost every instance, one or more driving errors trigger the accident. The well-trained operator understands his vehicle's limitations, the effect of his physical and mental condition, interaction with others, and the environmental conditions that can contribute to accidents. Drivers must be taught to compensate for such factors to prevent accidents.

Backing

Because of the high frequency of backing accidents, this subject also belongs in the driving training program. Although the results of backing accidents usually are minor in terms of vehicle and property damage, they can have serious personal injury consequences. The implications are that the driver involved has failed to exercise proper caution and has an attitude toward safety that could contribute to many serious incidents and accidents. Any time another vehicle or object is hit in a backing accident, the driver must be aware that a pupil could just as easily have been struck. Drivers should be taught that backing is to be avoided when possible, and should learn how to back safely when it becomes necessary.

Procedures to stress include: (*a*) getting out of the bus before beginning the maneuver and carefully noting the available clearance and all objects or obstructions, (*b*) backing from the driver's side, (*c*) backing slowly, (*d*) checking both sides continually as you back, and (*c*) using a reliable person to guide you.

New drivers should practice the driving techniques they are taught. The supervisor can only observe driving habits and respond to traffic situations by riding with them. By putting the driver behind the wheel and observing his driving performance over a prescribed course, the supervisor can evaluate the trainee's progress and readiness to transport pupils.

No transportation director should allow any driver to transport pupils until that driver has fully demonstrated an understanding of the principles of defensive driving and has acquired the driving skills necessary for safe, efficient operation.

Types of Training: Initial, Refresher, and Remedial

Before assembling any training material, the instructor should list the points trainees should learn and decide on their relative importance. The objectives of the training program should be to provide the driver with the knowledge needed to do the job, the skill necessary to do it properly, and an appreciation of the importance of the job and the need to do it safely.

Safe driving is not a simple skill. It requires the ability to make driving decisions quickly which should be acquired through planned training—not picked up haphazardly.

Each new driver must be thoroughly trained by a good training program that provides for development of driving skills to a high performance level. Good supervision will further refine and improve such skills.

The driver who completes the training course should:
1. Be able to maintain control over pupils on the bus;
2. Know procedures to deal with pupils who disobey established rules and regulations;
3. Understand schedules and know the flexibility permitted during adverse conditions or emergencies;

4. Be able to cope with emergencies that may arise during the course of duty;
5. Be qualified to administer first aid if needed;
6. Be able to operate a fire extinguisher effectively;
7. Know what to do if involved in an accident.

The amount of time needed for initial training depends on the selection program, the person employed, and the amount of usable skill and experience the person has. Adequate time must be allowed to develop the new driver's knowledge and skill to the degree necessary for effective job performance.

Refresher training

Periodic refresher training reinforces a driver's understanding of the policies, rules and regulations pertinent to operations. Also, it helps keep their performance efficient and safe.

Material covered in these classes will vary, but, in general, it should include the following:
1. Review of initial material as experience indicates it is needed;
2. Instruction covering the operation of new equipment;
3. Handling of new operating problems;
4. Changes in policies, laws, and regulations;
5. Periodic first aid refresher training;
6. Periodic fire extinguisher training;
7. Review of emergency evacuation procedures;
8. Review of vehicle inspection procedures;
9. Review of procedures to follow in the event of accident or emergency.

Remedial training

Remedial training can improve the performance of drivers whose records indicate that they have problems. The discussion technique is useful in such training. A description of an accident involving one member of the class, followed by a group discussion of defensive measures that could have prevented it, will help all to learn from the accident.

This type of training is indicated for any driver who:
1. Becomes involved in preventable accidents;
2. Fails to solve pupil behavior problems;
3. Abuses the vehicle;

4. Is discourteous;
5. Fails to operate reasonably close to schedule;
6. Is the subject of frequent complaints about attitude or performance;
7. Shows changes in personal habits that indicate personal problems;
8. Experiences changes in physical fitness because of the aging process or the consequences of illness or disease.

Psycho-physical Testing

Many psycho-physical and other tests are available and should be used to demonstrate to drivers their personal limitations or handicaps. Several qualities treated by these tests are discussed next.

Reaction time

Often, drivers do not realize the reaction time or distance that makes adequate following distance so important. This test emphasizes the importance of keeping an adequate distance between moving vehicles. A great help in preventing accidents is a visual demonstration of the distance a vehicle travels between the time the need to stop occurs and the time that braking effort actually begins. It is also useful to point out to older drivers that their reaction time may have increased and they must allow additional following distance to compensate for this change.

Distance judgment

A test of judgment of distance helps drivers recognize how well they can estimate the distance to approaching vehicles by comparing their positions with other objects. The ability to evaluate the distance and speed of approaching vehicles accurately is essential in such traffic maneuvers as passing a vehicle going in the same direction and entering a thoroughfare from a side road.

Glare recovery

Glare recovery is an important test for anyone who drives at times when headlights must be used. It reveals the time it takes for full vision to return after being subjected to the direct beams of car headlights at night. The distance traveled while the driver cannot see can be computed to emphasize this factor. Many drivers do not realize this hazard exists.

Tunnel vision

Some people have limited peripheral vision, called "tunnel vision." They can be taught to compensate for this limited sight by increased side-to-side head movement to observe all possible traffic conditions.

Such driver testing is needed to enable the supervisor to help each driver develop the compensating habits needed to drive safely. Drivers also should be impressed with the need to keep in good physical condition and to avoid things such as drugs, drug combinations and fatigue since they can adversely affect driving ability.

CHAPTER 7

Motivating the School Bus Driver

Motivation is the key to any safety program's success. Drivers must be motivated to police their own driving because their work environment makes direct supervision difficult.

The true test of the supervisor's skill is the ability to provide conditions that motivate the driver to maintain high standards. The following motivational methods and techniques can be used effectively by supervisors:

1. Make drivers aware of the high degree of skill they must acquire before qualifying to drive in your fleet.
2. Require remedial training for drivers involved in preventable accidents, and limit the number of accidents a driver can have and remain in your employ.
3. Demand that buses be cleaned inside each day, and cleaned outside as needed. Hold each driver responsible for any failures in this area.
4. Require neat appearance at all times. Drivers present a neat appearance and command more respect from both pupils and the public when uniforms are required.
5. Require drivers to be courteous at all times.
6. Appeal to the spirit of competition and publicly recognize those who do superior work.

High standards are challenging. Meeting them gives the driver a sense of pride in the job. Personal pride in their own skill makes drivers enjoy working in a fleet that is known for its high standards.

Set a Good Example

The supervisor should radiate dedication, pride, and enthusiasm in the transportation system. Your attitude and conduct should stimulate the safety consciousness of the drivers. Never do or say anything that might suggest you are not loyal to the system and its objectives.

Show Real Interest

Impart a sense of belonging to the drivers. Keep them informed of plans that involve them. Let them know periodically that they are meeting their objectives. Make them feel they are part of the team and that their personal efforts are necessary to achieve the goals of safety and efficiency. Let them know you welcome their suggestions. If their ideas cannot be used, explain the reasons; give them recognition for ideas that are used.

Encourage top management to use every opportunity to show personal interest in the drivers and the fleet safety program. Keep management aware of the importance of good buses, up-to-date maintenance facilities, and comfortable, adequate driver-room facilities.

Show your interest in the drivers by offering counsel and help if they come to you with personal problems. Let them know that you are always available for discussion of any problem.

Use Competition Effectively

Create job interest by appealing to the spirit of competition. Encourage each driver to compete with his or her own record to improve skills and performance. Many drivers enjoy the competition

Recognize Good Work

Most people appreciate recognition when they seriously devote themselves to their work. Drivers are no exception. Individual recognition of achievement through safe driver awards is a powerful incentive to good driving performance.

ANSWER SHEET

ST NO. _____ PART _____ TITLE OF POSITION _____
(AS GIVEN IN EXAMINATION ANNOUNCEMENT - INCLUDE OPTION, IF ANY)

ACE OF EXAMINATION _____ DATE _____
(CITY OR TOWN) (STATE)

RATING

USE THE SPECIAL PENCIL. MAKE GLOSSY BLACK MARKS.

	A B C D E		A B C D E		A B C D E		A B C D E		A B C D E
1	⋮ ⋮ ⋮ ⋮ ⋮	26	⋮ ⋮ ⋮ ⋮ ⋮	51	⋮ ⋮ ⋮ ⋮ ⋮	76	⋮ ⋮ ⋮ ⋮ ⋮	101	⋮ ⋮ ⋮ ⋮ ⋮
2	⋮ ⋮ ⋮ ⋮ ⋮	27	⋮ ⋮ ⋮ ⋮ ⋮	52	⋮ ⋮ ⋮ ⋮ ⋮	77	⋮ ⋮ ⋮ ⋮ ⋮	102	⋮ ⋮ ⋮ ⋮ ⋮
3	⋮ ⋮ ⋮ ⋮ ⋮	28	⋮ ⋮ ⋮ ⋮ ⋮	53	⋮ ⋮ ⋮ ⋮ ⋮	78	⋮ ⋮ ⋮ ⋮ ⋮	103	⋮ ⋮ ⋮ ⋮ ⋮
4	⋮ ⋮ ⋮ ⋮ ⋮	29	⋮ ⋮ ⋮ ⋮ ⋮	54	⋮ ⋮ ⋮ ⋮ ⋮	79	⋮ ⋮ ⋮ ⋮ ⋮	104	⋮ ⋮ ⋮ ⋮ ⋮
5	⋮ ⋮ ⋮ ⋮ ⋮	30	⋮ ⋮ ⋮ ⋮ ⋮	55	⋮ ⋮ ⋮ ⋮ ⋮	80	⋮ ⋮ ⋮ ⋮ ⋮	105	⋮ ⋮ ⋮ ⋮ ⋮
6	⋮ ⋮ ⋮ ⋮ ⋮	31	⋮ ⋮ ⋮ ⋮ ⋮	56	⋮ ⋮ ⋮ ⋮ ⋮	81	⋮ ⋮ ⋮ ⋮ ⋮	106	⋮ ⋮ ⋮ ⋮ ⋮
7	⋮ ⋮ ⋮ ⋮ ⋮	32	⋮ ⋮ ⋮ ⋮ ⋮	57	⋮ ⋮ ⋮ ⋮ ⋮	82	⋮ ⋮ ⋮ ⋮ ⋮	107	⋮ ⋮ ⋮ ⋮ ⋮
8	⋮ ⋮ ⋮ ⋮ ⋮	33	⋮ ⋮ ⋮ ⋮ ⋮	58	⋮ ⋮ ⋮ ⋮ ⋮	83	⋮ ⋮ ⋮ ⋮ ⋮	108	⋮ ⋮ ⋮ ⋮ ⋮
9	⋮ ⋮ ⋮ ⋮ ⋮	34	⋮ ⋮ ⋮ ⋮ ⋮	59	⋮ ⋮ ⋮ ⋮ ⋮	84	⋮ ⋮ ⋮ ⋮ ⋮	109	⋮ ⋮ ⋮ ⋮ ⋮
10	⋮ ⋮ ⋮ ⋮ ⋮	35	⋮ ⋮ ⋮ ⋮ ⋮	60	⋮ ⋮ ⋮ ⋮ ⋮	85	⋮ ⋮ ⋮ ⋮ ⋮	110	⋮ ⋮ ⋮ ⋮ ⋮

Make only ONE mark for each answer. Additional and stray marks may be counted as mistakes. In making corrections, erase errors COMPLETELY.

	A B C D E		A B C D E		A B C D E		A B C D E		A B C D E
11	⋮ ⋮ ⋮ ⋮ ⋮	36	⋮ ⋮ ⋮ ⋮ ⋮	61	⋮ ⋮ ⋮ ⋮ ⋮	86	⋮ ⋮ ⋮ ⋮ ⋮	111	⋮ ⋮ ⋮ ⋮ ⋮
12	⋮ ⋮ ⋮ ⋮ ⋮	37	⋮ ⋮ ⋮ ⋮ ⋮	62	⋮ ⋮ ⋮ ⋮ ⋮	87	⋮ ⋮ ⋮ ⋮ ⋮	112	⋮ ⋮ ⋮ ⋮ ⋮
13	⋮ ⋮ ⋮ ⋮ ⋮	38	⋮ ⋮ ⋮ ⋮ ⋮	63	⋮ ⋮ ⋮ ⋮ ⋮	88	⋮ ⋮ ⋮ ⋮ ⋮	113	⋮ ⋮ ⋮ ⋮ ⋮
14	⋮ ⋮ ⋮ ⋮ ⋮	39	⋮ ⋮ ⋮ ⋮ ⋮	64	⋮ ⋮ ⋮ ⋮ ⋮	89	⋮ ⋮ ⋮ ⋮ ⋮	114	⋮ ⋮ ⋮ ⋮ ⋮
15	⋮ ⋮ ⋮ ⋮ ⋮	40	⋮ ⋮ ⋮ ⋮ ⋮	65	⋮ ⋮ ⋮ ⋮ ⋮	90	⋮ ⋮ ⋮ ⋮ ⋮	115	⋮ ⋮ ⋮ ⋮ ⋮
16	⋮ ⋮ ⋮ ⋮ ⋮	41	⋮ ⋮ ⋮ ⋮ ⋮	66	⋮ ⋮ ⋮ ⋮ ⋮	91	⋮ ⋮ ⋮ ⋮ ⋮	116	⋮ ⋮ ⋮ ⋮ ⋮
17	⋮ ⋮ ⋮ ⋮ ⋮	42	⋮ ⋮ ⋮ ⋮ ⋮	67	⋮ ⋮ ⋮ ⋮ ⋮	92	⋮ ⋮ ⋮ ⋮ ⋮	117	⋮ ⋮ ⋮ ⋮ ⋮
18	⋮ ⋮ ⋮ ⋮ ⋮	43	⋮ ⋮ ⋮ ⋮ ⋮	68	⋮ ⋮ ⋮ ⋮ ⋮	93	⋮ ⋮ ⋮ ⋮ ⋮	118	⋮ ⋮ ⋮ ⋮ ⋮
19	⋮ ⋮ ⋮ ⋮ ⋮	44	⋮ ⋮ ⋮ ⋮ ⋮	69	⋮ ⋮ ⋮ ⋮ ⋮	94	⋮ ⋮ ⋮ ⋮ ⋮	119	⋮ ⋮ ⋮ ⋮ ⋮
20	⋮ ⋮ ⋮ ⋮ ⋮	45	⋮ ⋮ ⋮ ⋮ ⋮	70	⋮ ⋮ ⋮ ⋮ ⋮	95	⋮ ⋮ ⋮ ⋮ ⋮	120	⋮ ⋮ ⋮ ⋮ ⋮
21	⋮ ⋮ ⋮ ⋮ ⋮	46	⋮ ⋮ ⋮ ⋮ ⋮	71	⋮ ⋮ ⋮ ⋮ ⋮	96	⋮ ⋮ ⋮ ⋮ ⋮	121	⋮ ⋮ ⋮ ⋮ ⋮
22	⋮ ⋮ ⋮ ⋮ ⋮	47	⋮ ⋮ ⋮ ⋮ ⋮	72	⋮ ⋮ ⋮ ⋮ ⋮	97	⋮ ⋮ ⋮ ⋮ ⋮	122	⋮ ⋮ ⋮ ⋮ ⋮
23	⋮ ⋮ ⋮ ⋮ ⋮	48	⋮ ⋮ ⋮ ⋮ ⋮	73	⋮ ⋮ ⋮ ⋮ ⋮	98	⋮ ⋮ ⋮ ⋮ ⋮	123	⋮ ⋮ ⋮ ⋮ ⋮
24	⋮ ⋮ ⋮ ⋮ ⋮	49	⋮ ⋮ ⋮ ⋮ ⋮	74	⋮ ⋮ ⋮ ⋮ ⋮	99	⋮ ⋮ ⋮ ⋮ ⋮	124	⋮ ⋮ ⋮ ⋮ ⋮
25	⋮ ⋮ ⋮ ⋮ ⋮	50	⋮ ⋮ ⋮ ⋮ ⋮	75	⋮ ⋮ ⋮ ⋮ ⋮	100	⋮ ⋮ ⋮ ⋮ ⋮	125	⋮ ⋮ ⋮ ⋮ ⋮

ANSWER SHEET

SEP - - 2016

TEST NO. _____ PART _____ TITLE OF POSITION _____
(AS GIVEN IN EXAMINATION ANNOUNCEMENT - INCLUDE OPTION, IF ANY)

PLACE OF EXAMINATION _____ DATE _____
(CITY OR TOWN) (STATE)

RATING

USE THE SPECIAL PENCIL. MAKE GLOSSY BLACK MARKS.

Make only ONE mark for each answer. Additional and stray marks may be counted as mistakes. In making corrections, erase errors COMPLETELY.